PRAISE FOR THE WORK OF JERRY ELLIS

WALKING TO CANTERBURY

"In today's modern world we could all use a dose of Jerry Ellis's provocative writing and soul-searching. . . . No one provides better meaning to the wondrous world in which we live than the man best known for tapping into the sojourner that lies within all of our hearts. Like all masters, he will enlighten you with this grace and humility."

—JAMES A. PERCOCO
Author of *A Pasion for the Past:
Teaching History Creatively*

WALKING THE TRAIL

"Come along on the Trail with Jerry Ellis. You'll love every step of it."

—TONY HILLERMAN

"Ellis is wry and patient. The emotions that sent him on his journey are deep, and he treats them and his listeners with gentle respect."

—*The Boston Globe*

"Reading Jerry Ellis's account of his modern-day trek along the old Cherokee Trail of Tears is better than receiving a series of letters from a perceptive, generous-hearted, and imaginative traveler."

—DEE BROWN
Author of *Bury My Heart at
Wounded Knee*

"A remarkable journey of faith and endurance. By tracing the path of his Cherokee ancestors, Ellis discovers his past and its valuable connection to the current treasures of his heart and home."

—CRAIG LESLEY
Editor of *Talking Leaves:*
Contemporary Native American
Short Stories

"A meandering, informal, and always lively account in the mold of William Least Heat Moon's *Blue Highways* and other American 'road' books."

—*Library Journal*

"Peripatetic true confessions hook the reader with their very ingenuousness—a genuine American tale."

—*Kirkus Reviews*

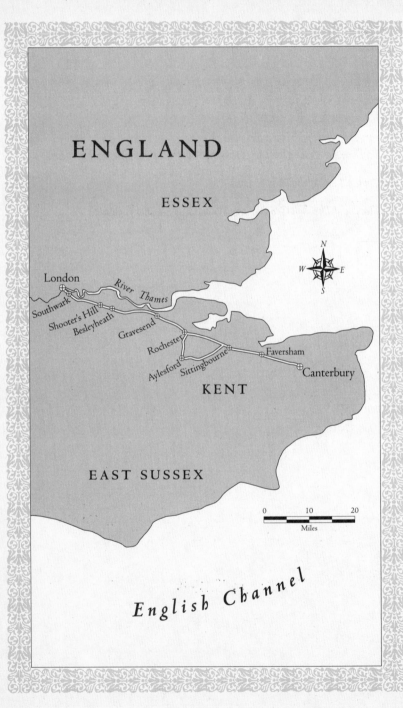

WALKING
TO
CANTERBURY

A MODERN JOURNEY
THROUGH CHAUCER'S
MEDIEVAL ENGLAND

JERRY ELLIS

BALLANTINE BOOKS
NEW YORK

For Debi

A Ballantine Book
Published by The Ballantine Publishing Group
Copyright © 2003 by Jerry Ellis

www.ballantinebooks.com

The photographs are reproduced by permission of the British Library.

Library of Congress Cataloging-in-Publication Data:
Ellis, Jerry.
Walking to Canterbury: a modern journey through Chaucer's medieval
England / Jerry Ellis.—1st ed.
p. cm.
1. England, South East—Description and travel. 2. Ellis, Jerry—Journeys—
England, Southeast. 3. Chaucer, Geoffrey, d. 1400—Knowledge—England.
4. Historic sites—England, Southeast. 5. Walking—England, Southeast.
I. Title.

DA670.S63 E45 2003
942.2'03—dc21
2002031167

ISBN 0-345-44706-9

Cover design by Beck Stvan
Cover photos © Angelo Hornak/Corbis

Book Design by Joseph Rutt

Manufactured in the United States of America

First Edition: March 2003

10 9 8 7 6 5 4 3 2 1

ACKNOWLEDGMENTS

First and foremost I thank *you*—the readers of my earlier books—for your support over the years. You have made me feel that what I write adds something to your life, and an author could ask for little more. My agent—Peter Miller, the Literary Lion—gets my grateful nod because he believed in this journey and the resulting book from the first day. My editor, Allison Dickens, has strengthened the book with her insightful suggestions, and Leslie Meredith, who commissioned the project, will forever be a crucial landmark in my life. I tip my hat as well to Sheila Hingley, the Canterbury Cathedral librarian, who assisted me with invaluable research.

AUTHOR'S NOTE

This book is based on my true-life experiences walking Pilgrims' Way, although the names and other details of certain individuals have been changed.

PROLOGUE

The year 1170, England: Four knights swung swords at Thomas Becket, kneeling before the Canterbury altar. One hit the stone floor with such force that the iron point broke off. Another cut Becket's skull in two.

While the knights looted Becket's home, the monks who had observed the murder mopped up the blood with cloth and prepared the body for the nearby crypt. Under his ecclesiastical robes, they discovered a hair shirt, a true sign of a dedicated monk, which was infested with worms and lice.

Yes, the monks agreed, Becket had the mark of both saint and martyr. Earlier that day he had asked his brethren three different times to flog him to show how he suffered for Jesus, the Holy Savior, and when the knights demanded that he pledge allegiance to the king of England, Henry II, Becket stood by the church: "God's will be done," he said, in his dying breath.

Neither Greek nor Shakespearean tragedy surpassed this fate of Becket, for he and Henry II were once best of friends— as entwined as a river to its banks. But when the king made Becket the archbishop of Canterbury, the highest papal post in the land, with the belief that his friend would obey the crown and suppress the power of the church, their friendship burned to ashes. Henry II wondered aloud if no one would rid his kingdom of this problem, and the four knights took his words as orders, mounting for Canterbury to right the wrong with iron.

The very night that Becket was killed, the miracles began. A townsman wiped blood from the cathedral floor and ran home with it to cure his paralyzed wife. In the weeks that followed, twenty more miracles were claimed, as believers began wearing ampoules of "the water of Thomas," which contained traces of Becket's blood. The cloth used by the monks to mop up the blood was mixed with water, which was sold for three hundred years following Becket's death.

Miracles even began to occur in France, Italy, and Germany. Canterbury monks—five had witnessed and recorded the killing—traveled to Rome to tell the pope himself what they had observed. Becket was canonized only three years later.

Henry II, directed by the pope, paid penitence by walking barefoot through Canterbury. Once inside the cathedral, the king knelt before Becket's resting place and was flogged by more than one hundred monks. He promised to build a monastery in honor of his slain friend and continued to kneel as the townspeople entered the church to behold that even the mighty crown of England could not escape the heavy foot of God.

Three of the knights who killed Becket paid penitence by trekking to the Holy Land. The fourth tried to cleanse his soul by creating a countryside maze, a symbol of man's pilgrimage through life. Such intricate networks of passages were sometimes built in churches so people could walk them in a matter of minutes.

Fifteen years after Becket's death, no less than seven hundred miracles were recorded in the presence of the saint's relics. In 1220 the body was moved from the crypt, where it had been since shortly after Becket's murder, to Trinity Chapel, a shrine glittering with jewels, gold, and silver. When the shrine was destroyed by King Henry VIII, 318 years later, one of those prized jewels, a blue diamond, was set in a ring that the king wore.

While a trip to Becket's shrine granted the most blessed nothing less than a miracle, it was said to help purify all, making shorter their obligated time in purgatory before entering the Kingdom of Heaven. For this reason, thousands journeyed to Canterbury each year. The number of pilgrims visiting the shrine in the Middle Ages was so great that their knees wore thin the stone floor where they prayed before the pink marble monument. They stuck their hands through its arched windows to touch the sacred coffin. It contained the body and lice-infested hair shirt, but the severed part of his head was now stored in a gold and silver reliquary in another section of the church known as the Crown of Saint Thomas.

But for medieval pilgrims to journey to Canterbury, sixty miles south of London, they risked their lives. Pilgrims' Way (see the frontispiece map) followed ancient Roman roads that led through thick forests with criminals ready to rob, rape, swindle, and murder.

A pilgrim in the Middle Ages also had to be on constant guard against witches, giants, Cyclops, fairies, and most certainly the Devil himself, who could appear in many forms, including in the very relics sold along Pilgrims' Way to protect travelers. One could buy such holy items as a piece of the rock where Jesus stood upon ascending to Heaven, straw from his manger, splinters from his Cross, his tears in a bottle, a feather from an angel, or even the tip of the Devil's tail. These medieval souvenirs were believed to have various curative or preventative powers.

No trinket or vial of holy water held the power of a visit to Becket's shrine, though. Becket's shrine held England's most treasured relics, and visitors filled the cathedral's coffers with offerings. Other churches competed with Canterbury for pilgrims' gold and silver by claiming that they, too, housed parts of Saint Thomas. How could the same relics appear in two places at once? Well, that simply further proved the power of relics to perform miracles by multiplying.

By the late Middle Ages, treks to Becket's shrine had become, for some, excuses to take vacations and see new sights. Geoffrey Chaucer was keenly aware of how these travels had mutated into a blending of the sacred and the secular. Addressing the complexity of such pilgrimages, he wrote *The Canterbury Tales*, one of the most enduring pieces of literature written in the English language. If an afterlife exists, one can't help but ponder whether Becket, seeing the events he set in motion, looked down on England from Heaven as he prayed or laughed until his sides hurt: royalty, power, politics, friendship, betrayal, murder, martyrdom, miracles, penitence, pilgrimages, theft, and classical literature—all of these elements interwoven are the makings of bigger-than-life history and drama.

I first learned of Pilgrims' Way as a senior at the University of Alabama, majoring in English. I had postponed the required course on Chaucer until the last semester because I dreaded having to read aloud portions of *The Canterbury Tales* in Middle English. Nonetheless, when I studied the *Tales*, they made me wonder what it would be like to walk Pilgrims' Way. Traveling, meeting interesting people, hearing their stories, and maybe even finding a miracle stirred my imagination.

During this same time I had fallen in love with a redhead in Oklahoma City, and some weekends I would hitchhike fifteen hundred miles round-trip just to spend Saturday night with her. Often those who gave me rides told stories from the deepest parts of their hearts. Some needed to confess to lighten their souls, while others longed for answers through conversation. A few just wanted to hear themselves talk and assumed that their stories entertained. Whatever their motivations, their tales revealed who they were. They and I were a bit like the characters in *The Canterbury Tales*, travelers who found fun, excitement, and sometimes meaning in sharing our lives.

In a way I became a professional pilgrim. By the age of twenty-six, I had thumbed enough miles to circle the globe five times and met people from all walks of life, including Mr. Universe and a group of the Hell's Angels. Through them I found a rare intimacy that fed my soul.

During those years I lived in Chicago, New Orleans, Oklahoma City, San Francisco, New York, Los Angeles, and Denver. I worked as a weight-lifting instructor, a carpenter, an artist's model, a waiter, a librarian, a journalist, a farmer, and a junk dealer. Thumbing from city to city, I sometimes told stories in exchange for meals from those who gave me lifts.

My life on the road was exhilarating, but it didn't quell the unrest within my soul, the feeling that I had not found my true calling.

The more I traveled, the more I came to realize just how much I loved my home in the Appalachian Mountains of Fort Payne, Alabama. While I had always felt a strong bond with my Cherokee ancestors, I found myself thinking about how home had been taken from them.

In 1838 seven thousand armed U.S. soldiers forced eighteen thousand Indians from their log cabins in the South. Four thousand Indians died as the soldiers marched them nine hundred miles (through the heart of winter) to Indian Territory, now Oklahoma. The dead were buried in shallow unmarked graves along this Trail of Tears.

I began to feel compelled to honor my Indian heritage by telling the world about the Trail of Tears. I wrote a screenplay. My contemporary protagonist, a Cherokee who had a vision that he must take a pilgrimage, walked the trail in reverse from

Oklahoma to Alabama to bring home the spirits of those who had died on the forced march. If he didn't fulfill his mission, he would never find peace.

Although the movie was never made, after six months of trying to sell the screenplay, I suddenly realized I had to become the protagonist in my own script. The story I had written was a map for my own mission in life. This was the way I could truly honor my ancestors—by walking their path and reliving their experiences of loss, exile, and resettlement. And I would show how their memories lived on.

From my hilltop I could see into the lush valley between Lookout and Sand Mountains with its meandering creek. Sequoya, the most famous of all Cherokee, lived near the stream in the 1820s, when he invented the Cherokee alphabet. His mother was Indian, but his father was a British officer. Sequoya was the only man in history to invent an alphabet by himself, the only alphabet invented in the past five thousand years. The giant redwoods in California were named after him, a man who had longed to empower his people with the ability to read and write that they might better protect their culture. While I would not write my own experiences on the Trail of Tears in Cherokee, I would protect and honor their spirits and culture with my writing.

In 1989 I sold almost everything I owned and took a Greyhound bus to Oklahoma to begin walking the trail. For two months I hiked from dawn until night and slept mostly in fields and woods, though strangers sometimes offered food and shelter. All along the trail, winding across seven states, people from all walks of life gave me items—an arrowhead, a silver cross, and other objects sacred to the givers. These gifts were meant as offerings to those who died on the trail in 1838 that they might rest in peace. But they were also a means by which those I met could be part of my journey.

When I returned home, I buried the offerings under a tall

red oak in a copse of trees fifty feet east of my cottage. I had built this cottage, named Tanager, over the course of two years, gathering stones and wood from the surrounding forest. These towering trees and the cottage were my cathedral. The burial site to which I returned my ancestors' spirits in the offerings I gathered became sacred to me.

Three hundred yards north of this burial site is another sacred place. Seven stones, as big as elephants' heads, form the shape of the Little Dipper. They were arranged by Indians during the Middle Ages—the very time when English pilgrims were walking to Becket's shrine. Sometimes I walk a narrow path to this Indian site and ask for guidance from the ancestors who created this configuration.

Living on ancestral ground has helped keep me in touch with my Cherokee heritage, and my walk along the Trail of Tears offered a remarkable fulfillment at that point in my personal history in 1989.

But the soul, like life itself, does not stand still. Just as the Trail of Tears reunited me with my Cherokee heritage, so I wanted to come face-to-face and soul-to-soul with my British ancestry. To do so, I felt that I needed to meet the descendants of those who had lived and died alongside my British ancestors. With one hand Cherokee and the other English, I perceived my walk on Pilgrims' Way as a means to climb higher in my family tree. My mission, however, presented an inner conflict. The English once had a hand in persecuting the Cherokee.

I arrived in England June 18, 1999, after flying from the United States. When I presented my passport to the immigration officer at Heathrow Airport, she studied me as if I were an international oddity. I wore tennis shoes, a blue cotton shirt, a brown leather jacket, and jeans. My hat was stained from years of sun, rain, and sweat. Dove and blue jay feathers stuck from one side of the hat, while a rattlesnake rattle rode snug in the back of the band. My backpack bulged with clothes, a camera, a journal, cooking utensils, a tent, toiletries, and personal items.

"On a hike?" she said, taking a closer look at the rattlesnake rattle.

"A pilgrimage," I said, hoping that the trek would be charged with extraordinary experiences. "From London to Canterbury. I plan to do it in the same amount of time it took medieval pilgrims. Seven days."

She now seemed all the more intrigued with my attire, which was notably different from that of a pilgrim in the Middle Ages. The only thing I had in common with Chaucer's pilgrims was my hat. Like mine, decorated with feathers and the snake's rattle, which I had collected on my walks, a pilgrim would have worn a big floppy hat, decorated with badges or shells to offer proof of his journeys. He might also have worn a "sclavein," which was a long, russet-colored tunic with big sleeves, sometimes patched with crosses. A soft pouch, a "scrip," would have hung from a leather belt strung over his shoulder. The pouch was small, to indicate that the pilgrim had little money or none at all. A rosary of beads might have dangled from his arm or neck, and he could have carried a wooden staff with a metal toe. Leather shoes probably covered his feet.

The pilgrim's dress was symbolic as well as practical. The staff defended the traveler against wild dogs and wolves, which represented the Devil. It also served as a third leg and suggested the Trinity as well as the wood of the Cross. The tunic, similar to the clothes Jesus wore, reflected the pilgrim's humanity. The medieval imagery became so ingrained into the British psyche that Sir Walter Raleigh used it two hundred years later in his poem "His Pilgrimage":

Give me my scallop shell of quiet
My staff of faith to walk upon;
My scrip of joy, immortal diet;
My bottle of salvation;
My gown of glory, hopes true gauge,
And thus I'll take my pilgrimage.[1]

Dressed in my modern pilgrim attire, I took a train from the airport to Victoria Station in London and there boarded the tube (British for subway) to Russell Square near the British Museum to look for an affordable bed-and-breakfast for the night. The sun was setting, and the streets smelled of Indian curry, Chinese food, and fish-and-chips. Red phone booths stood like monuments on the sidewalk, where two men wearing shoulder-length hair rocked their hips as each paraded with a blaring boom box on his shoulder. A bobbie (British for cop) at the corner motioned for two sleek black taxis to hurry on, and three teenagers on Rollerblades played follow the leader as the first jumped over a garbage can. No rain fell, but so many people carried umbrellas that it seemed a Mary Poppins party simmered in the approaching night's pot. My mouth watered just to walk new streets, and enchanting British accents fell on my ears like notes of an exotic song being born in the very air I breathed.

A pub's window revealed two women throwing darts, and the sound of a whacked tennis ball erupted from a small park. Images on televisions flickered inside shadowy apartments, and somewhere down an alley a cat shrieked. The enticing smell of perfume from a woman strolling in front of me lingered as a lone jet streaked the sky, its red wing lights blinking. The sights and sounds of modern London were in sharp contrast to the Middle Ages.

In the 1300s, if a renegade medieval serf could cross the Thames into London and stay here one year and a day without being caught by his lord, he became a free man. The city itself occupied only one square mile then. About thirty-five thousand people populated London, and they ranged from ragged serfs and students to members of the craft guilds (like carpenters and weavers), clergymen, and nobles. Regardless of whether they survived on scraps of cabbage snatched from the common marketplace or dined on roasted pigs in rooms hung with tapestries, all of the populace lived surrounded by the smell of open sewers. At sundown all were also locked within London when the walled city closed its gates.

William Fitzstephen, who died in 1190, was Becket's clerk and wrote a *Life* of the saint in which he described London at the time:

> London was walled ... and on the north side [has] pastures and a pleasant meadowland, through which flow river streams, where the wheels of mills are put in motion with

A walled city with musicians. (M.B. MS *Luttrell Psalter.* f.164v.)

a cheerful sound. Very near lies a great forest, with wood-land pastures, coverts of wild animals, stags, fallow deer, boars, and wild bulls. The tilled lands of the city are not of barren gravel but fat plains of Asia, that make crops luxuriant.... There are also about London on the north side, excellent suburban springs, with sweet, wholesome, and clear water that flows rippling over the bright stones; among which Holy Well, Clerken, and Saint Clements are held to be the most noted: these are frequented by greater numbers, and visited more by scholars and youth of the city when they go out for fresh air on summer evenings.

In the holidays all the summer the youths are exercised in leaping, dancing, shooting, wrestling, casting the stone, and practicing their shields; the maidens trip in their tim-brels [tambourines], and dance as long as they can see well. In winter, every holiday before dinner, the boars prepared for brawn are set to fight, or else bulls and bears are baited.

When the great fen, or moor, which watereth the walls of the city on the north side, is frozen, many young men play upon the ice; some, striding as wide as they may, do slide swiftly; others make themselves seats of ice, as great as millstones; one sits down, many hand in hand to draw

Men wrestling. (B.M. MS Roy. 2B
VII. f.161v. Queen Mary's Psalter.)

him, and one slipping on a sudden, all fall together; some
tie bones to their feet and under their heels; and shoving
themselves by a little picked staff, do slide swiftly as the
bird flieth in the air, or an arrow out of a cross-bow.
Sometime two run together with poles, and hitting one
the other, either one or both do fall, not without hurt;
some break their arms, some their legs. . . .[2]

Night had fallen when I checked into a third-story room at
the Avalon Hotel, overlooking a grove of trees in a public park.
A lone figure strummed a guitar as he perched atop a bench
near the tallest tree. A car horn sounded, and two cooing pigeons fluttered from my windowsill.

My tiny room, reached by a narrow flight of squeaky wooden
stairs, smelled of freshly ground coffee, which perplexed me
until I discovered that the bag of Guatemalan in my backpack
had spilled. The bathroom was across the hall, but my room
had a washbasin, hot and cold water, and a mirror on the wall.
A television, receiving only three channels, sat atop a table next
to a chest of drawers. Two cups, decorated with hand-painted
red tulips, rested on the table with a porcelain pot and tea bags.
Though as modest as my budget, the room felt cozy, safe, and
warm. The £25 (about $40) for the night included a full break-
fast, one I planned to make good use of before embarking on
my pilgrimage the next morning.

Most medieval pilgrims sought food and shelter in monasteries, where the monks gave freely and, when they obeyed the

Benedictine rule, even washed the travelers' feet. But often there were more pilgrims than there was room, and the pilgrims were forced to sleep outside on the ground or in an inn, where as many as three or four people shared a bed for a penny apiece—a whole day's wages. Such medieval inns were infested with rats and fleas, and innkeepers were notorious for serving spoiled food and cheating their patrons. Robbery was easily committed after putting a pilgrim to sleep with a drugged drink, concocted by mixing equal parts of seed of henbane, darnel, black poppy, and dried bryony root, which were pounded into a powder and added to ale.

The characters in *The Canterbury Tales* gathered in Tabard Inn the night before beginning their pilgrimage, and within minutes of checking into my hotel room, I took a subway to the site of the inn. It was located in Southwark, which was a red-light district in the Middle Ages. Today it is a collection of shops, pubs, and offices.

A real place in the Middle Ages near the foot of London Bridge, Tabard Inn burned centuries ago. Now only a plaque in a stone wall informs passersby of its existence.

Just up the street a sign designating The George pictured a knight in armor on horseback slaying a dragon. The Globe Theatre was only blocks away down by the river, and Shakespeare himself frequented The George, the only pub in the same block where the Tabard Inn once stood.

A cobblestoned alley led me beneath The George sign to a courtyard bustling with more than a hundred people, their ale-drinking tones blowing off workweek steam. Most of the party crowd hoisted glasses over wooden tables, but others appeared happier to stand so their whole bodies could talk.

I eased through courtyard elbows into the pub to get a drink and eyeballed the bartender to see if he was anything like Chaucer's Harry Bailey, the tavern's host in *The Canterbury Tales*.

A seemly man our Hoste was withalle
For to been a marshall in an halle [palace overseer].
A large man he was, with eyen steepe;
A fairer burgeis was there none in Chepe—
Bold of his speech, and wise, and well y-taught
And of manhood him lackede right naught.
Eek thereto he was right a mirry man.... 3

Harry Bailey persuaded the twenty-nine pilgrims to agree to spice up the journey to Canterbury with the twists and turns of stories they told one another. Many real pilgrims had loved to spin whoppers along the road. After all, in that pre–printing press era, storytelling was a chief source of entertainment. Each of Chaucer's pilgrims promised to narrate two tales en route to Becket's shrine and two more while returning to London. Harry Bailey would go with them and judge who told the best story. The winner was to receive a meal in his tavern paid for by the other, less persuasive pilgrims. But since Chaucer never completed his *Tales* (they end when the pilgrims spot Canterbury in the near distance), Bailey never had a chance to pass judgment.

Chaucer adapted many of his tales from stories that had already been written by other authors; "The Clerk's Tale," for example, was taken from a story by Petrarch, but he developed them far beyond the originals, copied by Petrarch's scribe.

The modern-day bartender in The George wasn't anything like the gregarious Harry Bailey. No, he was shy, with manners that said he'd prefer to be home with a good book rather than on the road with a bunch of chatty and competitive pilgrims. The glass of ale he served me, however, didn't disappoint.

In the Middle Ages ale was considered a healthy drink, and it was common for a man to consume a gallon per day. Women who made it in their homes were called "brewsters," "alewives," or "polewives." They already had the needed items in their homes for brewing—ladles, vats, pots, and straining cloths. The brewing process took several steps requiring long waiting periods between them, during which the women could continue with their other household chores. In the first step, barley was soaked for several days before the water was drained off. After the barley germinated, the dried malt was ground and hot water was added. Herbs and yeast were mixed in last. In this pre-preservatives era, the ale had to be consumed within days, before it soured.

When an alewife's creation was ready to be sold, she put a large pole with a brush fastened to it outside her door. The local ale taster, a "conner," was employed by the government to sample the brew to ensure it met certain standards. Many brewsters, however, chanced being fined by not notifying the conner. They sold the ale under the table to their neighbors.

"I'll have another ale," I said to the bartender, who took my glass and soon returned with a full one.

"I overheard you talking to the bartender," said a woman with red hair a few minutes later. "Are you really walking to Canterbury?"

She stood six feet tall, with the longest nose I had ever seen on a man or woman. Yet, somehow, it gave her an exotic beauty. Her head seemed to follow directions from her nose, as if it orchestrated every word that came from her mouth.

"Yes," I said. "I leave from this very block in the morning. It's where Chaucer's pilgrims departed."

"A modern *Canterbury Tales*," she said. "How delicious. Jack must hear this. Jack?" she called to a man at the far end of the bar who wore a gold earring. "Come meet this American. You have things in common."

"In that case," said Jack, as we shook hands, "perhaps I should run."

I liked Jack instantly. In his thirties, he wore a leather jacket. His eyes beamed with curiosity.

"He's walking to Canterbury," said the woman, who announced that her name was Alice.

"Jack is a walker, too," said Alice.

"Don't, Alice," he said.

"But not your typical walker," Alice added.

"Are you a long-distance hiker?" I said.

Alice's trophy nose pointed to Jack, her eyes coaxing him.

"No," said Jack, "I'm not one for testing endurance."

"Oh, come now, Jack," said Alice. "Live a little on a Friday night. Spill the beans."

"Yes," I said, "what kind of walking do you do?"

"It's just a game I play with myself," said Jack.

I couldn't determine if his discretion arose from modesty, embarrassment, or a desire to make me ache a bit to discover how he played his game.

"What's the game?" I said.

He sipped his ale.

"Straight-line walking," he said. "First, I have to be out of London so I have a little room. Then I point myself in one direction, away from the roads and streets, and begin walking in a straight line."

I thought he was pulling my leg but didn't mind in the least.

"The whole purpose of straight-line walking," Jack continued, "is to see where it will take you out of the ordinary. It gives you a whole new perspective sometimes, letting you see the folly of boundaries. I've walked through hedgerows, into clothes hanging on lines, and into a few gardens where I wasn't welcomed."

"Like that cabbage patch," said Alice.

"Yes," said Jack, "I once ended up among cabbages confronted by the farmer who raised them. I tried to explain my game. But he cherished a life of neat little rows, and people of that nature fail to see the beauty of drawing new lines in one's life just to see what will happen. He threatened to have me arrested if I didn't pay him for the cabbage he claimed I stepped on. It was a puny little cabbage at that, had a wormhole and looked more like a brussels sprout. Oh, did he take offense when I told him that. He was the exception, however, because most people I've met have shown tolerance, if not fascination. One lady made me lunch."

"Oh, yes, the pâté," said Alice.

"She stopped me right before I walked through her fish pond," said Jack.

"How'd you invent such a game?" I said, thinking that his story was as odd and whimsical as the tales Chaucer's characters told.

"You've never worked in an office at a routine job," he said, "or you wouldn't have to ask. Straight-line walking is a cure for the nausea of repetition."

I had not stepped on any cabbages in all my years of travel, but I fully identified with Jack's straight-line walking. As everyone should, Jack marched to the beat of his own drummer at the direction of a strong inner compass. His story made me feel more comfortable around him, so I revealed that besides re-creating the pilgrims' journey, I was also on the lookout for miracles.

"Hundreds of miracles were said to have happened at Becket's shrine," said Alice. "Do you think you'll find one there for yourself?"

"I'm not ruling anything out," I said.

"Belief in a miracle sounds more American than British in this day and age," said Jack matter-of-factly.

"Why American?" I said.

"Because in your country," he said, "you still believe in the great American dream. Anybody can become anything if he wants to badly enough. Right? It seems to me that's the equiva-

lent to seeking a Middle Ages miracle. For example, I've watched
the Academy Awards on the telly and seen Oscar winners first
thank God for their statue, or what it represents. They're tickled about the miracle that has just happened. God has blessed
them. But what about all the others who were competing for
the same award, not to mention qualified actors who couldn't
even get work? Does that mean that God was indifferent to
them? Don't misunderstand; I enjoy the entertainment either
way. It's just that personally I don't believe in miracles or God."

I was surprised to learn that Jack was an atheist, and that
pushed me back a few inches. Almost everybody I had met in
America believed, one way or another, in a Higher Power, and I
had come to rely upon that as a common bond with my countrymen, fragile as it sometimes was.

"How does a belief in miracles relate to the American
dream?" I asked.

He sipped his ale.

"As a culture," said Jack, "America is the child of England and
is yet in its youth. It can behave like one as well. On the other
hand, Mother England is quite old. Old and tired, I'm afraid.
We could use a good dose of American vitality."

True, I thought, my country has an energy and ingenuity
that give it indisputable charisma and wealth. Yet a double-
edged sword rode in the sheath of Americana. America can be
an adolescent pumped full of hormones, with more energy and
ego than a true desire for understanding itself or others. How
many generations will it take before a greater sense of humility
becomes a part of the American psyche?

But if England is old and tired, I could not see it in Jack's
impish eyes. His straight-line walking sparked my imagination.
I departed The George questioning whether some of my own
renegade ways were rooted in my British genes as well as the
Cherokee.

*   *   *

Back on the streets, I started walking to my hotel. Big Ben's giant hands told time in the near distance, and Westminster Abbey towered against the night with its heavenly steeples. The Thames reflected moonlight as the tide shifted, just as it had done when Chaucer lived here.

Geoffrey Chaucer, an only child, was born in London between 1340 and 1343. He was fortunate, because most infants died during the Middle Ages. In keeping with the thirteenth-century *De proprietatibus rerum*, written by the Franciscan Friar Bartholomew the Englishman, the newly born Chaucer would have been bathed in a "mixture of ground roses and salt." A finger, dipped in honey, was rubbed against his lips to encourage him to suck. If Chaucer got sick, his wet nurse took medicine—not him. She or Chaucer's mother chewed meat before giving it to the baby. At night he was wrapped in swaddling bands to make certain that his arms and legs grew straight.

Chaucer was born into the emerging merchant class, which at the time had the dignity of belonging to a growing middle class. His mother, Agnes Copton, was a member of the court, and his father, John, owned land and buildings in London, Middlesex, and Suffolk. Just beyond the city wall at Aldgate, he owned more than twenty shops.

Chaucer's father was also a notable winemaker. The business occupied the same grounds as the family home, located in the Vintry Ward on Thames Street. Houses didn't have street addresses in the Middle Ages and were located by landmarks. A stream, the Walbrook, bordered the Chaucer home. Large by the standards of the age, the house had wine cellars and a shop. Behind these a yard kept chickens and ducks, and a garden grew vegetables and herbs.

The herb vervain was sprinkled on the stone floors of the family rooms, located over the shop, because it was believed to promote happiness. Other herbs—like lavender, orris, meadowsweet, Cupid's-dart, costmary, and lemon balm—were also crushed and scattered on the floors because they were aromatic. Kitchen and seasoning plants included winter savory, leek, cardoon, samphire, chive, small-leaved basil, and red valerian. Medicinal herbs were avens, Saint-John's-wort, hollyhock, birthwort, marshmallow, meadow clary, licorice, comfrey, and feverfew. Rituals sometimes accompanied the herbs' harvest. Some were picked only at sunrise, while others were gathered when facing the east.

The inside walls of Chaucer's house were painted or whitewashed and hung with woven wool tapestries, depicting nature, military battles, or religious scenes. The heavy oak furniture was carved. Colorful cushions, often embroidered with heraldic symbols, were sometimes placed in chairs. The beds were grand, canopied with elegant covers, which were closed over and around the beds when family members retired to sleep, to keep them warm as well as for decoration. Fireplaces provided heat, and candles gave light. Servants were on hand to cook, clean house, wash clothes, tend to the garden, and run errands.

Chaucer's mother and father had inherited much of their modest wealth from relatives who had died from the Black Death (also known as the pestilence or the plague), which appeared five times in Chaucer's life over the course of fifty years. Its symptoms were undeniable: First came a boil on the arm or thigh that swelled to the size of an egg or apple within three days. Other boils, as many as twenty or thirty, also erupted from the flesh and would burst to make the victim weep as he shivered and sweated with a fever reaching 104 degrees Fahrenheit. The whole body ached as if it were being crushed in a tightening vise. Depression and internal bleeding were accompanied by the vomiting of blood. Before dying, usually within five torturous days, the sufferer was in agony. His groans could be heard a block away.

Chaucer first observed the Black Death in 1348, when he was between five and eight years old. The putrid smell of the thousands of rotting and burning bodies permeated London, and just beyond Chaucer's window, people collapsed on the street. Thieves who robbed the fallen soon found that they paid the ultimate price for their new riches. They quickly developed symptoms. Almost half of England—1,250,000 people—died in the first outbreak of the pestilence in 1348–1349, and two hundred thousand villages across Europe were destroyed.

England first heard of the Black Death in 1346 through rumors of horrible and strange deaths in the East. Unknown to those in the Middle Ages, the pestilence was caused by *Yersinia pestis*, a bacterium carried by infected fleas, which lived on *Rattus rattus*—a black rat that traveled on ships. The term *Black Death* originated from the blood that erupted from a victim's boils and turned black as it dried. The disease took three forms. The septicemic type infected the bloodstream and killed before the common symptoms appeared. The bubonic type was spread by contact with a victim's sores or bites of infected fleas. The pneumonic type was spread by air via droplets from respiratory infection, coughs, or sneezes.

The pestilence followed the trade routes, especially those dealing with Eastern spices and silk. The Black Death raced across England among a people who were already vulnerable to disease because of malnutrition. It had rained almost daily in the summer and autumn of 1348, and the chief crops of wheat and oats had rotted in the fields.

Paranoia over becoming infected with the Black Death and a lack of knowledge of what caused it swept through London, blazing with all the volatility of human emotions. Brothers and sisters, husbands and wives, stayed many feet apart when they spoke, and relatives often didn't visit one another at all. The pope's physician, Guy de Chauliac, put it this way: "A father did not visit his son, nor his son his father. Charity was dead."[4]

Some mothers who had once longed with all their hearts to give life now saw their nursing babies' lips as potential contaminants and stopped feeding them.

While bonfires of corpses lit the London nights, bells rang out in churches as people fell to their knees to pray. Candles, some as tall as the churches themselves, burned around the clock in hopes of warding off the death. The pope, residing at Avignon in 1348, was so afraid that he sat between two blazing fires, sweating as if the Devil were breathing down his neck.

In the midst of the chaos and fear, a quote by Saint Augustine was often repeated: "Nothing is more certain than death, nothing less so than the hour of its coming."

Some medieval Londoners believed that the death was caused by putrid air, contaminated by astrological forces. Planets were in the wrong positions, or lunar eclipses had frowned on man. In France King Philip VI requested that the medical facility at the University of Paris try to determine what caused the Black Death. The doctors said the conjunction of Saturn, Jupiter, and Mars in the fortieth degree of Aquarius that had occurred on March 20, 1345, helped give birth to the pestilence. Others in England speculated that the earthquake of 1347 had released deadly gases from deep within the earth or from hell itself. Swamp water was suspected, as was manure. Some said lepers or even the English themselves were responsible. Jews were accused of poisoning wells.

People flocked to doctors for advice on preventing the disease. The physicians urged them to avoid contact with the sick or to hold their breath when around them. Other doctors, charging hefty fees, got rich from advice they knew was worthless. In *The Canterbury Tales*, Chaucer reports the deceit and greed of the Physician, who made his riches during the pestilence. Mountain air was considered good. Carrying apples with herbs was recommended, as was ingesting powdered emerald. Mixing white wine with water strengthened the body. So did good

Bloodletting. (B.M. MS Luttrell Psalter. f.61.)

food, massage, and chastity (sex made the body hot and thus vulnerable). Bloodletting by a physician, however, was the most popular weapon against the death because it was believed to rid the flesh of impurities.

Many people's terror drove them to hysteria. Wrote Boccaccio, perhaps the greatest chronicler of the plague, "They maintained that an infallible way of warding off this appalling evil was to drink heavily, enjoy life, sing and gratify cravings whenever the opportunity offered, and shrug the whole thing off as one enormous joke."

Just as Boccaccio wrote *The Decameron*, tales told by nobles who fled Florence for the Italian countryside to escape the Black Death, Chaucer wrote *The Canterbury Tales* to reflect England in an era that was steeped in the inescapable threat of the plague. Just beneath the surface of Chaucer's festive pilgrims lurked death. The Cook in *The Canterbury Tales* had a pus-filled sore on his leg, a reminder that, at any moment, the plague could start anew. Indeed, some of the gaiety and gallows humor among the fictional pilgrims traveling to Canterbury was disguised pain.

Medieval Christians were taught that they should always be ready to pass from this world at any time, but the death—pounding at the door night and day—had turned the abstract into the real. The majority felt that the pestilence was God's punishment for their sins. Penance and prayer were the only true cure and prevention. The surest penance was a pilgrimage to Canterbury.

The Canterbury Tales is Chaucer's most famous literary achievement and was written when he was in his forties. But when he was only twenty years old, he wrote his first important poems—*The Book of the Duchess* and *Legend of Good Women*. He translated *Roman de la Rose*. By the year 1380, he had completed *The House of Fame* and *Parliament of Fowls*. *Troilus and Criseyde* earned Chaucer the reputation of being the "philosophical" poet.

Writers in the Middle Ages didn't usually keep diaries, and Chaucer left only one autobiographical account. On October 15, 1386, he appeared in the Court of Chivalry as a witness for Sir Richard Scrope, in a dispute with Sir Robert Grosvenor over the right to display arms. Stenography didn't exist in the Middle Ages, but a clerk recorded Chaucer's deposition in an abbreviated script. Chaucer gave his age as "forty and upwards," which is the key reference historians use to date Chaucer's birth, 1340–1343.

Q: Did you ever hear any objection or challenge made to the said Richard, or to any of his ancestors, by Sir Robert Grosvenor or by his ancestors or anyone in his name?

A: No. But one time I was in Friday Street in London, and as I was walking along the street I saw hanging outside a brand new sign that had those arms on it, and I asked what household that was that had those arms—of Scrope—hung outside it, and somebody answered me and said, "Oh, no, sir, they're not at all hung out there for the Scrope arms, nor painted there for those arms, but they're painted and hung up there for a knight from the county of Chester, and that man is named Sir Robert Grosvenor." And that was the first time I ever heard of Sir Robert Grosvenor or his ancestors, or anyone having the name Grosvenor.[5]

Chaucer spoke English, Latin, and French. His *Tales* were to be read aloud to listeners who could grasp subtlety, satire, and literary allusions, even though not all the characters en route to Canterbury were educated. Chaucer's storytellers reflected the roles and characters of their time: the Knight, the Squire, the Yeoman, the Prioress, accompanied by a nun and three priests, the Monk, the Friar, the Merchant, the Clerk, the Sergeant of Law, the Franklin, the Haberdasher, the Dyer, the Carpenter, the Weaver, the Carpet Maker, the Cook, the Shipman, the Doctor of Physic, the Wife of Bath, the Parson, the Plowman, the Miller, the Manciple, the Reeve, the Summoner, the Pardoner, and the Host.

Exhausted from the transatlantic flight, I turned down the covers on my bed at the Avalon Hotel and collapsed into the glorious kingdom of sleep.

The next morning I awoke recharged, downed breakfast in record time, slipped into my pack, and started hiking toward Canterbury, sixty miles southeast of London. I planned to sleep in my tent in meadows or woods along the way whenever the fancy struck or lodging wasn't available. I could cook meals by a campfire as I wrote in my journal about the people I met and the stories they told me.

Crossing the Thames into Southwark to the site of Tabard Inn, I took my first step on Pilgrims' Way. Also known as Watling Street in Chaucer's time, it was built during the Roman occupation in the first century A.D. The morning Chaucer's festive pilgrims departed Tabard Inn, Harry Bailey awoke them with the reliability of a restless rooster:

> Amorrwe whan that day began to springe
> Up rose our Host and was our aller cock,
> And gadred us togidre in a flock;
> And forth we ridden . . .

Pilgrims' Way soon led me from London's urban world into the English countryside, dotted with villages and farmhouses. Everyone I met gawked as though each wanted to come along. I suspected that with a forty-pound pack slung on my shoulder, they pictured me as the archetypal traveler, conjuring up thoughts and fantasies about a life of adventure. With each step I felt closer to that place where a journey becomes an odyssey, where beauty and wonder become landmarks as constant as the earth beneath one's feet.

In the Middle Ages this same countryside was spotted with market towns of no more than 150 people, manor houses, churches, and monasteries with fields and patches of woods between the landmarks. Along today's trail boys played cricket as their bats hit against balls like the crack of whips. A man threw a stick for his Irish setter, and a mother pushed twins in a stroller. A postman on a bicycle rang his bell as he passed an elderly man bent over a walking stick.

I waved at some who stared, but all waved back, as through that most ancient language, we entered each other's lives just long enough to remember how quickly things can pass us by. I liked that they seemed to guess what I was doing, where I was going.

The June day was unusually warm for England, and sweat dripped down my face as a red double-decker bus lumbered past. Yellow roses lined the tidy yards of two-story brick houses, some with carved marble faces centered over the doors, so life-like that they seemed to envy my ability to move on.

Rising and falling with grassy meadows and hills, the landscape beyond the village unfolded before me like a colossal and manicured flower garden. Sheep grazed. Rabbits hopped. Ravens squawked atop fence posts. The Thames flowed to the east, and seagulls drifted overhead.

As I hiked onward, the leather medicine pouch in my pocket, gently rubbing against my thigh, reminded me further of my dual heritage. I had made it in 1992, the year my father died. His ancestors were both British and Cherokee. We were exceptionally close, and his loss devastated me for months. On the day my mother and two sisters and I gathered to bury him, I placed a pouch like mine between his weathered carpenter's hands. It contained, among items too sacrilegious to name, some of the peas he was planting in our garden when he collapsed with a heart attack. It also held feathers of a dove, the bird sent from the Spirit World to tell listeners that they are not alone and that they are loved. I hoped that my father's medicine pouch, like my own, would give our souls strength and guidance in our journeys here on earth and beyond the grave. My Indian ancestors believed that some medicine could even empower a person to see spirits and ghosts.

I certainly hadn't spotted anything supernatural on Pilgrims' Way up to that point. But the cobblestoned sidewalk led to a wooded hill only two hundred yards ahead, and something about the tree-lined rise seemed out of the ordinary. The hill seemed to summon me. At first I thought I was simply awed by the beauty of the trees and the shade they could offer from the sun. The promise of a cool rest hastened my steps.

Climbing the hill, I began to feel as if the woods were pulling me. The sensation was so odd that I stopped walking with the hope that stillness would become a door to understanding.

I wasn't sure what to make of the feeling but started walking again feeling even more intrigued. By the time I reached the summit, my lungs were burning, but my anticipation out-weighed the pain.

I discovered a trail, only a foot wide, leading from the side-walk into the trees. Golden sunlight bathed the path for fifteen feet before it vanished over a bank into shadows. I wondered if following it would invade private property, but I saw no KEEP OUT signs, and intuition urged me forward.

The footpath led into a world vastly different from the one I had left in London that morning. Though I could still hear cars and trucks buzzing down London Road, I no longer saw them as I walked deeper into the woods.

Vines wrapped around trees, and ferns three feet tall grew here and there as if I had stepped into a prehistoric kingdom. I smelled the moist earth, centuries of decayed vegetation. Crick-ets chirped. A lone frog, hidden among the green, croaked.

Then the leaves of a huge oak rustled. It had fallen with such force that it had knocked the top off a smaller tree. Its roots had pulled out of the ground and now dangled in the air like black snakes.

Saddened that something so majestic had been downed by a storm, I walked slowly toward it, stepping more gently than be-fore, as if entering some ancient holy passageway into the earth's secrets. I placed my nose to a crack in the giant fallen trunk and inhaled a sweet and sour exotic scent.

I propped my pack against the trunk and sat on the ground ten feet away. A fern spread over my head, and the entire woods seemed like a shelter where I could hide from the world to find my most treasured memories or discover new thoughts. A breeze that rustled through the leaves seemed to whisper even more than sanctuary. I felt on the threshold of something extraordinary.

Ten minutes after sitting near the fallen tree, I still couldn't shake the feeling that I was on the threshold of something important. At the very least, the woods offered a sense of home, a refuge from the scorching sun, and a good place to cook lunch. Hiding my pack in thick vines, I walked back toward a small grocery store I had passed earlier.

My body was so relieved to be shed of the heavy pack that I found myself whistling. When I encountered a man on the sidewalk, he eyed me like an oddity. Seconds later, however, he began to whistle as well. We turned the air into music.

Nearing the grocery store, I beheld London in the great distance. Buildings that had towered over me that morning seemed now mere chess pieces.

The city disappeared behind trees as I neared the bottom of the hill and approached a small grocery store surrounded by houses. Across the street stood a church, and a white wooden cross, ten feet tall, rose from the grassy lawn. A crow squawked atop the roof and lifted its wings each time it called out.

I entered the store, and a plump man just ahead of me loaded his basket with frozen TV dinners. When he answered his ringing cell phone, he leaned against the freezer. His huge stomach shook as he laughed. Squeezing past him down the narrow aisle, I eyed lamb, pork, and beef in the glass-covered cooler. They, like the phone and the microwave oven that sat atop a sandwich counter, offered a sharp contrast to the mindset of the Middle Ages, which I was carrying around with me on my pilgrimage. Back then wood-burning fires cooked all meals, and meat hung in open-air markets surrounded by buzzing flies. Dogs and cats licked blood that dripped to the ground. Only feet away, in the same bustling thoroughfare, a man could have an aching tooth pulled by a butcher with a pair of pliers, while strapped in a chair with ropes to help him endure the pain.

A box of plastic forks on a shelf reminded me that most medieval folks ate with their hands or used a knife. If they dropped the leg of a roasted swan, dipped in mustard, or the breast of a

heron on the rat-tracked floor, they had only to make the sign
of the cross to cleanse it.

Sturgeon and whale were considered to be "royal fish," fit for
kings and queens. "Puddyng of purpaysse" was made by stuffing
a porpoise with its own blood and grease combined with oat-
meal, salt, pepper, and ginger. The fish was then boiled in water
and afterward placed in a broiler till it became crisp on the outside. "Gaylyntyne" was a sauce made with galingale (a spice
from the roots of the cypress tree), white bread crumbs, cinnamon, ginger, salt, and vinegar, poured over meat, poultry, or
fish. Flowers were picked fresh from the garden and sprinkled
on a cherry pudding called "chireseye."

While the poor drank ale, the rich preferred wine, which was
brought from English-ruled Bordeaux. But the wine had to be
consumed young because thirteenth-century winemakers had
no effective technique for corking bottles. Wine older than a
year was undrinkable. Peter of Blois wrote of wine he tasted at
Henry II's court: "The wine is turned sour or mouldy-thick,
greasy, stale, flat and smacking of pitch. I have sometimes seen
even great lords with wine so muddy that a man must needs
close his eyes and clench his teeth, wry-mouthed and shudder-
ing, and filtering the stuff rather than drinking."

I placed a can of ale in my shopping bag and added a head of
garlic, a chicken breast, a small bag of rice, and an apple. I had
to wait in the checkout line for several minutes but didn't mind,
since I spent the time studying the English money, which was
so new and exotic to me.

In the Middle Ages each town had its own mint, which made
silver pennies as thin as communion wafers. Any minter who
cheated on the amount of silver he put in each coin ran the risk
of severe punishment, as stated in the laws of Edward the Elder in the Coinage Regulations: "14. Thirdly, that there be one
money over all the king's dominion, and that no man mint

except within port. And if the moneyer be guilty, let the hand be struck off with which he wrought that odense, and be set up on [nailed to] the money-smithy; but if it be an accusation, and he is willing to clear himself, then let him go to the hotiron, and clear the hand therewith with which he is charged to have wrought that fraud. And if that ordeal should be guilty, let the like be done as is here ordained."

I left the store, climbed the hill, and pulled my pack from the vines. I gathered dry sticks, built a tiny fire within a circle of stones, pulled two lightweight pots from my gear, and soon had lunch cooking.

I had not cooked over an open fire the past year, and doing so now seemed to awaken a dormant part of myself. The fire's popping and crackling were the thumps of a drum and the jingles of a tambourine. It was the music of the journey that stretched before me, and I started to feel a freedom that only the open road can give.

I unzipped a pocket in my pack and removed a porcelain urn, as small as a saltshaker, which had come to America in the late 1700s when my British kin arrived. Hand-painted, it pictured a boy and girl somersaulting down a golden field while their parents sat on the ground having a picnic. At special spots along my walk, like this very place where I now cooked a musical meal, I planned to gather ancestral soil and place it in the tiny vessel. When I returned home, I would bury it near my cottage under the oak with the items people had given me along the Trail of Tears. The urn's contents would be homage to my English pilgrimage. I had already gathered my first thimbleful of soil outside Westminster Abbey in London because Chaucer was buried there in 1400, establishing Poets' Corner.

When a bird called out, I raised my eyes from the soil I had just now added to the urn and spotted a magpie, black and

Catching bees. (B.M. Stowe 17. f.148.)

white as a zebra, sitting on a limb over a meadow that bordered the woods. The field was brilliant with red poppies swaying in the wind.

Dozens of honeybees buzzed from poppy to poppy. Honey was the chief sweetener in early medieval England, since sugar had not yet entered the country. It was so prized that taxes could be paid with it. If a swarm of honeybees landed in the thatched roof of a Christian, he tried to convince it to stay with a prayer:

Sit down, sit down, bee!
St. Mary commanded thee!
Thou shalt not have leave,
Thou shalt not fly to the wood.
Thou shalt not escape me,
Nor go away from me.
Sit very still,
Wait God's will![6]

Beeswax made the best candles, and a wealthy household often burned one hundred pounds of wax nightly. The wax was also used as a healing balm for burns and cuts. Pagans were not to be outdone by Christians when it came to charming such a treasured commodity as the honeybee. As they threw grit over a swarm of bees, they spoke their spell:

Stay, victorious women, sink to the earth!
Never fly wild to the wood.
Be as mindful of my good
As each man is of food and home.[7]

"Busy as a bee" was first recorded by Chaucer in the *Tales*: "For aye as busy as bees been they." The buzzing of bees over the poppy field was broken by the sound of voices and rattling metal. Three boys on bicycles rolled down the footpath in the woods.

"Look," one of them called out. "Someone built a fire."

They slammed on their brakes.

"They're cooking their lunch," said another.

"I know garlic when I smell it," said the third boy. "I'd rather eat burned rubber."

They spotted me when I started toward them. Only one waved back.

"I'm from America." I said, hoping to reassure them. "On a pilgrimage to Canterbury."

"By foot?" said the one who found the garlic disgusting. "Canterbury is almost all the way to the ocean. Don't you have a car?"

"Back in the United States," I said.

"Can't you rent one here?" asked the second boy.

"You don't understand," said the only boy who had returned my wave. "A pilgrim can't ride. He must suffer. Isn't that right, sir?"

His eyes were so intelligent and intense that they made me wonder just how much the boy knew about suffering. Children

during the pestilence were afraid to even look into one another's eyes for fear of catching the death.

"My feet have hurt a little today," I finally said, "but I like to
walk."

"I suffer going to school," said the garlic critic.

"My sister makes me suffer," said the other boy who hadn't
waved.

"If I don't get this milk home to my mum," announced the
garlic critic, "it'll be worse than school and your sister put
together."

He pedaled down the footpath followed by his friend. But
the one who had waved didn't budge. He eyed my hat as if he
wanted to know its secrets.

I took it from my head and held it out so he could better see
it. "A friend gave it to me fifteen years ago."

"I wasn't born then," said the boy. "My parents hadn't even
met."

I eased the hat closer to him, encouraging him to take it. He
finally gripped it as his eyes widened at the snake rattle.

"The rattlesnake once saved the Cherokee from being cooked
by the sun," I said.

He stared at the rattle as though it were now alive. "How?"
he asked.

"It threatened to bite the sun if it didn't go higher into the
sky," I said.

He looked hungry to know more.

"If a Cherokee killed one rattlesnake," I continued, "he might
be forgiven. But if he killed another, hundreds of snakes would
chase him until he lost his mind."

Fear flickered in the boy's eyes. "We don't have rattlesnakes
in England. I don't think we do. What are all these feathers?"

I told him how the dove was sent from the Spirit World and
that the blue jay was the bird of good luck.

"A good-luck bird," he said, more to himself than to me. Lost in wonder, he appeared tempted to touch the feathers as if he wished good luck would rub off on him.

"What's your name?" I asked.

"Allen, sir," he said, as he returned my hat with his eyes still on the feathers. "What's yours?"

Answering him, I placed the hat on my head. He studied my backpack before turning to the flames that cooked my meal. "I wish I could walk wherever I wanted to," he said, eyeing the fire as if he wanted to add a stick and make it blaze higher.

"Why?"

"It looks like fun," he said. "Jesus walked wherever he went. I think he did. If he got too tired, I guess his disciples carried him. They were good mates. My father says Jesus was just a magician, but my mum says he was the Son of God."

"What do you think?" I asked, intrigued that he thought about such complex things.

"I don't like it when my parents argue," he said.

"But I mean about Jesus?"

"A magician couldn't heal people," he said.

Children in the Middle Ages were taught as modern Christian children are. They all heard about the love and kindness of Jesus. His teaching that children are special has comforted them for two thousand years.

But the medieval church was filled with hypocrisy, becoming rich and powerful on the backs of the poor it professed to love. It sponsored the Crusades in the East, killing thousands of Christians and non-Christians in the name of God, and practiced the kind of persecution of native peoples that it would later bring to the West.

Still, a part of me never stopped wanting to believe that people could love one another as Jesus said we should and looking for a real miracle worker walking the face of the earth today.

"Do you believe in miracles?" I asked the boy on the bike.

Straddling his seat, he studied me as if he didn't have the slightest doubt. "You and I are miracles, aren't we?"

He spoke with such strong conviction that goose bumps covered my arms.

"I have to go home now," the boy said. "I hope you have a good walk, sir."

He started to pedal away.

"Wait," I said.

He stopped. I removed my hat and pulled one of the three blue jay feathers from the band.

"The good-luck bird," he said, as his eyes got big.

I gave him the blue feather, and his smile was so genuine that it made me feel I was the one in luck, having been pulled in by this cathedral of woods to meet this boy.

The bike rattled as he vanished down the trail, and I hoped the feather would lift him as high as me.

I ate lunch, extinguished the fire, slipped into my pack, and started down the footpath past the fallen tree toward Canterbury. The magical forest path offered me a sense of home, but the pilgrims had feared the woods and traveled as groups for protection. Medieval forests teemed with packs of wild dogs, boars, and wolves as well as an assortment of criminals. They planned their crimes in taverns and retreated in times of danger to their wooded hideouts, where womenfolk, both "morts" (married) and "doxies" (unmarried), gave them food, drink, and sex.

Criminal names reflected their questionable talents. "Demanders for Glimmer," mostly females, held out their hands swearing losses from fires. "Freshwater Mariners" claimed to be victims of shipwrecks. "Abram Men" begged, pretending madness. "Dumbers" acted dumb. All were thieves, but "Hookers" (sometimes called "Anglers") were less subtle. They carried long sticks with hooked wire ends to snatch shirts, pants, and bedclothes from open windows.

A Letter-Book of Henry IV, dated 1412, recorded the punishment of a false pilgrim:

On the 20th day of July, in the 13th year, William Blake-
ney, shetilmaker [shuttlemaker], who pretended to be an
hermit, was brought unto the Guildhall, before Robert
Chichele, Mayor, the Aldermen, and Sheriffs, for that,
whereas he was able to work for food and raiment, he, the
same William, went about there, barefooted and with
long hair, under the guise of sanctity, and pretended to be
an hermit, saying that he was such, and that he had made
pilgrimage to Jerusalem, Rome, Venice, and the city of
Seville, in Spain; and under colour of such falsehood had
received many good things from divers persons, to the defrauding, and in manifest deceit, of all people.

And he was asked how he would acquit himself thereof.
Whereupon, he acknowledged that for the last six years
he had lived by such lies, falsities, and deceits, so invented
by him, to defrauding of the people, under the colour of
such feigned sanctity, and that he never was in the parts
aforesaid; which was also found out by the Court. And
therefore, it was judged that the said William should be
put upon the pillory for three market-days; and he was to
have, in the meantime, whetstone hung from his neck.
And precept was given to the Sheriffs to do execution
thereof.[1]

Out of the woods, I descended the hill where I had cooked
lunch and followed the trail leading back to the sidewalk along
London Road, which was buzzing with cars and trucks. Though
I preferred to walk a footpath through woods and meadows, I
found myself enjoying the sidewalk almost as much, now that I
felt the journey was really getting under way. I spoke to everyone I met, and each returned my greeting as if it was the most
natural thing in the world. It finally dawned upon me that they
did so, at least in part, because I was smiling, not only at them

but at myself as well. My armor was falling to the wayside. That innermost door we so often keep locked was starting to open.

With each step forward, I began to feel a bond with the landscape. Rolling green meadows dotted with farmhouses, as far as the eye could see, seemed to become part of me. The smell of freshly cut hay drifted in the breeze, and an apple orchard hung heavy with fruit. A tiny stream, rippling with minnows, sang an ancient misty song.

Stone walls three feet high were not mere fences to mark property boundaries and hold in horses and sheep. They were the blood, sweat, and tears of the medieval men and women who had made them and who rarely lived beyond their forties or fifties.

Like the soil itself, the rocks in the walls glinted with pieces of flint—some as big as cantaloupes. When the sunlight caught them, they glowed like darkened amber, as if some form of life within longed to surface. I knelt by one such wall and placed my fingertips to the flint just as the fence builder had done when he placed the stone. It was a fragile connection, but in that moment on my first day's walk, it seemed like a kind of lifeline to my British ancestors through the most common denominator—the earth itself.

I slipped from my pack and sat in the wheat field just beyond the wall. I was tired, and the rest was refreshing and allowed me to envision those who raised wheat here in the Middle Ages. Bread was the staple of life then, and a cake—made from wheat—was planted in the soil each spring along with the sown grains as a pagan prayer for a good crop. In 601 Pope Gregory the Great—founder of the Gregorian chant—wrote a letter of instructions to the missionaries in England concerning such pagan rituals:

And because they [new Christians] have been used to slaughter many oxen in the sacrifices to devils, some solem-

nity must be substituted for them on this account, as, for
instance, that on the day of the dedication, or of the na-
tivities of the holy martyrs whose relics are there deposited, that they may build themselves huts of the boughs
of trees about those churches which have been turned to
that use from temples, and celebrate the solemnity with
religious feasting, no more offering beasts to the devil, but
killing cattle to the praise of God in their eating, and returning thanks to the Giver of all things for their suste-
nance; to the end that, whilst some outward gratifications
are permitted them, they may the more easily consent to
the inward consolations of the grace of God. . . . For there
is little doubt that it is impossible to efface every thing at
once from their obdurate minds because he who endeav-
ors to ascend to the highest place rises by degrees or steps
and not by leaps.[2]

July was the hungry month. Last year's crop was gone, and
the new one was not yet ripe. When this happened, farmers
ground acorns, beans, and peas into flour or searched the woods
for beechnuts, which were usually considered pig food. But
any kind of meal was better than nothing to a people whose
seventh-century ancestors had experienced such a severe famine
that some—in groups as large as fifty—committed suicide by
gripping hands and jumping from a cliff so high that their
bones shattered on impact.

The church had convinced some that lack of food could
bring them closer to God, that fasting cleansed the body as well
as the soul. The tradition of Lent called for forty days of fasting ending at Easter, a time when most pilgrims—including
Chaucer's fictional ones—traveled to Canterbury.

A strong wind blew the two-foot-high wheat all around me,
and I was reminded that the pre-Christian British had viewed
this new religion and its traditions, such as Lent, with great

suspicion. When, in A.D. 597, King Ethelbert of Kent received the first priests, Augustine and forty companions sent by Gregory the Great, he demanded that they meet outside, wanting the wind to blow away any spells they might try to cast on him. Bede wrote of this event:

> Some days later the king came into the island and, sitting in the open air, ordered Augustine and his companions to be brought into his presence. For he had taken precaution that they should not come to him in any house, lest, according to an ancient superstition, if they practiced any magical arts they might impose upon him, and so get the better of him. But they came furnished with divine, not with magic, power, bearing a silver cross for their banner, and the image of our Lord and Saviour painted on a board; and singing the litany, they offered up their prayers to the Lord for eternal salvation both for themselves and of those to whom they came.[3]

Retrieving my pack, I gave one last nod to the stone wall before moving on. A hawk, circling overhead, seemed to follow me. Its short, shrill sounds floated through the breeze like the notes of an agitated flute. When the bird dived toward tall weeds, it took my breath. Seconds later its wings flapped as the hawk soared skyward with a baby rabbit dangling from its claws. In the Middle Ages, pet falcons were so prized that their masters often took them to church, where the birds sat upon their shoulders. Anyone caught stealing hawk eggs could be fined or sent to prison.

The smell of fish-and-chips made me lick my lips as Pilgrims' Way led from the countryside into the town of Shooter's Hill, where I discovered two men playing a version of bull and ring in the backyard of a two-story house, covered with ivy. Played in pubs in Chaucer's world, the game's aim was to swing

*Horseman with hawk. (B.M. MS.
Lutrell Psalter. f.159.)*

a metal ring, which hung from a rope attached to the ceiling, onto a hook on the wall. A bull's horn, used for the hook, was embedded in the nose of a bull's head hung on the wall. Sometimes other animals, like boars or stags, were used.

The two men playing bull and ring in the backyard had fastened a rope to a tree limb. Their hook, embedded in the trunk, was a railroad spike a foot long.

"You'll have to do better than that to beat me," said one, as the other's ring hit the side of the tree.

"*Aha*," said the underdog, "so you want me to play with my eyes open?"

Aha was first recorded in *The Canterbury Tales*, and William Safire, in his February 17, 1997, column "On Language" in *The New York Times Magazine*, called this expression "one of the great, unappreciated and deliciously nuanced words in the English language."

The metal ring dinged against the spike as I walked on and

soon spotted a theater poster on the side of a video store next
to an Internet café. It advertised a play in London and pictured
a man and woman naked in bed. Theater in the Middle Ages
focused on miracle plays. Jesus was resurrected from the tomb
and lifted to clouds in the ceiling by weights and pulleys. Devils
and angels leaped from trapdoors. Noah's flood flowed over
characters from overturned casks of water backstage. Thunder
boomed from barrels of stone turned by cranks. Audiences
squirmed and yelled when John the Baptist was decapitated.
Ox blood gushed from a fake corpse's head.

The plays were produced by guilds that moved from town to
town, staged on wheeled platforms. They attracted knights and
ladies as well as peasants, monks, and students. Criers announced
performances a day in advance. Though the play's theme was always religious, it reflected the harsh realism of medieval life.
An actor portraying Jesus often stayed on the cross for hours as
he moaned and recited verses. Masks, horns, and forked tails
designated devils, whose body suits were covered with horse-
hair, and they sometimes jumped into the audience to pinch
and bite onlookers.

A block beyond the theater poster, I passed a man at the street
corner playing a guitar for tips. He sang "Imagine," by John
Lennon, and I dropped a coin into his hat. His self-employment
sprang from an old tradition. Medieval minstrels performed for
the court, but others—called "gestours of disours"—scraped together a living on the streets. Stories, poems, and gestures accompanied their music.

A man wearing a black tie sat on a bench near the guitar
player and worked a crossword puzzle in the newspaper. He
looked as challenged by the pastime as those who liked to solve
riddles in Chaucer's world. Hiking on through the town and
back into the countryside, I entertained myself by recalling some
of those same riddles.

A moth ate a word. To me it seemed, A marvelous thing
     when I learned the wonder
That a worm had swallowed, in darkness stolen, The song
     of man, his glorious
Sayings, a great man's strength; and the thieving guest, Was
     no whit wiser for the
Words it ate.

The answer, a bookworm, always made me grin. But the answer to the next one was a little slimy. I recited the riddle as I
approached a farmhouse where a dog, in the front yard, wagged
his tail.

My house is not quiet, I am not loud; But for us God
     fashioned our fate together.
I am the swifter, at times the stronger, My house more
     enduring, longer to last.
At times I rest; my dwelling still runs; Within it I lodge as
     long as I live.
Should we two be severed, my death is sure.

The dog gave the oddest look when I told him the answer to
the riddle was a fish. But his tail kept wagging as I hiked out of
sight and down a hill to recite aloud a third riddle, which had
survived from the eleventh century in the Exeter Book:

I am a strange creature, for I satisfy women . . .
I grow very tall, erect in bed,
I'm hairy underneath. From time to time
A beautiful girl, the brave daughter
Of some fellow dares to hold me
Grips my reddish skin, robs me of my head
And puts me in the pantry. At once that girl

With plaited hair who has confined me
Remembers our meeting. Her eye moistens.[4]

The answer, an onion, wasn't what moistened my own eyes by the time I reached the town of Besleyheath. Windblown rain pounded my face. Night was only an hour away, and I planned to spend the night in a B and B. But the two I found were both full. The owner of the second one suggested I try the Swallow Hotel.

I pushed on with my head lowered against the cool, wet wind. The streets were black with umbrellas as a bobbie blew his whistle, motioning a car to hurry on. Two teenagers with red hair and pierced lips leaned against a doorway. One smoked a cigarette. The other, with a silver chain around his boot, puffed a cigar. Pigeons cooed on the ledge overhead.

Entering the Swallow Hotel, I felt welcomed by the warm lobby. The smell of freshly baked bread drifted from the restaurant, and my mouth started to water.

I should have realized something was wrong, however, when the hotel clerk frowned.

"I'm sorry," she said, "but a bus full of Scots just checked in to take the last rooms."

A drop of water fell from my hat.

"I wish there was something I could do," she said. "You really look tired. Why don't you have a seat in the lobby and rest awhile. The food here is rather tasty."

I took a seat and fished my map from my backpack. It was several miles to the next town, and even if I walked there, I couldn't be sure I'd find a vacancy.

"Walking, are you?" a voice said, with a Scottish accent.

I raised my head from the map to behold a man in his early seventies, his face as full and whimsical as that of W. C. Fields. Just looking at his face made me feel I had found some shelter from the rain.

"Yes," I answered the man, who said his name was Frank. "I'm walking to Canterbury."

He wore a suit with medals pinned to the jacket. They made me think of badges made of lead, bought as souvenirs by Becket shrine seekers. They pinned them to their floppy hats and clothes to prove they had traveled to Canterbury. Entrepreneurs, producing and selling the badges, adapted the idea from earlier kinsmen who had gone on pilgrimages to Santiago de Compostela, in Spain. There they gathered scallop shells and sewed them to their hats.

The scallop shell symbol arose from the Golden Legend. One version of the story (*Leyenda de oro*) was recorded by Jacobus de Voragine in 1228. The apostle James had traveled in Spain to convert others to Christianity. When he sailed home to Judea, he was beheaded by Herod for preaching that Jesus was the Son of God. The saint's disciples placed him on a boat without a rudder, and it miraculously survived the sea to land on the shore of Galicia, in Spain. The disciples beheld a man dressed as a bridegroom riding a horse, which raced into the waves and vanished. They assumed both died. But they soon rose from the ocean's depth, scallop shells dangling from them. In another version of the myth, a bride saw her love and his horse sink into the sea. When she called on the power of Saint James, the bridegroom emerged alive with the shells hanging from his clothes.

The body of Saint James was brought ashore and placed on a stone, which softened to become a sarcophagus around the body. The disciples asked Lupa, a local queen, to welcome the saint. She sent them to the king of Spain, who—as she had hoped—put them in jail. In the night angels released them. The king repented, and the disciples converted his whole city to Christianity.

When the disciples returned to Lupa, she offered them oxen to carry the body of the saint into the mountains to a tomb. She thought they would destroy the disciples. But when they made the sign of the cross over the animals, they became as gentle as lambs. Encountering a dragon, they killed it with the same sign.

Dante called the Milky Way the "Way of Saint James." Folklore said that the Milky Way stars were the souls of dead pilgrims en route to their destination. A shooting star was a pilgrim who had slipped from the path. When this happened, someone on earth was obligated to quickly say, "Dios te guía [God guide you]."

"I'm just now returning from a pilgrimage of my own," said Frank. His wondrous musical dialect performed magic on my ears, sounding of bagpipes on the heather-covered highlands of Scotland.

"Where have you been?" I asked, removing my wet hat to place it atop my backpack on the floor.

"Normandy," said Frank.

Two more men about Frank's age appeared in the lobby, both wearing suits adorned with medals. One with gray hair rode in an electric wheelchair.

"Come say hello," said Frank. His voice resonated through the whole lobby as he explained my mission.

"Aye," said the one who called himself George. He sat on the couch to sandwich me between him and Frank. "We make our trip every year and sell raffle tickets to pay for the ride."

"I never fired a shot myself in the war," said Frank. "I was a builder, but George was in the thick of it."

"Aye," said George, "the first regiments hit the beach at seven, and mine was licking the seawater at seven forty-five. The sand was soaked with blood, bodies everywhere."

George's eyes reflected such kindness that it was difficult to imagine that he had once been a fierce fighter. In the Middle Ages the most honored soldier was the knight. Originally the word meant anyone who fought or was a farmworker of free birth. But the knight became known as a professional soldier with extraordinary powers. His plate armor weighed fifty-five

Knights jousting. (B.M. MS. Roy. 10. E. IV. f.65v.)

pounds, and his lance was eighteen feet long. He could lose an arm or his head with a single blow from a battle-ax. In the fourteenth century, the biographer of Don Pero Nino wrote of knights: "They expose themselves to every peril; they give their bodies to the adventure of life in death. Moldy bread or biscuit, meat cooked or uncooked; today enough to eat and tomorrow nothing, little or no wine, water from a pond or a butt, bad quarters, the shelter of a tent or branches, a bad bed, poor sleep with their armor still on their backs, burdened with iron. . . ."

Chivalry was the knight's pledged word to a duke, an earl, a count, a baron, or a marquis, and the great emphasis put on it came from a time when the only form of government was the pledge between lord and vassal. Christian knights believed in the theory that all of them were brothers. If a knight broke his oath, he was charged with treason.

In exchange for the knight's services as a prized soldier, he was granted land, falcons, weapons, and horses. The battle horse, a "dexterarius," was the knight's most important possession, and from it comes the expression "to mount one's high horse." The word *champion* comes from the field (*campus* in Latin) where knights defended their honor, and what American hasn't eaten the Breakfast of Champions?

When a knight was not hunting or fighting or being entertained by dice, chess, backgammon, songs, dances, and pageants, he thrived on jousting tournaments. They could last an entire week and drew throngs of spectators, including prostitutes, food vendors, wealthy merchants, artisans, and members of the court.

Because of the violence and glory in the sport, the Dominicans denounced it. Knights were often killed during tournaments, and the church considered this the sin of suicide. But their judgments fell on deaf ears. Even the threat of excommunication didn't stop the sport. Audiences craved the excitement as much as the knights. Flags and ribbons fluttered. Trumpets blew. Nobles, who had bankrolled the knights, placed bets. Pickpockets, working the crowd, rejoiced.

Knights who had fallen from grace sometimes beat their armor into chains, which they wore around their necks and wrists to show just how low they had sunk from the heights of chivalry. To redeem themselves, they went on pilgrimages.

Though George had fought at Normandy and probably killed several men, his eyes—as he sat next to me—didn't suggest that his pilgrimage back to that once bloody beach had been one that sought redemption. They spoke of a man who believed in ideals, just like the Knight in *The Canterbury Tales*.

A KNIGHT there was—and that a worthy man—
That fro the time that he first began
To riden out [go on knightly expeditions], he loved
    chivalrye,
Trouth and honour, freedom and curteisye.
Full worthy was he in his lordes were [war],
And thereto had he riden, no man feere [farther]. . . .

"Ours hasn't been a pilgrimage of sorrow," Frank told me.

"Not with Frank Atkinson on the bus," said George, as he nudged me with his elbow.

"Oh, you got to laugh at life," said Frank, as he, too, nudged me with his elbow, as if competing with George. "See where I skinned my nose?"

He pointed to a scab on its tip.

"That's where the ground jumped up to kiss me one night," Frank continued.

"Aye," said George, "the ground has poor vision in the dark, for who would kiss the likes of an Atkinson otherwise."

Both old men nudged me with grandfatherly elbows. For a moment I thought I beheld them when they were as young as the boy who had received the good-luck feather. In that rare moment I realized with new clarity that I was right in the middle of life's journey, and that filled me with a subtle and private joy that made me thankful just to sit for a while feeling the touch of the elders. My regard for their age was respect for my generation in the years to come.

But I became puzzled when Frank reached into his pocket. He pulled forth a magnifying glass.

"Anytime someone in our group asks how my sexy nose is faring," said Frank, "I just tell him to take a good look for himself." He hurried the magnifying glass over his scab, and it enlarged into a scaly red monster. "Oh," Frank added, "the ground is a powerful kisser."

All three men laughed with such abandonment that it lifted me higher into my heart.

"That day on the beach in Normandy," said George, when the laughter died, "I thought I would be killed, with so many in my regiment falling all around me. But when I got to Holland and only two of the thirty-five in my group had survived the battle, I somehow knew that I would make it through the whole war."

George's voice was tender, as if battle had taught him just how fragile human beings can be. His eyes again brought to mind Chaucer's Knight.

And though that he were worthy, he was wis,
And of his port [bearing] as meek as is a maide.

He never yet no villainy ne saide
In all his life unto no manner wight [was never rude].
He was a veray, parfit gentil knight.

"Holland is where I got shot," said Ernest, who sat in the wheelchair. "I was nineteen when I lost the use of my legs."

"He walked on sticks till a few months ago," said Frank. "Now we can't turn our backs to him."

"Aye," said George, nudging me again. "He's become a regular speed demon in that hot rod of his."

The lobby began to fill with Scots wearing medals as they made their way into the dining room.

"I never knew Frank Atkinson not to be first at a table of food," said a plump Scot.

Frank held up his magnifying glass. "I'll be keeping a close eye on you at dinner," he said, "just to make sure you don't get more than your share."

As the festive Scots marched to the evening feast and I studied Frank's fun-loving grin, I began to better appreciate the depth and complexity of their pilgrimage to Normandy. They were returning from the site of the greatest horrors of their lives, and yet they, like Chaucer's pilgrims in the shadow of the Black Death, were able to turn the journey into a celebration of life.

I suspected, however, that if I knew the Scots better—on a deeper level—I would have uncovered greater sorrow from the war peeking from their hearts. In the aftermath of the Black Death, some British, as well as other Europeans, channeled their grief and shock into art, embracing the comic and the satirical: paintings depicted dancing skeletons, shrouded in black, as they beat drums, inviting all to join the ultimate party. This festive imagery, embracing death as part of life lived to its fullest, is rampant in the modern-day costumed merrymakers at Mardi

Gras, which ends the day before Lent begins, and in the Day of the Dead, celebrated in Mexico.

"Join us for a bite, lad," said George, as he nudged me one last time before rising to head for the restaurant.

Ernest rolled his wheelchair beside George, and I was surprised to find Frank still seated with the magnifying glass in his hand. "I never fired a shot in the war," he said, after everyone had disappeared into the dining room. "I was a builder."

I wasn't sure if he had forgotten that he had already told me this or if he repeated himself in an attempt to say more between the lines.

"A builder is as important as a fighter," I said.

He gave me a searching look and finally nodded. "Our group is getting smaller every trip. A few more years and we'll be just a few hairs on a dog's back. We lost Jimmy back in the spring. He was a good one, knew how to laugh at himself." Frank seemed to see his friend somewhere in the great distance.

"I've had a few friends die," I said. "Sometimes they say hello in my thoughts when I least expect it."

He raised his elbow, and I assumed he aimed to poke me again. But he placed his hand on my back. "Aye," he said, "you understand."

When the sadness eased from his eyes and he lowered his hand from my back, he got that funny look, as if he were about to raise the magnifying glass again. "I kept a little secret from the others," said Frank, "until Jimmy was being lowered into the ground. I had arranged for a trumpet player to hide behind a tree on the hill over the cemetery, and when I raised my hand, he began to play. Oh, it was sweet to watch everybody hear music as Jimmy went his way."

With night falling, I needed to go on my way as well and left the hotel to hike to the outskirts of town. With no certain room in the next town, I sought a place to pitch my tent, with thoughts of the Scots and especially Frank following me, the trumpet yet playing on that cemetery hill. I could even feel Frank's hand on my back and George's nudging-Knight elbow in my ribs.

I had walked more than fifteen miles that day up and down steep hills with a heavy pack, and my body was exhausted. I was relieved to find a spot that was ideal to pitch my tent, a giant wheat field with an oak standing in one corner far from a farmhouse. The field looked so much like the one where I had sat earlier in the day that I felt a kind of bond with tonight's wheat. It seemed to be waiting for me, to offer me a helping hand.

The lone tree looked much like the one near my cottage back home where I had buried the items given to me on the Trail of Tears. I had stood there the morning before I packed for my flight to London. I held the tiny urn and wondered what would happen before it was filled. England at that moment had seemed so far away.

But now, only forty-eight hours later, the bottom of the urn was covered with earth and a pebble, awaiting company. I was completing my first day's walk, my bridge to the journey that stretched before me.

I unzipped my pack and pulled forth my nylon tent as a dog barked from the farmhouse. A single light burned in an upstairs room, and a shadowy figure appeared at the window for several seconds before fading away.

My tent was green and blended well with the lush wheat as I drove its metal stakes into the earth beneath the tree. It had stopped raining, and in the great distance I beheld the Thames in the moonlight. With the heavens brilliant overhead, it was easy to imagine that I was living back when the Christians walked to Canterbury.

Those thoughts made me recall the stones in the sacred site

behind my home. I had no doubt that the Indians living during what is now called the Middle Ages had placed the stones in the shape of the Little Dipper as a means of reaching out to God. At the same time, pilgrims, my English ancestors, were beseeching the stars for miracles.

I removed my clothes and crawled into my sleeping bag, snug against the cool air.

My feet began to relax from the day's blistering hike, and I wiggled my toes just to feel the freedom from shoes. I turned my jacket into a pillow and wrapped my arms around it, seeking that place where dreams are born. The peace I then felt was like touching a lover I had wished for much too long.

Moments later I closed my eyes. How soothing it felt to rest my body and listen to the wheat waving in the wind, gently tapping my tent like ancestral fingers that had arisen from the very earth itself.

CHAPTER

3

Startled awake in the night, I groped to recall my location. Home? No, not there. Somewhere far from home. Then it came to me. I was inside a tent in an English wheat field south of London. But what had jolted me from sleep?

Sitting up, I became more alarmed. A light no bigger than an apple some fifty yards away floated just above the earth like a will-o'-the-wisp, a phenomenon in Chaucer's world thought to be the soul of a dead child.

The light grew closer. Opening my nylon tent door, I stuck my head into the cool air by the oak's trunk. A ghostly voice drifted over the wheat field, and my muscles tightened as I considered climbing the tree.

My eyes struggled to adjust, as the light grew brighter. My heart pounded, and I reached for my shoes. Seconds later, however, the voice proved to belong to a man who walked with a flashlight.

Following a path through the wheat field, his footsteps pounded the pebbled ground as he said, "It wasn't my fault, no matter what they say." His tone was as desperate and vulnerable as someone seeking redemption. When his path brought him closer, he added, "I'll do better next time."

I was tempted to call out, to ask what haunted him. Chill

A fox catches a rooster. (B.M. MS. Stowe 17. f.210.)

bumps covered my arms. The soul of a troubled stranger in the darkness was little less eerie than my thoughts of a deceased child floating like a will-o'-the-wisp over the earth. As he exited the field, his self-examination diminished to the sound of footsteps. The light grew dimmer and finally disappeared like a failed firefly.

Dawn, thankfully, replaced the ghostly night with the sun burning through the fog, drifting over the Thames. A rooster crowed from the nearby farmhouse as I got dressed and crawled from my tent.

Minutes before it rained yesterday, I had gathered dry twigs and stuck them into my pack. This morning I used them to build a tiny fire to make coffee beneath the oak. Waiting for the water to boil, I warmed my hands by the flames. A cow mooed from a distant pasture.

My body was still stiff from sleeping on the ground, and my legs were a bit sore from the first day's walk. But the aroma of perking coffee soon charged the morning air with new adventure on Pilgrims' Way.

I poured my first cup of coffee when the rooster crowed again. He sat atop a fence post some fifty yards away, his red and greenish-blue feathers shiny in the sunlight. His proud head was held high like Chauntecleer—the rooster in "The Nun's Priest's Tale."

A povre [poor] widow, somedeel stape [advanced] in age
Was whilom dwelling in a narrwe [small] cottage,
Beside a grove, standing in a dale.
This widwe, of which I telle you my tale,
Sin thilke day that she was last a wif,
In pacience lad a full simple lif. . . .
    A yerd she had, enclosed all about
With stickes, and a drye ditch withoute,
In which she had a cock heet [named] Chauntecleer.
In all the land, of crowing nas [none] his peer:
His voice was murrier than the murrye orgon [organ pipes]
On massedayes that in the chirche gon;
Well sikerer [more accurate]was his crowing in his lodge
Than is a clock or an abbey orlogge [chiming steeple clock].

Chauntecleer lived with seven hens. His favorite was Lady Pertelote.

    This gentil cock had in his governaunce
Seven hennes for to doon all his plesaunce,
Which were his sustres and his paramours—
And wonder like to him as of colours.
Of which the fairest hewed on hir throte
Was cleped fair damoiselle [noble young lady] Pertelote:
Curteis she was, discreet, and debonaire,
And compaignable, and bare hirself so faire
Sin thilke day that she was seven night old

That trewely she hath the hert in hold
Of Chauntecleer, locken in every lith [locked in every
    limb].

"I had a horrible dream last night," Chauntecleer confessed one dawn to Pertelote. "A creature like a dog or wolf
chased me."

"Don't be silly," Pertelote said. "Dreams mean nothing. Something you ate upset you. Take a laxative and you'll be fine."

"Maybe," said Chauntecleer. "But I'll remind you of the
story of two pilgrims who traveled together into a town where
only one found a room in an inn. The second slept in a barn
and appeared in a dream to the first one to say that he was being murdered. The first pilgrim dismissed the dream as foolish-
ness but later dreamed that his friend called out again, saying
his body was being dumped in a dung cart just beyond the city's
gate. The next morning the first pilgrim found his companion
dead in the cart. And let's not forget another tale where a sailor
dreamed he and his friend would drown if they set sail the next
day. The friend ignored him and died when the ship sank."

Lady Pertelote still wasn't convinced that dreams amounted
to a hill of beans, and Chauntecleer turned his attention to
a butterfly. That's when a fox sneaked up on him. The cock
started to flee when the fox said:

"Gentil sir! Alas, where wol ye gon?
Be ye afraid of *me*, that am your freend?
Now, certes, I were worse than a feend
If I to you wold harm or villainye.
I am not come your conseil for t'espye [to butt into your
    business],
But trewely, the cause of my cominge
Was only for to herkne how that ye singe.

For trewely, ye han as mirry a stevene
As any angel hath that is in hevene. . . ."

The fox asked the cock to sing as the rooster's father used to
do, and Chauntecleer's vanity overpowered his premonition.
When he closed his eyes and began to crow, the fox grabbed
him by the throat and ran. Pertelote and the other hens cried
out in such rage that all the animals in the barnyard, along with
the farm's widow and two daughters, began to pursue the fox.

"I'm surprised that someone as clever as you," said Chauntecleer, fearing for his life, "would not yell something smart to
those chasing you."

When the prideful fox started to shout an insult to the pur-
suers, his mouth opened wide enough for Chauntecleer to fly
to the top of a tree. The fox's sweet words then failed to budge
the cock.

Thou shalt namore thurgh thy flatterye
Do me to sing and winken with mine eye.

I finished my coffee, put out the fire, and stuffed my tent
into my pack, thinking that pride and vanity come in many
forms in the world of man. Beware the danger of the distract-
ing butterfly as much as the crafty fox. Some dreams are whis-
pers from the soul.

The path of last night's ghostly stranger appeared as I hiked
across the wheat field. His tracks in the mud were as fresh as his
voice in my memory. Though I hadn't seen his face, it seemed
to contain the face of every man who had ever wrestled with
his conscience in the night. It haunted me in a comforting way
because it reminded me that I was not the only one who had
ever done such a thing.

After yesterday's rain, today's air was fresh, and everything
that grew from the earth seemed to celebrate its green. There

wasn't a cloud, and the sun glistened on moist meadows where horses grazed. A colt kicked and ran as if playing with an imaginary friend, and I was lifted to see such a spontaneous creature. His head shot up and down as if nodding to life itself, and his tail swished the air like a thousand threads. Any single strand could've royally sewn the loose button on the top of my shirt.

The soreness in my legs vanished as I hiked on, and the weight of my pack didn't bother me as it had yesterday. I relished the workout, the burning in the calf muscles and the back of my thighs. No longer dependent on a car, my body was taking on a new meaning.

It was Sunday, and church bells rang across the English countryside when I spotted a neighborhood store next to a pub. I had planned to enter the store just long enough to buy some bread and cheese. But once inside, I fell under its intimate spell.

Too small to house an elephant, the store swelled with Englishmen because it was the only place nearby selling groceries that morning.

"You're out of luck," said Herbert, the store's owner, to a customer who had asked for a can of kidney beans. "I sold the last one yesterday to Mrs. Allison."

"Are you sure?" said the customer, a man in his forties who held a toy terrier as if it were too precious to walk upon all fours.

Herbert searched his shelves again. "Still empty," he said.

"The wife had promised to make chili today," said the dog carrier. "I've looked forward to it all week and have half a mind to knock on Mrs. Allison's door."

"I think she was having them for dinner last night," said Herbert, who seemed to know everybody's business in the neighborhood.

"A widow her age should not gobble a whole can of beans," said the customer. "Now I suppose we'll have to eat in the pub." The tiny dog barked as his master stepped from the store.

"He waits till the last minute for everything," Herbert said. "But I do wish I had more beans."

Two giggling girls rushed into the store and dropped money on the counter.

"Same as yesterday?" said Herbert.

"Yes, please," said the taller child. Her earring was a golden dolphin.

Herbert fished two pieces of candy from a jar and handed it to the girls, who began to giggle. They raced back to the sidewalk.

"I have a boy about their age," said Herbert. "Today is his birthday."

"Having a party?" I said.

"If there's a pint of ale in England," Herbert said, winking. "Oh, yes, there's enough balloons in our house right now to float it to Scotland." He eyed his watch. "If my worker doesn't get here soon to relieve me, I'll be late for the cake. I almost wish my son would be late as well. He's growing up much too fast. Seems only last week he was playing with stuffed animals. Now he wants a pistol after seeing some horrible American movie. Boys little older than himself carried guns and shot each other. What's all this plague of violence in the United States, anyway?"

Herbert's observation awoke disturbing memories about the murders of John F. Kennedy, his brother Bobby, Martin Luther King, and John Lennon. It also hit closer to home. Years ago in New Orleans, my lover had been shot in the back and paralyzed from the waist down as she walked near Tulane University. The police later discovered that the teenager who shot her did so as an initiation into a gang. Recently I had come to sleep with a loaded rifle next to my mountain bed in Alabama because violent crime had become common in a community that was once more peaceful than most. Herbert was right. A plague as real

Longbowmen at practice. (B.M. MS. Luttrell Psalter. f.147v.)

as the one that swept through Chaucer's world now infected American society.

Handguns did not exist in the Middle Ages. Cannons, shooting bolts, were rarely used because they often blew apart, killing more users than foes. The crossbow—made of sinew, steel, and wood—also fired bolts and had such frightful penetrating power that the church banned it, to little avail, in 1139. It had to be cocked by the archer's placing his foot in a stirrup and a hook fastened to his belt. Slow and heavy to carry, the weapon was transported to battle on a wagon.

The longbow, adapted from the Welsh and used by the English against the Scots in the highlands, was the most deadly weapon. A skilled bowman could shoot as many as a dozen arrows per minute, compared to the crossbow's two or three. The longbow had a range of three hundred yards, and in 1337 Edward I—preparing to fight France—forbade on pain of death any sport except archery. Any man who manufactured the longbow and its three-foot arrows was freed of debts. The longbowman dominated military power at sea as well as on land. On ships the archers fought from high towers called "castles."

Even the famed knight, labeled by an anonymous poem as a "terrible worm in an iron cocoon," feared the longbow because it could penetrate his chain mail, which covered most of his body. Prone to rust, the chain mail was cleaned in a rolling barrel of sand and vinegar. His helmet alone weighed seven to eleven pounds. In addition to the lance, his weapons included a two-handed sword, an eighteen-inch dagger, a battle-ax equipped with a spike, and a club-headed mace with razor-sharp ridged edges. Martial abbots and bishops swung such a mace, believing that it excused them from the rule forbidding clerics "to smite with the edge of the sword."

The largest medieval weapons, used to attack castles with walls sometimes twelve feet thick, were the mangonel, the ballista, and the trebuchet—powered by torsion, tension, and counterpoise. The mangonel consisted of twisted ropes pulling a beam, which, when released, hurled a fifty-pound stone as far as two hundred yards into a high curve. The ballista was like a giant crossbow, shooting bolts and javelins point-blank. The trebuchet, a slinging machine, acted a bit like a child's seesaw. One end was loaded with enormous weights, while the other end, pulled down by force, housed the weapon. When the weighed end was freed, it sent the weapon—sometimes even a rotting horse or plague victim—on its hurried way.

A weapon several stories high, the "movable tower" was a wooden structure covered in raw hides or metal plates to protect it against fire. Often assembled near the attack site, it rolled on wheels and released a drawbridge for its besiegers when it reached castle walls.

"Mining" was another method used to overpower a castle. A tunnel was dug till it hit the wall, and then its supporting stones were replaced by wooden beams. When they were set on fire with straw and brush, the wall would collapse to create an opening into the castle.

In 1224 the chronicle "Annals of Dunstable" recorded the use of weapons by the forces of Henry III to capture Bedford Castle:

On the eastern side were a stone-throwing machine and two mangonels, which attacked the new tower every day. On the western side were two mangonels, which reduced the old tower. A mangonel on the south and one on the north made two breaches in the walls nearest them. Besides these, there were two wooden machines erected ... overlooking the top of the tower and the castle for the use of the crossbowmen and scouts.

In addition there were very many engines there, in which lay hidden both crossbowmen and slingers. Further, there was an engine called a cat, protected by which underground diggers called miners ... undermined the walls of the tower and castle.

Now the castle was taken by four assaults. In the first the barbican was taken, where four or five of the outer guard were killed. In the second the outer bailey was taken, where more were killed, and in this place our people captured horses and their harnesses, corselets, crossbows, oxen, bacon, live pigs and other things beyond number. But the buildings with grain and hay in them they burned. In the third assault, thanks to the action of the miners, the wall fell near the old tower, where our men got in through the rubble and amid great danger occupied the inner bailey. Thus employed, many of our men perished, and ten of our men who tried to enter the tower were shut in and held there by their enemies. At the fourth assault, on the vigil of the Assumption, about vespers, a fire was set under the tower by the miners so that smoke broke through the room of the tower where the enemy were; and the tower split so that cracks appeared. . . .[1]

Medieval weaponry was a child's slingshot compared to today's threat of nuclear and biochemical warfare, capable of destroying the whole human race. But that Sunday morning, as locals came and went from the cozy store, weapons and violence in any form seemed a million miles away.

The store's customers eyed my pack and me as though I were a traveling window with a fresh view. Welcoming their eyes, I said hello not only to be friendly but also to hear their voices return the greeting. Each was musical in its own distinct British way, and every new person added to a universal song. It was Albert, in his sixties, however, who hit notes that made the whole little store vibrate with wonder.

"Swan matches?" said Herbert.

"All others are imposters," said Albert, as he nodded to me as if passing a law.

Herbert handed him a box of Swan, which pictured the graceful fowl. Simply holding the matches made Albert beam as if their awaiting flames would light the flight of a magical bird. He was clean-shaven, and his gray bushy sideburns would have made Elvis himself take an admiring look, as they stretched halfway to his flat chin. His white shirt had been newly pressed, and his suit coat had a single speck of lint on the right shoulder. Albert stood so close to me that I could have blown the lint away with a quick, strong breath.

"What makes those matches so special?" I said, after telling Albert I was on a pilgrimage to Canterbury.

"My boyhood rides on the back of that swan," said Albert, handing me the box. He motioned that I should take a close look.

I couldn't see him on the bird's back, but I sure saw the swan in Albert's soft eyes and humble face.

"My aunt rides on that swan with me," Albert added to his riddle. "She always lit her cigarettes with Swan matches, and she's the one who taught me how to roll tobacco. That might not seem like much at first glance, but she had been hit by a truck and had only one arm."

"She rolled cigarettes with *one* hand?" I said, visualizing Albert when he was a child looking up at his one-armed aunt.

He pulled a pouch of tobacco from his coat and poured some onto a piece of rolling paper. His five manicured fingers pushed, pressed, squeezed, and twisted with loving care till a cigarette appeared out of thin air. Sealing it with his tongue, he held it up as though to confirm it was the genuine article.

"You got some fancy fingers," I said, feeling that I, too, had gotten to take a ride atop that swan's back. "Could I trade you some of my own tobacco for that cigarette?"

Albert looked intrigued but perplexed.

"It's a Native American custom," I said, thinking that the exchange might give me more than he could dream.

"I've never smoked any Indian tobacco," said Albert, offering me the cigarette.

I opened my pack and dug past my journal and camera, down into jeans and shirts. Albert looked on as though we had entered a subterranean world. His eyes grew bigger yet when a leather bag appeared, holding a red stone pipe and tobacco. I placed Albert's cigarette inside the bag and gave him some of my tobacco. Raising it to his nose, he sniffed, smiled, and stuffed it into an old box of Swan.

After Albert eased the box into his coat, he paid Herbert for the matches and a "scratch pad," a chance at the national lottery. "It's for my dad," said Albert. "He's bedridden, and I buy him one every day. It's his only hope of a miracle."

A woman walking with a cane bought a plastic bottle of ketchup and a half pint of whiskey, when Albert was almost out the door. Then he turned and eyed me up and down as though searching for something as subtle as the lint yet atop the shoulder of his coat. I stepped closer to him, where sunlight shined on the store's floor, casting our shadows across each other.

"If I were a young man," said Albert, "I'd walk with you to Canterbury."

Something close to his heart flickered in his eyes, and I wondered if he thought his walking to Canterbury would help heal his bedridden father.

"A part of you is going with me," I said, as my hand motioned "your swan."

His lips parted, but no words came. In his nod, however, he spoke plenty before heading out the door. He was almost to the corner when he removed the box with the tobacco and again raised it to his nose. Moments later Herbert's employee—a woman in her early twenties with the tattoo of a rose on her neck—raced into the store to apologize for being late. Herbert dashed off to his son's birthday party.

If his son had lived during the Middle Ages, he would have gone "a-ganging" every spring with the rest of the villagers. On "gang-days" boys learned the village perimeter by being ducked in boundary creeks and having their bodies rubbed against landmark trees and rocks. Most died in the same village where they were born and rarely left those perimeters.

Villagers lived in rectangular houses called "halls" that ranged in size from fifteen square feet (a bay) to four or five bays. Animals, living in the same dwelling, slept in one end of the hall but were free to come and go through the house's door. The thatched roofs—made of straw, broom, heather, or reeds and rushes—offered homes for wasps, hornets, spiders, and birds. They rotted quickly from rain and caught fire easily. The walls—made of sticks and clay—were so fragile that robbers could "break in." Small windows invited light from the sun and moon, and the floor was packed earth, covered with straw or rushes. A fire of wood or peat burned in the center on a raised stone hearth, vented through a small opening in the roof. The house was perpetually smoky because a fire burned all day as milk, water, and porridge simmered in iron kettles. At night a ceramic lid with holes covered the fire. Beds were straw pallets placed on the floor.

Meat, baskets, and bags dangled from rafters to escape mice and rats. Chairs were rare, and most families dined seated on benches at a trestle table, easily put away at night to make more room. "Maslin," a mixture of wheat and rye or barley and rye, was baked into loaves of bread weighing four pounds. Poorer families economically favored pottage over bread as the principal food because it didn't have to be ground and avoided the miller's exaction. Barley grains intended for pottage were first allowed to sprout before being dropped into the boiling pot. Salt pork or bacon fat, along with garlic and onion, were added for flavor, as were cabbage, leeks, and parsley. Raw fruit, considered unhealthy, was sometimes even cooked in the soup. Ale was the chief drink. Though medieval diets were healthy, being high in fiber and low in fat, they lacked protein, lipids, calcium, and vitamins A, C, and D.

Medieval villagers bathed in a barrel with the top removed and repeatedly used the same water. Men bathed first, followed by women and children. The babies were last, and sometimes the water had become so dirty, says folklore, that it gave rise to the expression "Don't throw out the baby with the bathwater."

In rare cases a peasant owned pewter dishes, brass pots, and silver spoons. Wooden chests housed his table linen, towels, bedding, and clothing. Earthenware bowls, wooden spoons, and jugs sat in cupboards.

A man wore a short tunic with a belt. His stockings reached to his knee, but hose stretched to a cloth belt at his waist. Gloves protected his hands, while a hood covered his head. His leather shoes had wooden soles. Wimples sheltered women's heads and necks and sometimes flapped in the wind like the wings of giant butterflies. The church frowned upon women, especially married women, revealing their forehead and hair because it was considered too worldly. Belted at the waist, long woolen gowns adorned women, whose underclothing consisted of linen.

A well-to-do peasant trimmed his tunic with fur from a fox or squirrel and might wear long, narrow, pointed shoes. If he chose to dress like those living in London, he could sport a woolen hat with a band decorated with feathers. Fashionable women, uncensored by the church, sometimes decorated their hair with wreaths of flowers called "chaplets."

Men wore beards, but mustaches were scarce. Hair fell to their collars and was groomed with a comb, made of wood or horn. Mirrors, always handheld, came from glass or polished metal.

Toilets, when they existed at all in the villages, were mere trenches. As often as not, the call of nature was simply answered by retreating "a bowshot from the house." Moss and hay were used as sanitary paper.

A "toft," or front yard, accompanied each house and was enclosed by a fence or ditch to contain the animals and their pens as well as barns or sheds for storing grain. The "toft" extended to a "croft" behind the house, where a garden grew along with fruit trees. Most peasants drew water from a communal well, which was often near the church—the only stone building in the village.

In the Middle Ages in England, more than 90 percent of the population lived in rural villages, and lives depended on the soil. Prosperous peasants tended a "yardland" or a "half-yardland" (thirty or fifteen acres)—enough land to support their families. But "cottars" held only five acres or less and had to work for their wealthier neighbors to make ends meet. Over half those in villages were cottars.

Whether half-yardlanders or cottars, most peasants were nonfree—villeins or serfs. Two to three days weekly—"week's work"—throughout the year, they were obligated to labor for their lord. If their daughter married, they paid their lord a fee. To sell their livestock, they had to ask permission. They were not protected by the royal courts as free men were. The lord,

Threshing wheat. (B.M. MS. Luttrell Psalter. f.74v.)

judge of the manorial courts, imposed his will upon them as he saw fit.

By the thirteenth century, a serf could give the lord money instead of labor, but either payment amounted to half of the serf's weekly efforts. Manor custom books detailed what the lord expected in services. The serf knew how much land he was to plow, how many oxen he could use. Special rights were also negotiated between the lord and a tenant. At Christmas the serf could give his lord a hen in exchange for deadwood in the forest. He could mend a fence for the right to fish in the lord's pond or dig a ditch to gather some hay from the lord's field. At Easter tenants gave their lord eggs.

When crops demanded it, the lord could order both free and unfree to abandon their own work and labor for him, reaping, mowing, and plowing. Such work services were called "boons" or "benes." The lord rewarded their efforts. "Alebidreap" boons gave them ale, while the "waterbidreap" boons offered them water. "A hungerbidreap" required that the workers bring their own food. When the lord furnished food—fish, meat, soup, bread, and cheese—he piled it high in celebration. He also gave the workers a "sporting chance." If mowers could catch a sheep released in the field, they could roast it. Haymakers received the biggest bundle of hay they could lift with their scythes.

Though in theory a lord owned all land, tradition dictated that a serf could pass his holdings on to his heir, accomplished through a ritual performed by the lord's steward or bailiff. He offered the serf a stick. When he accepted it, he was considered to be in possession ("seisin") of the holdings as if the right had traveled through the wood from the lord to the tenant. If a serf left the village, he was required to pay a fine and yearly fee while he was away. He also lost his land.

Villagers met in assemblies to create bylaws to govern their agricultural lives. A bylaw of 1329 read: "No one shall take in outsiders or natives who behave themselves badly in the gleaning [gathering the grain after the reapers were finished] or elsewhere.... Also, no one may tether horses in the fields amid growing grain or grain that has been reaped where damage can arise. Also, no one may make paths, by walking or driving or carrying grain, over the grain of another to the damage of the neighbors or at any other time."[2]

While men made the bylaws, the parish priest reviewed the laws of God in Sunday sermons. For his religious services, he was to receive the crop of every tenth acre, offerings on feast days, and earnings from the "glebe," church land cultivated by tenants or by the priest himself. When a serf died, he was expected to leave his "second-best beast" to the priest.

Some priests abused their positions and stored corn in the churches while cattle grazed in the churchyard. Archbishop of Canterbury John Peckham ordered medieval parish priests to preach at least four times a year.

Slipping back into my pack, I exited the little store that Sunday morning and heard more church bells. They were so far away that the ringing came and went with gusts of wind.

Hiking toward the next town, Gravesend, I followed a sidewalk alongside a cemetery where tombstones stood as solid and certain as death itself. The Anglo-Saxons who invaded England buried their dead with personal belongings. Men were put to rest with swords, and women were buried with needles and thread.

Among the hundreds of graves before me, a single person stirred. His red hair blew in the wind as he walked to a tombstone shaped like an angel, forever frozen with her wings spread. When he knelt over the grave, he removed a plastic bag from his pocket and emptied its contents atop the mound, where grass concealed it.

The man was in his late forties or early fifties and kept kneeling by the grave as I walked closer along the edge of the cemetery. I couldn't help but stare.

When he noticed me, I felt uneasy—as if I had violated a precious moment. But he smiled, studying my pack and feathered hat.

"I'm on a pilgrimage to Canterbury," I called out.

He left the grave and joined me by the iron fence surrounding the cemetery.

"American?" he said, as though that might explain my mission.

Freckles dotted his balding head.

"My ancestors were English," I said. "English and Cherokee. Didn't mean to startle you."

"I was just on the way to have lunch with some friends," he said. "I visit them every Sunday after I come to my wife's grave. She died fourteen months ago."

"Sorry," I said.

His fingers snapped.

"Just like that, she was gone. We had been riding bicycles. She was hot and wanted some ice."

He fidgeted with his gold wedding band.

"I told her I'd race her home," he said. "We hadn't pedaled

ten feet and she collapsed. Doctor said it was a stroke. Dead at forty-five."

"I hope there's an afterlife," I said, "where we can see those we love."

"My wife was a religious person," he said, "but I've never believed in fairy tales. I enjoyed her while she was alive. Better mind this hot sun yourself carrying a heavy pack."

His story seemed to have flown out of nowhere like a tortured bird released from a cage. Just as suddenly, he wished me a safe journey and walked on, as though he might've had second thoughts about revealing something so personal.

I moved on as well but couldn't get him off my mind. Returning to the cemetery, I wandered among the tombstones to the one shaped like an angel with spread wings. There atop his wife's grave, among thick grass, rested cubes of ice. They melted under the sun, seeping into the earth like a cold drink of water. I started to touch them but decided that such an act would invade the man and his wife. Somehow I could see her lips moments before she died, craving ice as she and her husband raced home. Then I saw his lips when he had told me she died. I hoped that they had kissed the morning of the tragic bike ride.

Even a mile from the cemetery on Pilgrims' Way I could still see the melting ice, as if the sun followed me to rattle the story a little longer in my brain. Then I tried to just hear the widower's tender words: "I enjoyed her while she was alive." No small wonder, I thought, that Chaucer's themes of love and death in *The Canterbury Tales* have endured more than six hundred years. They're as timeless and universal as hunger and thirst. I would never again view cubes of ice in the same way.

The landscape rolled before me like giant green waves, foaming with white daisies. They flowed over me, washing me head to toe with the smell of freshly mowed hay and plowed earth.

That afternoon a valley appeared to my right, bordered by a white chalk cliff with lush vines dangling from it like green waterfalls. Ancient farmhouses with stone fences loomed in the near distance, and I suspected that the cliff had once been a landmark for "gang-days" in the Middle Ages. Whether or not boys who grew into men had ever had their bodies rubbed against the white stone to learn village boundaries didn't matter. I wanted to mark my journey with the cliff and hiked down into the valley.

I removed my pack as well as my shirt and pushed my shoulders and arms into the base of the cliff. I admired its solidness, its mammoth size, and most of all its age.

Most of the cliff's surface was hot from the sun, but in a shaded area it cooled my cheeks when I eased them against it. My forearm rubbed against the rock; it became scratched and started to bleed—just a few drops. Sweat ran into the cut, and it stung. I liked that the stone took me closer to my flesh, formed in part from the DNA of medieval ancestors who once walked the very earth I now traveled.

The flesh-to-cliff experience excited me as though it released a primal force within. I felt like climbing a tree or trying to scale the cliff. But I had been a weight lifter for more than thirty years, and instead I turned to a stone as big as a basketball. Lifting it, I held it overhead against the blue sky as a private cry to the world that I was alive, "a-ganging" with the rock. Unlike a village's perimeter, however, my spirit had no boundaries. The pilgrimage was giving it fresh air, and my soul was taking deeper breaths.

The next thirty minutes I sat on the ground and wrote in my journal about the day's experiences as birds sang from the overhead limbs. The inviting spot tempted me to spend the night there. But I was hungry, had no food, and decided to push on to Gravesend—less than an hour away. I was grateful not to be a serf, to have no lord breathing down my neck. When Easter came, I'd give my eggs to whomever I chose. Or eat them myself.

Gravesend sat atop a small hill overlooking the Thames to the east, and brick houses lined the street. On a sign saying POCAHONTAS IS BURIED HERE, someone had scratched "And so are my dreams."

The sun was setting, and the air, blowing off the Thames, was cold when I spotted a BED-AND-BREAKFAST sign in a window. A man in his twenties with a gold earring sat on the porch, a suitcase by his side.

"Nobody home?" I said.

"Not just now, mate," he said. "I've been waiting an hour."

Two men in their forties relaxed twenty feet away on a bench in the yard as they smoked pipes. Their bikes, strapped with travel bags, leaned against an iron fence surrounding the two-story house. They eyed me as though trying to decide my mission.

"How long have you been waiting?" I said.

"Fifteen minutes," said the taller one, who wore a short blond beard and horn-rimmed glasses. "Fifteen minutes too long. We have traveled all day and are a little tired."

"You're not British," I said, trying to place his accent.

"Swedish," he said.

I told them my name, where I was going.

"We must talk," said Anders, who wore the beard. "We're on a pilgrimage as well, headed to France."

"Yes," said his friend, Kai, who was clean-shaven. "We are sailors on the same ocean. We must compare maps before the sea monsters get us or we fall off the edge of the world."

The men's eyes beamed with intensity, intelligence, and playfulness.

"We will have dinner together," said Anders, as if taking control.

I was not used to anyone's making plans for me, and so shortly after meeting, but my Cherokee heritage had taught me long ago that any encounter on a journey might appear for a reason. Embarking on this trek, I had promised myself not to fight my instincts or my fate.

"Dinner sounds good," I said, "but let's not wait here. I saw some pubs down near the river. Maybe they rent rooms overhead."

Anders and Kai made an exchange in Swedish. Though I didn't understand a word, their expressions, tones, and body language spoke of a strong friendship. It warmed me but also made me a tad envious. Two years earlier my best male friend from New York was driving to visit me in Alabama when he died of a heart attack along the way. I missed him, a decorated marine and photographer for *Life* magazine.

"Yes," said Anders, "let's look for lodging down by the water."

Kai's impish eyes twinkled, and just like that we became a trio on Pilgrims' Way. Putting away their pipes, they pushed their bikes alongside me as we hiked down the hill toward the Thames, where a freighter worked its bulky way upstream.

We found rooms at a tavern called "The Mermaid." The crash of billiard balls mingled with laughter and music blaring from the jukebox.

"Don't worry about the noise," said the barmaid, as she escorted us up three narrow flights of squeaking wooden stairs. "The pub closes early tonight."

She was in her thirties, radiated sensuality, a love of life, and lingered at the door of my room just long enough to hint that she was hungry to meet someone new.

"I've never hiked to Canterbury," she said, "but sometimes I walk down by the river to write poems."

"I bet you've written some beautiful things," I said, taking a much closer look at her eyes. Longing for tenderness, they seemed to say that she had secrets to tell—if only the right person would listen.

"Not always so pretty," she said, lowering her head. Her honesty gave her face more beauty than she could've imagined. "I've got to get back to the pub. Maybe you'll come down later?"

She started down the stairs, and I listened from my open door. I hadn't before known that the squeak of stairs could be so inviting, suggestive.

My room was little more than a bed, but its window— elegant with white-lace curtains—offered an intimate view of the river. It was so close that I felt as if I could reach out and touch it, make the water ripple in the soothing golden light of sunset.

The bathroom was just down the hall, and I was relieved not to bathe like medieval men and women in a barrel. The hot shower did more than just wash away the day's sweat and dirt. It revived me, transforming skin into a newly found luxury.

Anders, Kai, and I found a restaurant. Dusk was falling, and two candles' flames danced atop our table while the smell of curry spiced every item on the Indian menu into a mouth-watering dilemma. Before the food even arrived, we were as busy as Chaucer's pilgrims trading stories. The Swedes, skilled in the art of listening, squirmed when I spoke of once eating live bugs with Indians in the mountains of Mexico.

"What a pity we don't have any insects to nibble on this evening," said Anders.

"I didn't say I liked eating the bugs," I said, "but it would have been impolite to have refused the invitation."

"As a Buddhist," said Kai, "I'm offended that you may have eaten my grandmother."

I shrank an inch.

"He's not a Buddhist," said Anders.

"No," Kai said, with that certain impish look in his eye. "And if one of those bugs was my aunt, I hope you did eat her."

Our conversation turned to how we got hooked on travel.

"I ran away to New York when I was teenager," I said. "I was suffocating in my hometown."

"Americans are restless because it's in their genes," said Anders. "Your country was settled by Englishmen and other Europeans who were not happy in their birthplaces."

"Americans are often searching for something," I agreed, questioning if he had hit upon a profound truth. Perhaps my wanderlust stemmed from my English roots, and my strong sense of home came from my Cherokee blood.

Anders's father was dead. And Anders didn't get along with his mother, who lived alone, occupying a single room in a mansion.

"My mother's father was a doctor," said Anders, "and she was spoiled. She has no true understanding of how to show love. She can't help herself and will always stick the knife in and twist it when she has the chance with me."

Most men I had met did not speak so openly, and Anders's confession humbled me. He spoke seven languages and was a college professor, teaching philosophy and economics.

"Some people don't understand how the two subjects are fins on the same fish," he said. "They think economics is graphs and numbers. But I try to teach my students to see how they can live life to its fullest, to do all they can with what little they have. That's why Kai and I are on this journey. Travel and meeting people are how you learn about yourself, the quality of your life, and how you might improve it."

Kai, the father of two teenage boys, was a professional artist. He had recently turned from painting seascapes to doing portraits.

"People are more difficult to paint," he said. "The more

interesting ones have such depth of feeling that their faces won't stay still. I get lost in their eyes alone. But this is a hard time right now for me to focus. It hasn't been long since my wife left me for another man."

Neither anger nor self-pity eroded Kai's voice, but his eyes couldn't hide the scars.

In the Middle Ages the church viewed marriage as the will of God to create children rather than to enjoy flesh. But of course, sex was on people's minds. Male theologians considered females to be the evil seducers. After all, they argued, hadn't original sin itself sprung from a woman? Eve had caused Adam to lose Paradise by eating from the Tree of Knowledge, condemning mankind to a life of pain and sorrow.

Medieval women who plucked their eyebrows were considered the most seductive. It was believed that demons in purgatory stuck "hot burning awls and needles" into holes produced by plucked hairs.

Though the use of chastity belts has been exaggerated, husbands did sometimes protect "their treasures." The technique evolved from the Moslem practice of padlocking the labia and came to England via the Crusades.

An unmarried woman didn't have many options to support herself. She could remain a virgin and join a nunnery to give all her love to God, "the spouse of the soul." She might become a "spinster" and operate a spinning wheel. Or she could become a prostitute in London, where she was required to wear a striped hood.

The majority of women, however, did marry and could do so when they turned twelve.

Boys had to be fourteen. Some couples simply made promises to each other while holding hands in the woods—or making love in a hayloft. Without a witness, however, trouble came when either person—usually the man—disavowed having made such an agreement. In such cases the betrayed could sue the other. In 1217 in the Constitutions of Richard Poore, bishop of Salisbury, it was forbidden that "anyone encircle the hands of a young woman with a ring or rush or any other material, vile or precious, in jest in order to fornicate with her the more freely, lest while he [or she] thinks he jest he avoid the honors of marriage." It wasn't until the sixteenth century, however, with the Catholic Church's Council of Trent, that witnesses were required.

Marriage was, in large part, a business arrangement made between families to keep property in the family. A man could usually not marry without his father's approval, because it meant that the elder was passing land from himself to his son. This was a monumental rite of passage for both father and son. The father was accepting the twilight of his life, and the son was embracing his adulthood.

The marriage ceremony had two parts and began at the church door, just as the Wife of Bath bragged: "Housbondes at chirche door I have had five." With friends and family gathered around the bride and groom, the priest would ask if anyone knew why the couple could not lawfully be joined. Then the groom would announce his dower, which was usually land to be given to his wife in the event of his death, and/or the gifts the bride's father gave. The groom then placed gold or silver and a ring on a shield or book along with pence to be given to the poor.

Next the priest asked the couple if they would have each other as man and wife. They answered, "I will." That's when the bride's father gave her to the groom, who took her right hand in his. The ring was then blessed and sprinkled with holy water. The groom took the ring from the priest and placed it on the bride's middle finger, because it was believed in medieval England as it had been in Rome that a vein runs from the heart to that finger.

The groom's gift of money and ring to the bride was his "wed," or pledge, to fulfill the marriage contract. The ceremony was a "wedding."

With the wedding over, everyone retired from the church door to the inside altar. A nuptial mass was held, and after the "Sanctus," the care-cloth, a pall, was placed over the couple as they knelt in prayer. Any children the bride had out of wedlock could be held under the cloth as well for them to become legitimate.

After the mass the pall was removed, and the priest gave the groom the kiss of peace. The groom in turn kissed the bride. A feast with bride-ale followed, and the groom was expected to give a ball to the first who requested it. In 1268 near Ferrybridge, Yorkshire, William Selisaule stopped a newly married couple and asked for the customary ball, which the groom did not have. He gave a pair of gloves as a pledge for it. Later that day men from the village of Byram demanded a ball, and the groom explained he had already promised it to another. A fight with hatchets and bows and arrows broke out between drunken members of the wedding party and the Byram men. Several were injured, and one was killed.

When a serf married, his lord received "merchet," a fine or fee often paid by the bride or her father. Depending on the serf's wealth, the merchet ranged from six pence to four pounds. "Leirwite" was a fine paid for premarital sex, and "childwite" was the money given for bearing a child out of wedlock.

The aristocracy often disturbed the church when it sought grounds for divorce because the marriage had proved to be barren or disappointing. Divorce among peasants, however, was rare unless bigamy occurred. The peasants tended simply to separate, obeying the terms of the church court.

Any English couple married for a year who could truthfully swear that they had not argued and did not regret the marriage could come to Dunmow in Essex to win the Dunmow Flitch, which was a side, or flitch, of bacon. While the Wife of Bath did not qualify for the meaty prize, she certainly did not perpetuate the medieval theologians' doctrine that woman was the source of mankind's pain and sorrow. On the contrary, she said, "Allas, allas, that ever love was sinne."

One of the two candles' flames atop our table had died since we arrived at the restaurant almost two hours earlier, and the sorrow in Kai's eyes about his broken marriage had long ago been replaced with a playful twinkle. From time to time he appeared to doodle on a napkin. When he handed it to me, I did a double take.

The sketch of my face didn't look like the person I usually saw in a mirror. It was older, harder. The wrinkles that had started to arrive only a few years earlier were more pronounced. I usually thought of myself as a bird—my Cherokee name was Crane at Creek—but Kai's drawing depicted a face that looked more like a turtle's head. I questioned whether, like Chauntecleer in "The Nun's Priest's Tale," I was blinded at times by vanity. Well, I told Kai, if I am truly more a weathered turtle than a sleek bird, maybe I could at least outrun some cocky flop-eared rabbit.

"When my children were small," said Kai, "long before they could read, I would tell them stories by placing my drawings in the woods behind our house. My wife and I would watch them go from tree to tree to learn what would happen next."

It was dark when we returned to our rooms over the closed pub, and I already dreaded saying good-bye to Anders and Kai the next day. I would miss their sense of humor, their honesty, and their picking up the next dinner bill.

I placed Kai's sketch in my journal and stepped to the window overlooking the Thames. In the shadows along the shore, someone bent over to lift a shell or rock and threw it into the water. I couldn't tell if it was a man or woman but thought of the barmaid who said she went there to write poems, ones that weren't always so pretty.

Sometime in the night, the sound of squeaking stairs aroused me.

CHAPTER

4

A foghorn awoke me snug in bed at The Mermaid the next morning. Last night's dinner conversation with Anders and Kai made me eager to see them. They were kindred spirits, the wind under a fellow traveler's wings.

Stepping across the hall to the Swedes' door, however, I discovered that the only breeze they offered at this early hour came from their snores. I left a note on the floor: "Gone for coffee. Be back soon."

Hitting the street, I hoped to discover a bakery that smelled of freshly baked cinnamon rolls. My wish became sugar in the rain when all doors said CLOSED.

I ended up in front of McDonald's with minutes before it opened. A middle-aged woman wearing baggy, wrinkled clothes stood nearby, rubbing her hands together. Her gloves were threadbare, and her hat sported a plastic red flower.

"Cold," she said, in the icy breeze blowing from the Thames. "Cold."

"Yes, it's chilly," I said, thinking how warm my bed had been last night. I wondered where she had slept.

"I was born cold." She had lost some teeth. "My mum was the same. Always shivering."

A worker unlocked the door. The woman dashed to a table

and scooted a chair near Ronald McDonald. He towered over her, smiling as if they had waited all night to rendezvous. A mother and young son took the table nearest her. When the boy sat on the clown's foot, the forever-cold woman's eyes saddened. Toying with her hair, she bit her lips as though to cage words of jealousy.

Bigger-than-life plastic clowns didn't decorate medieval pubs, but fools—the seeds of modern-day clowns—entertained kings and queens in the Middle Ages. Some of the earliest European records present the fool as a "nebulo," or a nobody in the feudal hierarchy. Neither freeman nor serf, he was a social outcast and required to sit at a separate table when he wasn't performing.

The fool's identity depended on his relationship with his master. Because the fool was a nobody, the king could grant him favors without arousing jealousies at the court. The king could also withdraw his favors as quickly as he granted them or banish the fool from the castle with the snap of his fingers. Living in such social limbo, however, gave the fool rare freedom and subtle power. He got to know the king in ways no one else did and could say things to him that no one else dared. After all, his job was not only to amuse—by showing life's folly—but also to remind the king of man's harsh nature, which was easily forgotten when surrounded by a court of yes-men. The fool Golet, much aware of man's evil, saved the life of William of Normandy when he informed him of assassins' approach.

The Latin word *follis* meant "fool" and had the original meaning of an air-filled bag, giving rise to the bladders or "baubles," which were the fools' scepters. The scepters varied but often consisted of sticks with a fake fool's head on top and an exaggerated phallus on the bottom. The heads were adorned with cock's combs to suggest the sexuality and silliness linked to the rooster (hello, Chauntecleer), and their tiny ears were those of an ass. Tongues often stuck insultingly from the mouths. A fool—he sometimes jumped naked over fires as he farted—

could shake his scepter in the face he chose and let the observer decide if he intended to confront his mind, his sexual desires, or create the age-old conflict between the two.

The fool's wooden sword was used as a phallus in mock battles to satirize knights or males in general. As often as not, however, the fool needed the wooden prop as a real defense against those who took severe offense at his humor. Any fool who pushed his master too far could end up in prison or the madhouse, with only the tiny head on his scepter to console him.

The medieval fool could be of two types. One was the innocent or the retarded, and the other was the clever or the counterfeit. Retarded fools were believed to be in touch with supernatural powers. Clever fools, who could also act as poets and minstrels, stirred human emotions to help their audiences transcend daily reality.

According to folklore, in 1340, at the French court of Philip VI, no one but an unnamed fool had the nerve to inform the king that Edward III at Sluis had destroyed his fleet.

"Those cowardly Englishmen, those chickenhearted Britons," said the fool.

"How so?" Philip asked.

"Why, because they had not courage enough to jump into the sea like your own sailors, who went headlong from their ships, leaving them to the enemy, who did not dare to follow them."

Dwarfs, once believed blessed by the gods in Egypt, were cherished as fools who could bring good luck in medieval England. In 1249 Eleanor of Provence, Henry III's wife, kept a dwarf fool named Jean, who had been discovered on the Isle of Wight. Only three feet tall, the fool had a special place in Eleanor's heart, since she had grown up in the company of entertainers. Her father, Raymond Berengar IV, count of Provence, was a famed troubadour poet.

Most fools in the Middle Ages were male. Artaude du Puy,

a woman fool in 1337 who attended Jeanne, the queen of Charles I of France, was one of the few exceptions. But whether male or female, a medieval entertainer who did not find security as a fool, through either alms or wages, struggled to make a living in a world where many considered his occupation questionable if not downright corrupt. As early as 750 the archbishop of Mainz, Lull, writing to Gregory of Utrecht, warned him of "worldly delights," which included spicy foods, drink, fancy clothes, falcons, hawks, grain-fed horses, baying hounds, and "buffoons." In 789 Charlemagne forbade the clergy to own "jokers." One of the greatest sacrileges of the entertainers was to dress like a monk or a nun or any other member of the clergy.

But during the Feast of Fools, begun in the eleventh century, even the clergy celebrated folly. During this time the "nobodies" in the church had a chance to become somebodies. On December 28, a boy bishop was selected from the choir and altar boys to preach a sermon, as if truth could come only from the "mouths of babes" and fools.

As early as 1220, however, the Feast of Fools encountered trouble. Old shoes instead of incense were burned on the altar, and buckets of water were poured over the Fool Precentor, who was also called the Fool Bishop or Fool Abbot. By the end of the fourteenth century, the clergy had suppressed the feast in England, though elements survived in the celebration of the Twelve Days of Christmas, when Lords of Misrule were chosen to oversee manorial households, schools, and courts. Folly during the Christmas season has endured in England ever since.

As late as the 1940s in America's Deep South, a remnant of the Feast of Fools survived at Christmas. Teenagers in the Appalachian Mountains gathered, sometimes fifteen or more to a group, to paint their faces or don masks before visiting neighbors to "act the fool" in Dry Sitting. During the game the fools were not allowed to talk but would simply sit and make faces

while their hosts tried to guess who they were. On the surface
the game was nothing more than silliness, but when examined
with a closer eye, it probed the ancient philosophical question
posed by the Caterpillar in *Alice in Wonderland* and wiser court
fools throughout history: "Who are you?"

A fool in England's Middle Ages, even a successful one,
could be forced to question his identity when he grew gray and
unwanted. A letter dated January 26, 1536—written by Thomas
Bedyll to his chief about his visit to Croyland Abbey—stated
that he had found a young fool, "not past fifteen," who could
replace the king's old fool, "Sexten."

In the late Middle Ages, death itself was sometimes portrayed as a fool, suggesting that it both outsmarts and survives
mortals as it drags them to their graves. The fool's immortality
is seen in the modern clown, when he is knocked in the head
with a hammer and recovers seconds later as though he had
simply paused to ponder his silly fate. Who hasn't watched the
death-defying slaps, jabs, punches, and falls of a Three Stooges
movie and thought that Curly, Moe, and Larry were the biggest
fools on earth? Still, their supernatural powers intrigue and entertain as they confront us with our own frailty of breakable
bones and hearts. Today's presidents might make excellent use
of an insightful and brave fool, but the closest we come to that
in the modern world are late-night television comedians such
as David Letterman, Jay Leno, and the performers on *Saturday
Night Live*.

When I left McDonald's, the woman who adored the towering
plastic Ronald still sat by his side as if they were committed till
death do them part. I returned to The Mermaid, where the
Swedes were brewing tea in the kitchen cramped with their
bikes and someone's socks dangling from a line, strung over the
table. Kai spread strawberry jam on toast, and Anders poured

a bowl of "Swiss-Style Muesli." I told them of the shivering woman's romance with the clown.

"The poor too often lead us to our own inner riches," said Anders, as though recalling a lecture he had given to his philosophy and economics classes.

True, the three of us were wealthy that morning. But our now going separate ways was a poor thought. When they finished their meals, we exchanged addresses, and they strapped their bags onto the bikes. I slipped back into my pack.

We dropped our keys to The Mermaid onto the table, sprinkled with crumbs from Kai's toast, and ducked the dangling socks as we exited the kitchen. They pedaled beside me to the outskirts of Gravesend, and it became time for the countryside to carry them away like some gigantic wave.

"I've never had a reason to visit America till now," said Anders, adjusting his glasses as if to keep composure. Kai simply nodded, with that impish twinkle dancing in his eyes.

"I've been to Sweden," I said, "but it was many years ago, and I had no friends there then. I'd like to go back."

"If you meet God on your pilgrimage," said Anders, "tell him we said hello."

"And to please send cash," said Kai. "You have my address."

The Swedes had almost disappeared around a grassy curve, when they circled back. At first it seemed that they had forgotten something. But it soon became clear that they simply wanted one last close look. So did I, and we savored one another's eyes without reservation before they turned once again to vanish beyond the curve of no return.

Melancholy tapped on my one-man door for the next mile but went its shadowy way when an entertaining fence post appeared. A piece of paper, twice as big as my hand, had been tied to it. On it was the sketch of a floppy-eared rabbit that ran as fast as the wind. It grinned like a trickster—signed "Kai."

The Swedes' playfulness inspired me to reevaluate the day,

Stealing cherries. (B.M. MS. Luttrell Psalter. f.196v.)

and even the sky seemed more inviting. It hung over me like some colossal cape, and the sun was a golden brooch. It was so warm by noon that surely even Ronald's gal was cozy on some park bench, her frayed gloves cast aside.

A flock of white pigeons flew from a barn loft and circled overhead like a turbulent cloud of snowflakes. When they landed atop the barn, a few of them strutted and cooed as though to brag of their feathery feat. If my delight had been grain, they could've feasted for a week.

A roadside plum tree flourished with so much ripe fruit that the limbs bent as if gravity itself beckoned for a taste. I pulled a plum and stuck it to my lips. Juice as warm as a lover's mouth ran down my chin, and I couldn't image anything on earth tasting sweeter and more exotic. Eve had not caused herself and Adam to lose Paradise at all. It was alive and well right there on Pilgrims' Way.

Halfway through the day, I stopped under an oak to rest. I poured water from my canteen onto a washcloth and placed it to my burning face. A breeze cooled the skin, and I removed my shoes and socks to bathe my feet as well.

As I massaged my sore heel, a piece of black flint several feet away by the edge of a cornfield caught my eye. No bigger than my index finger, it was partially covered by earth and looked like an arrowhead. I had found hundreds of Native American artifacts over the years, and the idea of now finding one made by an Englishman hundreds or thousands of years ago thrilled me, connecting me to my British heritage in a new way.

Lifting the flint from the soil, I saw that it wasn't an artifact at all. But my discovering the stone had opened another door. I hadn't walked with bare feet on the ground in years and never in England. Somehow it felt right that the soil rubbed my skin, like slipping into a favorite shirt that had been put away and forgotten till that moment.

Only six feet inside the cornfield, the earth was yet moist from the rain three days ago. Sticking my toes into the mud, I became a kid again. Then the oddest thing happened when I beheld my footprint. For a moment it belonged to someone else long ago. I was walking through the past and the present at the same time. Someone yet unborn would one day stick his bare foot where mine had been.

A crow landed atop a tree thirty yards away as I put on my socks and shoes. It squawked and lifted its wings as though saying something important. Medieval men and women often kept jays and magpies, called "pies," caged in their homes and taught them to imitate human speech. Nightingales and larks were treasured as songbirds.

A pet bird belonged to Hugh of Avalon in Burgundy. He came to England in 1180 to help Henry II atone for the murder of Becket by forming the monastic order of the Carthusians and its house at Witham, in Somerset. He later became the bishop of Lincoln and resided at the manor of Stow, where a swan followed him from dawn to dusk like a guardian angel. If anyone, including monks, came near the bishop, the swan attacked them. The bishop, on the other hand, could stroke the bird as if it lived for his touch.

Chaucer himself was an avid bird-watcher and writes of birds more than five hundred times in his collective works. His most famous bird story appears in "The Manciple's Tale." Phoebus, a famed warrior and a great musician, loved his wife more than anything on earth. He would do anything to please her. But sometimes he was overpowered by jealousy.

Phoebus kept a white-feathered crow in his home, which could repeat anything he heard. One night when Phoebus was away, his wife slept with her secret lover. Upon Phoebus's return, the white crow told him all that he had observed.

Phoebus flew into a rage and murdered his wife. When he realized that she was gone forever, he turned on the "little bird that told him." He jerked out all its white feathers, replaced them with black ones, and took away the crow's ability to talk and sing. Then he kicked him out.

Today's crow continued to squawk with such passion that it seemed half of England was being cautioned not to repeat everything that it heard. Certainly such advice is just as wise in the modern world as it had been in the Middle Ages. No matter how sophisticated a person's palate, his foot in his mouth rarely passes the taste test. Though Chaucer developed the story of Phoebus, he didn't originate it to further his favorite theme of the relationship between men and women. It came from the tale of Apollo and Coronis in Ovid's *Metamorphoses*.

A whole flock of squawking crows flew overhead as I approached the town of Rochester. My canteen had dried up over an hour ago, and I was thirsty and hot.

"Could I trouble you for some water?" I called out to a woman who pulled weeds from flower beds in her front yard. She offered a curious stare, and I explained my trek.

"Right you are," she said. "We can spare a drop of water."

I filled my canteen from a faucet in her yard and learned that Helen had recently retired as a hairstylist.

"If you cut hair like you raise flowers," I said, "you made a lot of people happy."

"You are kind," she said. "Do you like flowers?"

"I have a garden back home," I said, thinking that both she and I had continued a hobby passed to us from medieval ancestors.

"Oh, do take a closer look, then," said Helen, leading me among her geraniums, foxgloves, and petunias. "They're the last things I see at night and the first each morning." She had worn a tiny path among her flowers, as if making daily pilgrimages to them. "I've always loved to grow things, but especially now that I'm not working. I suppose they've taken the place of people. I take my scissors to them, too. Oh, dear me." A nervous little laughter revealed her false teeth. "See that house across the road? That's where Charles Dickens lived. They say his ghost sits on the wall at midnight. If you believe in such things."

"Do you believe such things?" I said.

She hesitated.

"When my sister and I were children, we saw one down by the castle," she said, pointing just down the road. "It was a knight without his head. My father said he lost it over a woman he loved."

She offered her nervous laugh again, and I wasn't sure if her story was meant to be sublime humor. After all, whether in the Middle Ages or in the modern world, who with an ounce of passion in his heart hadn't lost his head at least once over romance?

"I don't want to be a burden," said Helen, "but would you take something to Canterbury for me? Oh, it's a tiny thing."

She cut a red rose and handed it to me.

"Maybe you could light a candle when you get there and sprinkle the petals under it?" she said. "Oh, it's not a prayer for me but for my husband. He hasn't been feeling so well."

"Sure," I said, realizing that my journey then took on added meaning. "I'll do it for you."

She gave such an endearing look that I suspected she was about to ask me into her house to meet her husband, have dinner, and spend the night. But the invitation didn't flow as generously as her water.

I placed the rose petals in my pack and moved on, eager to see the castle. Reaching Dickens's stately two-story house, I paused before the wall where she said his ghost sat at midnight. Somebody—I assumed a kid—had written: "Know why Dickens ghost likes to sit here? He's hot for Humpty Dumpty and all the king's men."

Minutes later I became frozen in my tracks when Rochester Castle appeared, bordered by the river Medway. It was no less spectacular than childhood television memories of the Disneyland castle with roman candles showering red, yellow, and blue flaming balls over it. Tinkerbell, like some medieval fairy, might've soared over it with a magic wand at any second.

The turbulent history of Rochester Castle was no Disney fantasy. Built in 1130—just forty years before Becket's murder in the Canterbury cathedral—it housed three residential floors over a basement with surrounding walls 113 feet high. Its corner towers stood 12 feet higher. In 1215 a hundred rebel knights, foot soldiers, and bowmen had taken possession of the castle, and King John swore to overpower them. He sent orders to Canterbury to manufacture "by day and night as many picks as you are able." Six weeks later the digging had finally led his men to the edge of the castle wall. With plans to undermine it, John instructed justiciar Hubert de Burgh to "send to us with all speed day and night forty of the fattest pigs of the sort least good for eating to bring fire beneath the tower." To the groans of knights inside the castle, a large section of the wall collapsed when the lard blazed supporting timbers.[1]

A medieval castle household awoke at dawn on pallets in cellars and attics, while the lord and lady in the great chamber arose naked from a curtained bed. Knights, sleeping near their posts, relieved their "brothers" who had kept guard all night in towers and on the walls. Servants tended to fires in the kitchen and in the great hall.

A breakfast of bread with wine or ale followed mass in the

chapel. The lord, dressed in a long-sleeved tunic fastened with a brooch, met with stewards and bailiffs to discuss the day's business. The lady, also wearing a tunic and cosmetics made of sheep fat, talked with overnight guests or did embroidery. The chaplain or one of his clerks tutored the children, and knights and squires practiced their skills of war—mostly fencing and tilting. With lessons completed, the girls were free to pamper their dolls while the boys played with bows and arrows, horse-shoes, or tops and balls.

The castle courtyard buzzed with grooms, feeding horses and cleaning out stables. The forge blazed with oak as the smith made nails, wagon parts, and horseshoes. A laundress, us-ing a solution of wood ashes and caustic soda, washed table-cloths, towels, and sheets in a wooden trough. Domestic servants emptied chamber pots, thick with hay, which was used as toilet paper.

In some cases the latrine or "garderobe" was positioned in the castle wall. Other times it extended from the wall over a river or moat or emptied into a shaft leading to the ground. Rainwater diverted from gutters could clean such shafts, which at times presented a problem in defending a castle, since in-vaders climbed them. Henry III once sent orders ahead as he journeyed from one residence to another: "Since the privy chamber ... in London is situated in an undue and improper place, wherefore it smells badly, we command you on the faith and love by which you are bounden to us that you in no wise omit to cause another privy chamber to be made ... in such more fitting and proper place that you may select there, even though it should cost a hundred pounds, so that it may be made before the feast of the Translation of St. Edward, before we come thither."[2]

When a king or lord traveled, he did so with his bathman—who prepared the water—and his wooden tub, which was usu-ally placed in the castle garden in the summertime and by the chamber fire in the winter. He and his lady also traveled castle to castle with their bed, made from a wooden frame with ropes and strips of leather interlaced to create springs. These were then covered with a feather mattress, sheets, quilts, fur coverlets, and pillows.

A lord and lady who visited other nobles overnight were careful to make certain that they were not being watched during private moments. Owners and their stewards could use "squints" or peepholes hidden in castle wall decorations to spy on more than wayward servants.

A lord's steward, however, usually had far more important, if less tantalizing, business than being a voyeur. The "Seneschaucie," or "Stewardship," was a thirteenth-century manual that instructed the steward on managing the lord's estate:

> The seneschal of lands ought to be prudent and faithful and profitable, and he ought to know the law of the realm, to protect the lord's business and to instruct and give assurance to the bailiffs who are beneath him in their difficulties. He ought two to three times a year to make rounds and visit manors of his stewardship, and then he ought to inquire about the rents, services, and customs . . . and about franchises of courts, lands, woods, meadows, pastures, waters, mills and other things which belong to the manor. . . .
>
> The seneschal ought, on coming to the manors, to inquire how the bailiff bears himself within and without, what care he takes, what improvement he makes, and what increase and profit there is in the manor in his office, because of his being there. And also of . . . all other offices. . . . He ought to remove all those that are not necessary for the lord, and all the servants who do nothing. . . .
>
> The seneschal ought, on his coming to the manors, to inquire about wrongdoings and trespasses done in the

parks, ponds, warrens, rabbit runs, and dove-houses, and of all other things, which are done to the loss of the lord in his office.[3]

In 1226 Simon of Senlis, a steward of the bishop of Chichester, followed the manual when he wrote:

Know, my lord, that William de St. John is not in Sussex, wherefore I cannot at present carry through the business which you enjoined upon me, but as he comes into the Sussex, I will work as hard as I can to dispatch and complete in accordance with your honor. I sent to you 85 ells of cloth bought for distribution for the use of the poor. As regards the old wine, which is in your cellar at Chichester, I cannot sell to your advantage because of the over-great abundance of new wine in the town of Chichester. Further, my lord, know that a certain burgess of Chichester holds one croft which belongs to the garden given to you by our lord the king, for which he pays two shillings a year, which the sheriff of Sussex demands from him. Wherefore, since the land belongs to the said garden, and was removed from it in ancient times, please give me your advice about the said rent. . . .[4]

The steward later wrote:

Know, dearest lord, that I have been to London, where I labored with all my might and took care that you should there have ... wood for burning, brewing and repairs. Thanks be to God, all your affairs, both at West Mulne and elsewhere, go duly and prosperously. Also I have taken care that you should have what I judge to be sufficient quantity of lamb's wool for your household against the winter. . . . Speak also with Robert of Lexington about having beef for your larder in London.... If you think it wise, my lord, I beg that part of the old corn from West Mulne shall be ground and sent to London against your coming....[5]

A steward had to be constantly on his toes to make sure that household workers didn't steal from his lord. From Michaelmas (September 29) to Michaelmas, he daily listed what entered the castle and what left it. He had to know how many loaves could be baked from a quantity of wheat and see to it that the exact number was delivered to the pantler, who was in charge of the pantry. Meat as well as milk, cheese, eggs, wine, and ale had to be accounted for. The steward even kept tally of the castle's guests and what they required. The records of Prince Edward in June 1293 read: "There came to dinner John of Brabant, with 30 horses and 24 valets, and the two sons of the Lord Edmund, and they stay at our expenses in all things in hay, oaks and wages."[6]

In May 1265 a daily household account of Eleanor de Montfort stated:

On Sunday, for the Countess and lord Simon de Montfort, and the aforesaid persons [in the household]: bread, 2 quarters, wine, 4 sextaries; beer, already reckoned. Kitchen. Sheep from Everley, 6, also for 1 ox and 3 calves and 8 lbs. of fat, 12s. 2d.; 6 dozen fowls 3s.; also eggs 20d. flour 6d. Bread for the kitchen 3d. Geese 10, already reckoned. Marshalcy [stable]. Hay for 50 horses. Oats, 3 quarters and a half.

Sum 17s. 7d. [The daily wage of a thirteenth-century craftsman was almost 5 pence, and there were 12 pence in a shilling, 20 shillings in a pound.][7]

A steward was often a knight, which gave him the honor of sitting near the head of the dinner table with the lord and lady

and any ecclesiastical dignitary or noblemen who might be visiting the castle. The table, covered with an elegant cloth, was set
with knives, silver spoons, silver cups, dishes for salt, and "maz-
ers," or wooden bowls. A thick slice of bread three or four days
old, a "manchet," served as a plate for meat. The "manchet" or
"trencher" soaked up juices and was then eaten or given as alms
to the poor.

When a blown horn announced that the meal was to start,
servants called "ewerers" rushed to the table with basins and
towels. They poured warm, scented water onto the guests' hands
from ewers or aquamaniles of bronze or silver or enamel, sometimes designed as an animal's head so the water could flow from
the mouth. Following grace, the pantler brought bread and
butter. Wine, served by the butler, came next, along with soups,
stews, and meat, which was cut with a knife but eaten with the
fingers. Two people often ate from the same bowl. A man helped
a woman just as the younger helped the older. The best of manners was expected in all aspects of eating. No elbows on the table. No belching. No talking with mouths full. Hands and nails
should be kept clean at all times. Do not dip meat in the salt
dish. The mouth was usually wiped, especially before drinking,
on a large napkin draped over the shoulder.

The finer meals were creative surprises. Cooked pheasants
were served with their feathers to look as if the birds yet lived,
and some dishes were made in the shape of castles and animals.
Guests often brought their hooded falcons, riding upon their
wrists. Their hoods were removed when large pastries being
served released birds to fly about the hall, till the falcons—much
to the joy and excitement of the guests—snatched the birds
from midair. Each course ended with a "subtlety," which was a
sculpture made of papier-mâché, or sugar or marzipan, which
the guests sometimes let melt in their mouths.

Dinner was served at 10:00 A.M. and supper, eaten at sundown, could be a gluttonous affair. On Christmas Day 1252,

when Henry III's daughter married the king of Scotland, Matthew Paris recorded that "more than sixty pasture cattle formed the first and principal course at table . . . the gift of the archbishop."[8] Such feasts often served peacocks, swans, suckling pigs, boars' heads, and venison. Oysters, eels, crab, and crayfish were eaten as well. In 1230 the sheriff of Gloucester received this royal order: "Since after lampreys all fish seem insipid to both the king and the queen, the sheriff shall produce by purchase or otherwise as many lampreys as possible in the baili-wick, place them in bread and jelly, send them to the king while he is at a distance from those parts by John of Sandon, the king's cook, who is being sent to him. When the king comes nearer, he shall send them to him fresh."[9]

During the meal guests were sometimes entertained by "ystri-ones" (actors), jesters, or "jongleurs," which were professional minstrels singing in French. They moved about the table as they sang of love, nature, or the Crusades and played instru-ments that included lutes, harps, reed pipes, bagpipes, trum-pets, kettledrums, and cymbals.

When the meal ended, the guests washed their hands before dancing or playing chess or backgammon. The more adventur-ous and physical guests, however, preferred to play "hot cock-les," in which they struck a blindfolded player as he knelt. Amid the guests' laughter and his moans, he tried to guess who had hit him and knew too well in some cases by the lack of delicacy in the blows.

Just across the English Channel at the castle of Count Robert of Artois, guests were treated to more inventive entertainment than hot cockles. Garden statues squirted water on them as they walked past, and a trapdoor dropped them onto a feather bed. One room, upon the door's being opened, made the sound of thunder. Pressurized pipes "wet the ladies from below."

When a medieval castle's evening ended, servants carried

Men playing whip-top. (B.M. MS. Roy. 2B. VII, Queen Mary's Psalter. f.164.)

flaming torches to escort the lord and lady to their room. Thirteenth-century manuals advised them to bring the lord his robe, take off his shoes and hose by the fire, comb his hair, prepare his bed, put out the dog and cat, and make certain that his basin and urinal were set close at hand. Then they were to leave immediately that their "sovereign may take his rest merrily."

Crossing the bridge over the Medway River, as wide as the Mississippi River in some spots, I entered the green lawn of Rochester Castle, which now dwarfed me. No wonder medieval peasants stood in awe of their lord's power when they stood before such a mountain of stones. It looked as if it could swallow a man in one quick gulp.

But as I moved closer to the castle's entrance, my attention was diverted by four teenagers, sitting on the ground and playing cards. One with blond hair, dyed red on top as if he were a fun-loving fool at a medieval court, spoke first.

"You're new in town."

"Yeah, first time to the castle," I said. "Came to see the king. Can you introduce me?"

He ran his fingers, covered with rings, through his dyed hair.

"Would if I could," he said. Then his grin faded. "A king has no use for our kind."

His implication drew me closer than the castle's grandeur.

"What kind are you?" I said, moving his way.

All the teenagers' eyes livened.

"We're the Rochester outcasts," he said.

Outcasts of runaway serfs, pilgrims, vagabonds, entertainers, and lepers roamed medieval England. Each was required to carry a letter stating the purpose of his journey and could be fined if found without his papers.

"I've felt like an outcast a time or two myself," I said. "Mind if I join you for a little while?"

"No," said the blond. "There's room."

I sat on the grass.

"You don't act like most adults," said another boy, who introduced himself as Big Head.

"Is that good or bad?" I said.

"Most older people don't care what we think," he said. "They'd never dream of asking to sit with us."

"You look like fascinating company to me," I said.

The boys beamed, as if no one had told them that in a long time. Though I was more than old enough to be their father, I felt my own distant youth stir deep within.

"Is that part of a snake in the back of your hat?" said the boy who introduced himself as Chris.

I told them a little about my heritage and why I was on a pilgrimage to Canterbury.

"That's cool," said the blond, whose nickname was Red Top. "Wish I had the guts to take off on my own like that. I'd go to America."

"My father's off on a trip by himself right now," said Big Head. "He's traveling all over England on a motorcycle doing a scavenger hunt to join the Hell's Angels."

"If you're lucky, he'll not come back," said Red Top.

Big Head frowned.

"My father isn't always good to me," he said. "I've been homeless for several days now. Last night we all slept under those trees." He pointed to behind the castle.

"Some guy about your age came to our fire," said Chris. "He really got to us. He just sat there looking at the flames till he finally said he had brain cancer."

"Yeah," said Red Top, "he wasn't even mad about it. Just kept saying he didn't want to die yet."

"I was relieved when he left," said Scott, who spoke for the first time. "I have too much on my mind as it is already. My brother is in jail right now for stealing a car and goes to the judge tomorrow."

"Are all of you homeless?" I said.

"Oh, no," said Chris. "I live in an old folks' home. I like it there. Really old people are fun to be around sometimes. I make money by packing beans."

"I roof houses," said Scott. "But I'm out of work right now."

"I'm on the dole," said Big Head. "I guess that's something like welfare in the United States. I want to form a band."

"We're going to a concert in Glastonbury this weekend," said Red Top. "We've already rented a van for six of us. When we get to the festival, we'll find a hole in the fence and crawl in."

"We've got to be fast about it," said Big Head, as he crawled on his stomach a few feet as though instructing recruits.

"Be easier just to buy a ticket," said Chris.

"Yeah, but who's got the quid?" said Scott.

"Even if we had the money, I'd rather crawl though the fence," said Red Top.

Though I suspected the teenagers were showing off a bit, I loved their excitement. Chaucer was a teenager himself when he got a strong taste of excitement. Serving in the English army in France, he was captured while on a foraging expedition.

Records of the keeper of the king's wardrobe show that on March 1, 1360, while the army was in Guillon, the king gave £16 (or about $5,000 in today's currency) for his ransom.

"I definitely need further instructions on how to crawl through a fence hole," I said. "But right now I want to find a room for the night. Can you guys help?"

"Andy Snacks," said Red Top. "They'll rent you a room."

The very name of the place intrigued me.

"Andy Snacks?" I said.

"Just a few blocks from here," said Chris. "We'll show you."

The teenagers shot to their feet, and we were off. It was a beautiful match to walk through the center of Rochester with the kids. They seemed as delighted to be seen with the American pilgrim as I was to be escorted. Sometime between when I first met them and now, I had forgotten our age difference. It seemed that life's clock had but a single hand, pointing to the eternal moment.

"There," said Red Top, as he gestured toward a sign saying ANDY SNACKS over a restaurant door. Paint peeled from the building, and a window was cracked.

Then the four teenagers whispered among themselves. At one point Big Head gave me a wondrous glance, unlike anything I had ever seen before.

"It's settled," said Red Top, when the group came from its private street meeting. "We have a surprise for you tomorrow. Be at the castle grounds at noon."

"Surprise?" I said.

"You'll see," said Big Head, as if he couldn't wait.

As they strolled away, their laughter whetted my curiosity. Slipping from my pack, I entered Andy Snacks to the smell of a freshly baked pie. A dozen tables with red chairs sat empty as if the place were closed. But a hundred eyes seemed to study me as they peered out from snapshots on the wall.

"They're people who have stayed here," came a woman's

voice as she stepped from the kitchen. "I'm Joyce. My husband, Philip, and I are the owners."

A tall and handsome man in his sixties who I assumed was Philip stepped from the kitchen with a pot in his hand. He looked me up and down as though he wasn't sure what to think.

"I'm on a pilgrimage to Canterbury," I said, wondering if at this stage of my journey it wouldn't have been easier to wear a sign saying that around my neck.

"I didn't know people took pilgrimages anymore," he said.

"Sure they do, Philip," said Joyce. "Don't you remember the Italian a couple of years back?"

"If she was a pilgrim," said Philip, "I'm the pope at a brothel. Just because she was walking and wore dainty little crosses hanging from her neck didn't convince me."

"She did leave her room in a riot," said Joyce. "Balloons hung everywhere, and the bed smelled of wine." She hesitated but added, "She made friends with men quickly."

"If you rent me a room," I said, "I'll put all my balloons away before I leave."

Philip nodded, and Joyce searched among keys, dangling on the wall.

"All we have left is the red room," she said. "Do you mind red?"

I told her that the color was fine and took the key. Philip was giving directions to my room when a little man in his fifties stumbled through the back door with a mop and bucket of water.

"That has it," he said, as if washing his hands of the whole wide world.

"This is Charlie," said Joyce. "His room is near yours. He's lived here for several years now."

I offered to shake Charlie's hand.

"You can just call me Number One," said Charlie. "If you want to know the truth of the matter."

"Number One?" I repeated, to make certain that I had understood.

"Here," said Philip, as he took a framed poem from the wall and handed it to me. "This says it all."

I read the poem aloud:

ODE TO CHARLIE
I love me very much
I know I always shall
I never find me boring
I am my own best pal

Number One, strutting like Chauntecleer, took the poem from me and placed it back on the wall. Then he straightened it. And straightened it again. He was almost out of the dining room and into the kitchen with his mop and bucket when he turned to eye the "Ode to Charlie" one more time. Pleased that the poem was in its perfect place, he disappeared as the mop handle rattled against the bucket.

"He's like a child," Joyce said, lowering her voice.

"He's on the dole but blows it every payday on gambling," said Philip. "Just can't help himself."

"We find him little jobs here to help keep him going," Joyce added. "Now don't forget that your room includes a full English breakfast. Philip cooks it, and he's a whiz."

I had never felt more welcomed and at home more quickly than at Andy Snacks. Indeed, as I headed upstairs to my room, it dawned upon me that I had never felt safer than I had the past day or two. Something about England I couldn't yet put my finger on was introducing me to a new level of relaxation. It was as though stress I hadn't even been aware of before coming to England had been rubbed off my very skin when I pushed my shoulders, arms, and back into the "a-ganging" cliff outside Gravesend.

My sense of peace, however, faced a tricky test when I opened the door to my lodging. It was the reddest room I had ever seen. Even the curtains were red. It almost seemed that I was living back in medieval England under the care of John of Gaddesden. He was the physician to Edward II. The young Chaucer was an attendant to the king's son, Prince Lionel. When the prince became ill with smallpox, the doctor instructed that he be wrapped in red cloth in a room with red curtains and red carpet. It was believed that the red would lower the temperature of the patient by drawing the excessively red blood outward. Prince Lionel survived the smallpox.

John of Gaddesden also taught that being touched by a monarch could cure tuberculosis, which was called the "king's evil." That is, if his medicine made of weasel blood and dove droppings didn't work. He advised a patient with colic to wear a sealskin girdle (belt) with a whalebone buckle. For epilepsy he prescribed extract of cuckoo, mixed with boar's bladder and mistletoe, because he thought the bird had the same disease once a month. He was the author of a book with one chapter entitled "Disagreeable Diseases Which the Doctor Can Seldom Make Money By." No records confirm that Chaucer ever met John of Gaddesden, but he was certainly much aware of him. In his prologue to The Canterbury Tales, his "Doctor of Physic" knew well such authorities as Hippocrates and a long list of others, including "Gatesden."

Andy Snacks was closed for dinner. I ate at a nearby pub and lingered after the meal to write in my journal and *eavesdrop* on conversations around me. English law in the Middle Ages forbade houses to be built closer than two feet apart because rain dripping from the edge of the roof could damage the other's property. This part of the roof became known as the "eaves drop," and those who tried to hear what was said in the house next to them became known as "eavesdroppers."

By the time I headed back to the red room, most shops had

closed, and banners, stretched between the two-story brick buildings, flapped in the wind. Only a few people stirred, and I cherished the opportunity to take a close look at each one. One passerby resembled an American cousin of mine so much that, for a moment, I was awed—ready to ask, When did you get here? Funny thing, those carnival mirrors reflecting ancestral genes.

But the familiar stranger simply nodded, and we went our separate ways, save in the pilgrim's heart, where—I was learning—sometimes even a glance is a link to one's own meaning and purpose. Minutes later I crawled into the red room bed at Andy Snacks. When I closed my eyes, I thought of hearth and home—my little Alabama cabin so far away just now. But that did not make me long for my beautiful Cherokee mountains, where God himself seemed to live. No, he was also there on Pilgrims' Way atop the grand British mountain of human diversity.

I love me very much
I know I always shall
I never find me boring
I am my own best pal

CHAPTER
6

A beautiful morning tune swept through my red room at Andy Snacks, as if some enchanted bird perched in the hallway. It soon proved to be Charlie, Number One himself, whistling as he dashed downstairs.

The smell of sizzling bacon and perking coffee filled the air, and parted curtains revealed a sunny sky. Following a quick shower, I put on clean clothes and went down to the restaurant.

"Did you sleep well?" said Joyce, as if I had known her for years.

"Yes," I said. "There's a taste of home here."

"You didn't ask how I fared in the cold dark night," said Number One, as he poured himself a cup of coffee.

"Oh, Charlie," said Joyce. "You're such a baby. Did you rest well, too?"

"I'm not telling you," said Number One, as he winked. "Where's my breakfast, anyway?"

Philip stepped from the kitchen with an egg, as though he had just gathered it from a henhouse.

"I'll cook your breakfast, Charlie," said Philip, "just as soon as I'm done with John's."

"If it's for John," said Number One.

"Thank you, Charlie," said an elderly man who sat at a table fifteen feet away. White-haired, he fumbled with a pack of cigarettes.

"John is blind in one eye and can barely see from the other," Joyce whispered to me. "He's been living here for fifteen years."

"Are you whispering about *me*?" said Number One.

"No, Charlie," said Joyce. "Just mind your own sweet business."

"Makes me uncomfortable when people say things I can't understand," said Number One.

"Give me a light, Charlie?" said John, as he stuck a cigarette to his lips.

"*That* I understand," said Charlie, striking a match.

"I met a man a couple of days ago who rolled a cigarette with one hand," I said.

"Really?" said Number One. "I can't roll one with two hands. My blooming tobacco flies every which way into a big mess. John Wayne could roll with one hand. Him and all those other famous cowboys."

"They're just movie cowboys, Charlie," said Joyce.

"I used to be able to see movies," said John, puffing his cigarette.

"Philip and I liked the movies," said Joyce. "We met when we were only fifteen."

"I don't believe in romance," said Number One. "All women got little devils in their souls." His face turned sour, as though he were addressing the Wife of Bath herself.

"Oh, Charlie," said Joyce, "you just never met the right one."

"You can say that again," said Number One.

"I had a good wife till she died," said John.

"Do you have children?" I asked.

"A boy and girl," said John. "They've grown up and gone their own way now. Can't recall the last time they came to see me."

Philip returned with a plate of fried eggs, bacon, potatoes, and toast and placed it on the table in front of John. His fork, guided by one poor eye, groped to find its target.

"Want a hand, John?" said Number One.

"No," said John. "I feel adventurous today."

John hadn't shaved in a couple of days, and it saddened me that his children didn't visit him more often. On the other hand, he seemed lucky to have a home—one room though it was—at Andy Snacks, where Joyce, Philip, and Number One cared about him.

When Philip brought breakfasts for Number One and me, he pulled a chair to the table and joined us. Joyce had been right yesterday when she said Philip was a good cook, and I told him the same.

"Cooking gives me something to do," said Philip. "I couldn't stand the notion of just sitting around, racking my brains about how to spend the day."

Racking one's brains originated in the Middle Ages. The rack, an instrument of torture, was introduced into the Tower of London by the duke of Exeter in 1470 and was also called "Exeter's Daughter." The guilty person's ankles and wrists were fastened to the rack's rollers, which were tightened until they occasionally pulled them from their bloody sockets. The rack was abolished in 1640, but the term for struggling with one's thoughts to the extreme stayed.

"I was a carpenter before we took over Andy Snacks," Philip added.

"I was a laborer," said John. His weathered and scarred hands won my respect.

"I've never liked work of any kind," said Number One.

"What a surprise," said Joyce.

"Always like to build things," Philip continued. "My son and I tinker with used cars. Sell one now and then. My greatest pastime, though, is raising pigeons with my son. We keep them at his house. Oh, there's nothing more magical than to see a flock of racers released to hurry back home."

"I had a pigeon once," said John. "He would sit on my shoulder and coo."

I felt in excellent company because, like Chaucer and other medieval Englishmen, I was a great lover of birds myself.

"I'd eat a live pig before I'd let a messy bird sit on my shoulder," said Number One. His comment seemed a contradiction, since he could whistle as prettily as a bird.

"When you think about it," said Philip, "people aren't exactly the white lace on a ball gown, now, are they?"

"Don't want any people sitting on my shoulder either," said Number One.

"Oh, Charlie," said Joyce.

"I hadn't thought about that pigeon in years," said John, as if he suddenly saw the bird as close as his own hand. "But I can still hear him."

"Oh, you never forget what gets next to your heart," said Joyce, "no matter how many years pass."

"As far back as the building of castles," said Philip, "a breed of pigeon known as the tumbler was used to entertain royalty. I've raised them myself."

"They were something sweet," said Joyce. "They'd turn flips in the sky."

"And the cow jumped over the moon," said Number One.

"It's true," said Philip. "They're like acrobats."

In that wondrous Andy Snacks moment, I envisioned a flock of ancient tumblers over Rochester Castle. They brought *ooooohs* and *aaaaahs* from everyone at the court as the lord's fool ran among the guests to flap his arms like wings and turn somersaults before blowing a single tiny feather from his mouth.

"My pigeon couldn't do any tricks," said John. "I liked him just the same."

Somewhere in the midst of John's humbling pathos, Number

One's comic cynicism, Joyce's gracious hospitality, and Philip's charming speech, I decided to spend another night at Andy Snacks. Indeed, any thought of pushing on today down Pilgrims' Way after I was to meet the teens at noon on the castle lawn was now totally out of the question.

"I'd like to pay for a second night," I told Joyce and Philip after breakfast. When I offered the cash to Philip, he hesitated.

"You don't have to pay," he said with a fatherly tone.

"No," said Joyce. "It's our little way of helping you get to Canterbury."

Early pilgrims did not trek to particular shrines, as did those who walked to Canterbury. An Anglo-Saxon writer in the tenth century wrote of the penitential pilgrim: "He throws away his weapons and wanders far and wide across the land, barefoot and never staying more than a night in one place. . . . He fasts and wakes and prays by day and by night. He cares not for his body and lets his hair and nails grow freely."[1]

The Council of Macon in 585 decreed that a bishop found guilty of murder should pass the rest of his life in pilgrimage. Some Irish canons as late as A.D. 1000 required that anyone who killed a bishop's servant be condemned to perpetual exile. Lesser crimes—including incest, bestiality, and sacrilege—could require the offender to journey for twenty years. Archbishop Odo Rigaud, visiting the province of Rouen, regularly imposed pilgrimages on clerics and laymen for sexual misconduct. Acts of forgery, breaking sanctuary, and public irreverence toward the church were also punished with pilgrimages. Robert de Frechesne, guilty of seizing and imprisoning a cleric, had to journey to Saint Michael's Church in Rouen to recite fifty "Pater Nosters" and fifty "Ave Marias," fast for three days, and give five shillings to the poor. Roger da Bonito, after killing the bishop of Fricentro in 1319, was sent to Rome, Santiago, and Jerusalem.

The idea that a pilgrim should visit a certain shrine didn't become popular until the eleventh century. Many pilgrimages were self-imposed because people wanted to clear their consciences of sins and crimes even if no one else knew of the misdeeds. While the church's confessors were the principal decision makers on who should take a pilgrimage, they were not alone. The law courts could sentence a criminal to journey to a shrine, which saved the expense of feeding him in jail but added to the throngs of thieves already crowding the roads. The guilty who pretended to take a pilgrimage and only hid with friends or family or in some nearby village could be fined, locked in prison, or put to death, depending on the severity of the crime. Guilds and universities could also demand that a member cleanse his soul by trekking to a sacred site. So many lied about their journeys, however, that it became necessary for the pilgrims to return to their confessors, courts, and organizations with "testimonials," signed by members of the clergy caring for the shrine, to prove that they had been there.

Pilgrims often walked barefoot and wore chains or leg irons. A weapon used in their crime, such as a dagger or sword, was commonly fastened to the fetters. Medieval man believed that when the chains broke, God had forgiven him. A nobleman named Frotmund in 850 killed his father and took a pilgrimage with a crowd of other sinners to Rome, Jerusalem, and back to Rome. With his chains still intact, he traveled back to Jerusalem and Rome over the mountains of Italy and France, until the fetters finally broke in the church of Saint Marcellin at Redon. Skeptics attributed such feats to fraud or rusty chains, but this didn't stop the growing belief among thousands that God watched over shrines to deliver sinners. Charlemagne in the eleventh century was said to have written his sins on a piece of paper and had them wiped clean by Saint Gilles when the words disappeared.

In the Middle Ages people believed that disease of the body was caused by their sins, and masses journeyed to sanctuaries of the Blessed Virgin when they became ill with the "Holy Fire," which was caused by eating rye infected by a specific mold or fungus. Its symptoms were severe gangrene, sharp burning sensations, convulsions, and nervous disorders. In 1128 Hughes Farsit wrote:

This horrible disease spreads beneath the stretched blue skin, separating it from the bones and slowly consuming it. The pain and heat steadily increase until the victims long for death as their only hope of release. As the fever wastes the limbs, a raging fire burns the internal organs, yet it produces no heat and it never abates, however much the wretched victims pour cold liquids over themselves. . . . It was horrible to behold the sick and the recently cured, the sign of death still visible on their bodies and in their faces. Yet the mercy of God is even greater than the afflictions of men. When no human remedy could be found, . . . the sick, even as the fire raged inside them, took refuge in the benevolence and healing power of the ever-virgin Mother of God, and she did not disappoint them in their hopes.[2]

Disease was also seen as a result of the Devil's entering the human body. Peter the Deacon, the historian of the Monte Cassino abbey, claimed that he saw a devil flee from the mouth of an epileptic cured by Saint Benedict. Guibert of Nogent noted how the Devil behaved in his cousin's body when the arm of Saint Arnoul was used:

When the arm of the blessed martyr was laid upon him, the sickness shifted its ground and settled in another part of the body. Then the virulence was put to flight again and the whole arm pressed hard against it. The whole force of the disease ran up and down his face and limbs and finally flowed into the region of the throat and shoulders, the skin being a little raised like a mouse. Then gathering into a ball it vanished without pain.[3]

Fear of sudden death from the plague and burning eternally in hell inspired masses of pilgrims to travel to Rome in the Jubilee Year of 1350, a time when all confessed sinners were forgiven free of charge. As many as five thousand pilgrims entered and left the city daily and camped around fires at night. Boniface VIII established the jubilee in 1300 and had intended it to be a centennial event, but the first year was so successful, with two million pilgrims boosting the economy, that the jubilee was held every fifty years. Today it is celebrated every twenty-five years, and a sinner is cleansed, says the church, by simply walking through the doorway of one of four churches, where thousands crowd to kiss and rub the weathered wood as though it were the body of Christ himself.

Disease, guilt, and crime drove the majority of pilgrims to Canterbury and other shrines throughout Europe. But in rare cases citizens could be sent on such travels for simply not conforming. Henri le Kien, a painter of Tournai, was ordered to Rocamadour in 1428 because he "made a habit of insulting and criticizing other people ... and thus caused great dissensions and troubles." The disgruntled artist was "never to return to the city unless the citizens gather together in their guilds and districts to re-admit him."[4]

England never embraced the Inquisition as Europe did to punish those found guilty of heresy, but many of its victims were sent to Canterbury to repent. Though they were not required to wear chains and fetters, they were obligated to wear two large crosses made of saffron-colored cloth on their front and back. To remove the crosses brought severe penalties. The wearers were ostracized by other pilgrims and prevented from staying in inns or hospices.

While the spiritual depth of a pilgrimage varied from person to person, some professed not to care about the journey at all. They could even pay the court or the damaged party a fee and avoid the pilgrimage altogether. Once a sentence had been passed, the convicted had a few weeks to raise the money. If he was unable to pay the fine, however, he had to start walking to the appointed shrine. The farther away a shrine, the steeper the fine. In France a trip to Santiago and Rome cost the offender 12 livres (equal to about £12), but a pilgrimage to Saint Martin of Tours cost him only 3 livres.

Before a committed pilgrim took to the road, he made a will, asked his wife as well as his feudal lord for permission, and sought forgiveness from those he had wronged. Then he requested a blessing from his parish priest or monk. This blessing extended beyond the pilgrim's soul and covered his clothes as well as his staff, which was handed to him from the altar in a ritual that originated with knights departing on the first Crusade. For pilgrims to travel in masses was common, but a solo traveler won the most respect because it gave the pilgrim a greater opportunity to know God.

I departed Andy Snacks and headed toward Rochester Castle. Whether it was fate or luck that had led me to such a colorful and inviting place to spend the night and commune with others didn't matter. I simply knew, right down to my bones, that I was meant to be there. It was a home away from home, and as I walked through Rochester, I felt that I belonged in the town as well. That, in turn, inspired me to reach out to others with new vigor. When a man began to unload crates of fruits and vegetables from his truck for a street market, I offered to give him a hand.

"Are you mad as a hatter," he said, "working when you don't have to?"

"I need the exercise," I said. He studied me as though that

just wasn't explanation enough. "I usually lift weights at a gym, but I'm away from home just now, walking to Canterbury on a pilgrimage."

He eyed my Cherokee hat and then the heavy crates. He finally handed me a crate of apples, and as I told him a bit more about my purpose in coming to England, he began to let me into his life. Rex was an only child and had been born on the coast at Dover. He moved to the Rochester area because his wife wanted to be near her ailing mother, who had died the past year. His own mother was dead as well. His father was a commercial fisherman who had once caught a shark that had swallowed a child's toy metal dog.

"I was just a lad when my father cut that dog from the fish's belly, and it scared the hell out of me," said Rex. "He took it to the local pub, and they kept it in a jar of water like a pickle. The bartender asked tourists to guess what it was, and the villagers would nudge each other while they looked on."

"You pulling my leg?" I said, thinking that such an odd kind of story could have been told by one of Chaucer's fun-loving pilgrims.

"No, mate," he said. "It was a boring little village, and we were starved for diversion."

"Sounds like a story with a big moral?" My eyes teased.

"No, mate," he said. "My father and his friends didn't go to the pub to fill their pints with meaning."

Then for the first time Rex laughed—and laughed so hard that he hesitated to lift a crate of oranges. It was in that carefree zone that I saw his face flourish into an entirely different person than I had first perceived. It reminded me how often we all wear a mask till the right situation takes it from our hardened and oh-so-busy faces in this competitive modern world. In that rare moment, too, I thought how easily Rex and I could've passed each other by. I would have been but another traveler, and he would've been the deliveryman whose crates were in my way.

Rex had three children and a fourth who died at birth, something from which—if I read his tone and eyes correctly— he had never fully recovered. He had considered becoming a priest when he was a child. His mother had prayed for that.

"But when I got older," he said, "I came under the lovely spell of women. I think my mother understood."

His eyes shone as though that spell had done him right when he pulled his wallet forth to show a picture of his wife and kids. They were in their backyard, and the children held hot dogs on sticks over a fire. Rex's wife wore sunglasses and lazed in his lap as he held up a can of ale to toast the perfect picture.

When we placed the last crate on the sidewalk, Rex looked as though he wished there were more to unload. I felt the same way.

"If you need more exercise," he finally said, "my lawn could use a good mowing."

I started on down the street when he called my name. His hand released a red apple, which arched some ten feet before landing in my palm.

"I almost forgot," said Rex. "Do you know about The Friars over in Avion? It's a monastery only about ten miles from here, and I think they have rooms for people like you. Pilgrims headed to Canterbury spent the night there."

I had not heard of The Friars, and thoughts of meeting others on spiritual journeys as well as exploring a medieval monastery intrigued me. I couldn't help but wonder, too, if I had met Rex for this very information.

"I'll check into it," I said.

Walking on through Rochester, I ate the apple, not because I was hungry but because I wanted the encounter with Rex to linger. After all, it wasn't just an ordinary piece of fruit. It was another gift from Pilgrims' Way. Finishing the apple, I put its seeds in my shirt pocket.

Down by the river Medway, I used a pub's phone book to find The Friars' number. It rang twice, and—

"Hello, Brother John speaking," came the voice.

I had never been to a monastery and wasn't sure what to anticipate. But a part of me half expected to hear Gregorian chants in the background, so I was a little surprised when a cat meowed. That, or Brother John had the unique hobby of making animal sounds.

"Sorry," said Brother John. "The cat is on my shoulder. I'll just set him down. Very well, what can I do for you?"

"I'm an American on a pilgrimage to Canterbury," I said. "Do you have a place for me to stay tomorrow night?"

Medieval churches and monasteries had holes in their doors for mouse-catching cats to come and go, and I questioned if that was true today at The Friars. The cat meowed again, and the monk scolded.

"Yes, we'll have a place for you to sleep," said Brother John, without asking a single other question except for my name.

It seemed amazingly easy to reserve a room at the monastery. In medieval England the roads were teeming with thieves who dressed like pilgrims so they could enter monasteries and hospices, built by the clergy, to swipe anything they could carry and sometimes rape the nuns. I wondered where I would sleep there and if the monks at The Friars practiced the Benedictine rule of washing a traveler's feet.

With some thirty minutes left before I was to meet Big Head, Red Top, Chris, and Scott at the castle lawn, I found a sunny spot to lounge by the river. There I removed my shoes and socks and trimmed my toenails. They looked better, less like weapons, but I wasn't certain that even the most loving of monks would cherish them. Still, the thought of a holy stranger bathing another's feet made me hope that the Benedictine rule was yet alive and well at The Friars.

Wind gusted off the Medway and through the trees and openings in the castle. There it howled just as it did in the Middle Ages, and I studied the great stone structure as if it were alive, breathing and inviting me in.

When I entered the castle, it was as cool as a cave. All the timbers, twice as thick as telephone poles, that once supported the floors were long gone, and the holes where they had rested in three levels were like tombs, reminding that even the hardest and thickest oaks fall prey to time. That made me respect the endurance of the stones all the more and those who had placed them here almost a thousand years ago. How many people in today's world could say they've created anything that would last that long? Some of the stones had eroded to reveal various shades of pumpkin-orange, while others were as black as coal or as gray as a winter's day.

Gundulf, bishop of Rochester, who was also responsible for the Tower of London, began Rochester Castle in 1087. But the castle was completed by William de Corbeil, archbishop of Canterbury, to whom Henry I granted custody in 1127.

Winding stone stairs led past latrines, through decorated arched doors into the chapel, and past fireplaces up to the mural gallery, where minstrels once sang. Other times the gallery acted as an exercise court. In the center of the castle, a well shaft, as big around as a barrel, was reachable from all floors by use of a winch. Food was cooked outside the castle, down in the bailey, and reheated in the castle when it was served. Here and there in the walls' cracks where sunlight shined, renegade plants grew as if they wanted to soar above their earthly kin. Pieces of black flint, just like those dotting the fields along Pilgrims' Way, were sprinkled in the ancient mortar between the plants, and it seemed as if the very ground once had a mind and spirit of its own to create the artistic vision that now surrounded me.

The word *loopholes*, which modern English speakers use to denote narrow escapes, comes from the "narrow windows" in medieval castles through which knights once shot their arrows

toward enemies down below. Looking through a Rochester
Castle loophole, I beheld the Medway, which, at high tide, had
washed against the castle walls before modern man tampered
with the earthen banks. I felt protected here, inside a womb.
I wished that I owned the castle and that it was restored to all
its glory. Some nights I would sleep atop it to watch the moon
and stars and sip wine with the one I loved. Other nights I
would invite my friends to a feast. I would be happy to help
with the cooking.

The medieval fantasy faded when I noticed satellite dishes
on distant houses and cars on the bridge. A lone jet streaked
the sky. But at least for a few seconds, as wind whistled through
the stone loopholes and into my face, I had been a lord.

Exiting the castle, I became startled when fingers gripped
my shoulder from behind. I turned to find Red Top. Overnight
he had dyed part of his hair blue. He held a black scarf, blowing in the wind, and I wasn't sure what to make of his canary-
eating grin.

"I said we had a surprise for you," he said, as he raised the
scarf.

Big Head and Chris waved from the edge of the castle near
the woods, where they said they had slept two nights ago, when
they met the stranger with brain cancer. They looked as eager
as Red Top.

"What kind of surprise?" I said.

"First, I got to blindfold you," said Red Top.

The medieval game of "hot cockles" shot through my perplexed mind. I had zero interest in being blindfolded on my
knees as others punched me in jest while I tried to guess who
they were.

"Oh, come on," said Red Top. "It's nothing to fear. You
seemed fun yesterday."

Big Head and Chris motioned for me to get with the plan,
and I questioned why Scott wasn't with them. Was he hiding as

part of this game? Their smiles were hard to resist, but I had not been blindfolded since I was a child and didn't want to be cast into darkness now. Yet a part of me was intrigued to find the pilgrimage taking an unusual turn. It wasn't usually my nature to dodge the unknown.

"OK," I said. "I'm putting a lot of trust in you guys."

"Relax," said Red Top. "Enjoy the ride."

He tied the scarf over my eyes. Sunlight shone through the cloth, but I couldn't see anything. He took my arm and led me in the direction of Big Head and Chris. If passersby on the street noticed us, what in the world would they think? I became concerned that an alarmed observer might call the police.

"Watch your step now," came Big Head's voice.

"Yeah," said Red Top, as he slowed our pace to a near stop. "Lift your feet high."

"Where are we going?" I said, as my shoe scraped against what appeared to be a rock.

"That's it," said Chris. "Now lift the other foot."

"How about a hint?" I said.

"A hint," said Big Head. "Hmmm . . ."

"Here's a hint," said Chris. "The answer will soon be in your hands."

I was more confused than ever but guessed that we were now among the trees behind the castle. Bushes rubbed against my jeans, and twigs snapped beneath my feet. The smell of decaying leaves filled the air.

"Where's Scott?" I said.

"We thought he'd be here by now," said Chris. "He's with his brother at court."

I wasn't sure whether to believe Chris or not.

"Just a couple more steps," said Red Top.

I stumbled over something, but he braced me before I fell.

"Sorry about that," said Red Top, and then I thought someone laughed. "Now sit down."

I eased to the ground onto what I supposed was a blanket and started to remove the blindfold.

"No, no, no," said Big Head. "You haven't passed the touch test yet."

I could smell cigarette smoke and what seemed to be the remains of a campfire. For all I knew, the "outcasts" had led me into a circle of witches.

"Hold out your hands," said Chris. "Turn the palms up."

Now there was no doubt. Someone other than Big Head, Red Top, and Chris did muffle laughter.

"Shhhh . . . ," Red Top warned.

"Ready for the first touch test?" said Big Head.

"I hope so," I said.

Something several inches long that reminded me of a snake brushed against my palms, and as many as five people laughed. I felt more in the dark than ever.

"Did you like the queen's tongue?" came a male's voice I had never heard before.

"Oh, don't be crude," came a girl's voice. "He'll think we have no respect for her majesty."

At least seven or eight young people laughed.

"When was the last time she invited you to lunch?" came the voice that had first spoken of the queen.

"Knock it off," said Red Top. "You're interfering with serious business here."

"Oh, *doooo* forgive me," said the boy.

"Get ready for the second touch test," said Red Top.

"Don't do it so fast as last time," said Big Head.

"So time me," said Red Top.

"Just get on with it," said Chris.

I took a deep breath just as something warm, rough, and round like a pineapple slid though my palms. But this was no fruit. It had a belly.

"Want to make a guess?" said Red Top.

"A baby dragon?" I played along.

"Close," said Big Head.

Just as the creature was placed in my hands, someone untied my blindfold, and I almost jumped right out of my skin to find a squirming iguana. The kids—there were more than a dozen of them—roared as the lizard's tongue came and went from its mouth like an earthworm doing a slippery dance.

"OK," I said, as the creature tried to crawl from my lap. My face heated from blushing. "You got me."

A boy with a Mohawk haircut took the iguana.

"It's OK, Honey-Bunny," he said, placing the animal on his shoulder.

"You should have seen your face," Red Top said to me, when he finally stopped laughing.

"You were a good sport," said Chris.

"I told them you would be," said Big Head. "It was my idea."

"How can I ever thank you?" I said.

There wasn't a single face in the teen crowd that didn't beam. Each eyed me as though I had truly passed some kind of test, and I liked that as much as they seemed to have enjoyed the exotic lizard gag.

The iguana paled, however, in comparison to the creatures medieval man believed roamed the earth. The phisiologus, a "monstrous thing in the sea," was thought to be often mistaken by sailors to be an island, and they would build a fire upon it to cook their meals.

The ahuna was another sea monster that was thought to turn everything it ate into grease. It had no gullet but a belly. When other fish tried to eat it, it would withdraw its head into the belly. If it became hungry in the frightened state, it would eat part of itself rather than risk being eaten whole by the surrounding fish. The polippus looked much like a whale but had feet and could climb the sides of ships to snatch sailors to the bottom of the sea to eat them. On the other hand, the gentle and graceful pauus maris was the peacock of the sea, with the head of a bird and the body of a fish.

The barnacle tree was believed to thrive on the Isle of Man, where it grew barnacles that opened to reveal geese. Albert Magnus denounced the tree as false in the thirteenth century, but tales of the tree even flourished among herbalists in the eighteenth century. The zieba tree was said to grow bare-bosomed men and women who lived in bliss as they contemplated the beauty of nature.

The kids gave a loud cheer when Scott appeared on the path leading from the castle lawn. His fingers, high overhead, formed jubilant Vs.

"My brother didn't have to go to jail," he shouted. "The judge just gave him a lot of community work to do." He eyed the iguana and the blindfold on Red Top's lap. "I thought you were going to wait on me."

Big Head handed Scott a bottle of whiskey as he flopped to the ground, and he lifted it to his lips. When he finished, he passed the bottle to the girl, whose tongue had a silver stud in the center. Whenever she spoke, it reflected sunlight and looked like a shooting star. A boy with a freckled nose held her hand as though that very star had taken him to outer space more than once. Every time she glanced at him, she seemed to fall more deeply in love. A picture of them kissing had been screen-printed onto her blouse. It made a stark contrast to the medieval art of "orfrois," in which the more educated and talented girls stitched portraits of friends and lovers onto rich silk. As a signature, a girl would sometimes weave strands of her own hair into the delicate design.

"Oh, get that out of my face," she said, when Big Head dangled a large rubber penis. "I don't need a toy, thank you very much just the same."

"I bought it at the joke store today," Big Head said. "Red Top got the cards."

Other kids were playing poker with cards that pictured naked women doing things with their fingers that would arouse some and offend others. But for all the excited talk, I didn't hear a single word of profanity. Words like *fokkinge, cunte*, and *crappe* entered the English language in the Middle Ages when Dutch sailors came to England. *Bugger* derives from the medieval Latin *Bulgarus*, meaning "both a Bulgarian and a sodomite." The word originally referred to a Bulgarian and then to Bulgarian Heretics, an eleventh-century group of monks and nuns accused of practicing sodomy.

"I wore the penis sticking from my shirt pocket when I bought a cookie this afternoon," said Big Head. "The bakery clerk's eyes almost popped out."

Though all the teens were obviously full of hormones, I couldn't help but be amused. At least they showed honesty about their desires, as carnal as those of Chaucer's pilgrims as they journeyed to Canterbury. English sexual thoughts were even demonstrated with a little humor as early as the eleventh century in the *Exeter Book*, offering a riddle about a young man and woman who joined forces:

Monk and nun in the stocks. (B.M. MS. Roy. 10. E. IV. f.187.)

Both swayed and shook
The young man hurried, was sometimes useful,
Served well, but always tired
Sooner than she, weary of the work.
Under her girdle began to grow
A hero's reward for laying on dough.[5]

The answer: churn. Another riddle went:

I heard of something rising in a corner
Swelling and standing up, lifting its cover.
The pride-hearted bride grabbed at that boneless
Wonder with her hands, the prince's daughter
Covered that swelling thing with a swirl of cloth.[6]

The answer: dough.

As the whiskey bottle and the rubber penis were passed about the group, the silver-tongued girl curled up on a blanket and placed her head in her boyfriend's lap. His fingers eased through her hair.

"We're having an all-night party in a field down by the river starting at dusk," said Big Head, as he placed the rubber penis into his shirt pocket. "You want to come? You can camp out with us, if you want."

"Yeah," said Red Top. "Come along."

When seven or eight of the other kids said the same, I told them that I would at least come by to say hello.

"We'll tell some ghost stories," said Big Head.

"Ghost stories are for children," said the boy who had suggested that the iguana's tail was the queen's tongue. His nails were long and painted black, except for the tip of the index fingers. They were tipped with silver glitter. His nickname was

"Sir Pretty," and he reminded me of the Pardoner in *The Canterbury Tales*:

> A voice he had as small as hath a goot
> No breed had he, ne never should have—
> As smooth it was as it were late y-shave
> I trow he were a gelding or a mare.

"In honor of our American holy man," said Sir Pretty, "tonight I will tell my favorite story from *The Canterbury Tales*. I did a school report on that old hack Chaucer and know his work well."

Red Top, behind Sir Pretty's back, stuck his finger down his throat before saying, "Lovely." Big Head pulled his rubber penis from his shirt pocket and tapped Sir Pretty on the head.

"I hereby crown thee Storyteller of the Night," said Big Head.

Even Chaucer's festive pilgrims could not have topped these kids' spirits to party, and I would not have missed the all-night gathering for the world. Many hours later, when the sun set, I departed Andy Snacks and followed a map Big Head had drawn. It led me past the castle to the iron bridge with its lion statues and over the Medway down a narrow street. From there I followed a footpath almost a mile outside of Rochester to an abandoned farmhouse near the river.

The teens had already started a fire in a big field, and Big Head and Red Top walked out to meet me. Most of the same teens I had met at the iguana gag were there along with a few new ones. Some were eating pizzas, while others played bongo drums and a guitar. Several bottles of wine stuck from a paper bag, and a bottle of Jack Daniel's was passed around. Sir Pretty waved to me as his bracelet dangled over the head of the silver-tongued girl and her boyfriend, who cuddled near the flames. Chris and Scott were gathering firewood.

"Are you not worried the police will bust you?" I said.

"No, they never bother us here," said Red Top.

"No," Big Head echoed. "They don't like to walk this far."

When darkness fell, Sir Pretty stayed true to his word and began telling "The Summoner's Tale," a satire on the church about a friar who went from door to door gathering gifts in a bag in exchange for prayers he never gave. The Summoner— he had pimples and boils, and his breath reeked of garlic, onions, leeks, and strong wine—tells how the friar lectures a reluctant donor long and hard before the donor agrees to offer him a gift, a fart that is to be divided equally among all the friars at the convent. Sir Pretty quoted Chaucer line by line in modern English:

I never heard the like, or I'm a liar;
I think the devil stuck it in his mind.
And in arithmetic did no man find,
Before this day, such puzzling question shown.
Who could be able, now, to make it known
How every man should have an equal part
Of both the sound and savour of a fart?

Most of the teens and I groaned when Sir Pretty made the sound of a loud fart, but a few found it funny and began duplicating the coarse noise. He finally continued with the tale as his silver-glittered nails reflected the light of the campfire. The friar hurried to the nearby house of a lord to tell how deeply he had been offended.

"I'll pay him out for it," the friar shouted. "I can defame him."

The lord's valet offered a solution. He proposed that the donor be strapped to a thirteen-spoke wheel while a friar knelt at the end of each spoke. When the donor passed gas, he would turn the wheel, sharing the gift equally among the friars.

Sir Pretty ended the story by pretending to fart again, and the teens applauded. All except one did, that is. Having drunk too much, she was throwing up. That, or the tale sickened her.

"That's the best story in the whole lot," said the silver-tongued girl. "Not because it's so base, but because it mocks the church. It's just a kind of mafia. Priests and preachers are only legalized godfathers. And people who believe in God are just hanging onto false securities. You don't need that kind of illusion to be a good person."

The tale had not made me ill, but the sound of the girl throwing up got on my nerves. I walked down to the river. It was chilly away from the fire. Buttoning my jacket, I savored my own body heat as spotlights on the distant Rochester Castle made it glow like a medieval monument that even the great Sphinx itself might've eyed with envy.

The laughter of the teens soared over the river in the wind, but when it shifted, I could not hear them at all. Standing around the fire, they looked tribal—as if they lived long before Christianity came to England. One girl started to dance around the flames, and her pagan moves inspired the others to clap in beat, as if they were all one flesh and blood. When she removed her shoes and banged them like tambourines, the kids clapped louder yet.

"I don't believe the same as she does about God," said Red Top, when he and Big Head joined me by the water. "I don't believe in religion either. But there's a God or force or something beyond what we understand. Don't you think?"

"Yes," I said. "We can never fully understand, and that's why we're rightly awed. We can just try to be aware of it and respect it. It's a part of who we are, our own mystery and wonder of how we came to exist at all. I usually talk best to God when I'm in the woods or by a river like this one here. Sometimes I do it when I smoke."

"Smoke?" said Red Top.

"My Cherokee ancestors taught that our prayers rise to heaven in smoke," I said.

I reached into my jacket pocket and removed a bundle wrapped in cloth. I unwound it to reveal a red stone pipe eight inches long.

"I carved it at my home," I said. "It's from Pipestone National Monument in Minnesota. Native Americans can still quarry the rock there. It's been done for hundreds of years by many different tribes. When the Indians met there, they would put aside their weapons, their differences, to gather the stone. It's considered sacred, that it has medicine."

"Can I hold it?" said Red Top.

"Me, too," said Big Head.

"Sure," I said. "We can smoke it if you like."

"Yeah," they said, in perfect harmony.

Their fingers traveled over the red pipe as if it had something to give them through mere touch, while I dug a leather pouch from my jacket. It was meaningful to me because it had belonged to my father. He had blessed it before he gave it to me.

"What's this medicine you mentioned?" said Big Head.

I packed the pipe bowl with tobacco.

"It's what empowers you to stay in touch with your heart, the opening to the Spirit World," I said. "Most Indians find it in Nature, but it can come in different forms."

"Like medicine is God?" said Big Head.

"Something like that," I said, as I struck a match and lit the tobacco.

"Smells good," said Red Top.

"Yeah, smells sweet," said Big Head.

I passed the pipe for their lips to go "a-ganging" with the carved stone. They would, after all, probably remember this night down by the river's boundary for the rest of their lives. I knew I would just as surely as if the medieval peacock of the sea, the pauus maris, had appeared swimming up the moonlit river.

The wind had settled, and they watched the smoke rise in the night as if each had a private prayer on the way to heaven. Mine was already being answered, for Big Head and Red Top were medicine for me.

When the cup is full, there's no sense pouring more into it. Sometimes the same is true for the human heart. That's how it seemed with the night as well, as Big Head, Red Top, and I finished smoking the pipe down by the river. I promised to see them tomorrow before pushing on to the monastery and headed across the field toward Andy Snacks, the sound of the drums and the pagan yelps around the flames following me.

When I undressed for bed, my shirt smelled of the campfire. It seemed that the night's spirit clung to me as well, and I fell asleep feeling as though I had drunk from the Fountain of Youth. Anything and everything was possible.

The next morning I awoke feeling torn. A part of me was excited to hike on to the monastery, while another part didn't want to leave those I had just met. But I had promised myself to complete the trek in the same amount of days as did the medieval pilgrims, and hours were clicking away.

Before breakfasting at Andy Snacks, I bought pastries uptown. Returning to the B and B, I found Number One pouring a cup of coffee while one-eyed John, still unshaven, smoked an after-breakfast cigarette. Joyce and Philip were busy in the kitchen when I poked my head in and held up the box of sweets.

"I hope you like chocolate," I said.

"I'm a chocolate expert," said Number One.

"I don't think he invited you, Charlie," said Joyce.

Number One looked heartbroken.

"Oh, but I do invite you, Number One," I said. "And you, too, John."

Number One bit into his second pastry before the rest of us had finished our first.

"Are you sure you have to leave today?" he said, licking chocolate from his upper lip. "This éclair isn't too bad."

"The trail calls," I said.

"Payday isn't far off," said Number One. "I could show you how to win some money gambling."

Joyce and Philip rolled their eyes.

"Well," said Number One, "someday I'll strike it rich."

Philip wiped his hands and pulled an envelope from his desk drawer.

"I had the pictures developed I took yesterday," he said, and handed them to me. There was Number One straightening his "Ode to Charlie" on the wall and John showing a hopeful lottery ticket. One showed me writing in my journal, and in another Joyce was putting sugar in coffee.

"Welcome to the Andy Snacks family," said Philip, as he now taped my picture on the wall's sea of faces.

"How about my picture?" said Number One.

"Yours is already up there, Charlie," said Joyce.

"You can never get too much of a good thing," said Number One.

Slipping into my pack, I headed toward the party field by the river but became surprised to spot Big Head and Red Top in the center of town. Pieces of dried grass crowned their uncombed hair, and the rubber penis stuck from Big Head's shirt pocket as if it had become as much a medal as those worn by the medieval pilgrims.

"Must've been a late night," I said.

"We haven't slept," said Big Head. "Stayed up talking about God and medicine and all that."

"I was just on the way to say adios," I said.

"We were headed to see you," said Red Top. "Thought we'd walk with you for a while, if that's OK?"

The morning sun cast the shadow of Rochester Castle on the hill over the town as we started up it, and I felt a hint of loss when we stepped from its huge cool shade, because I might never walk in it again. The subtle grief, however, was soon dispelled by the enthusiasm of my all-night truth-seekers.

"Do you believe in ghosts?" said Big Head.

Accounts of ghosts in the Middle Ages centered on those who claimed to have seen dead relatives. They appeared to their loved ones to ask for prayers, almsgiving, and masses in their names to help speed their departure from purgatory on to heaven. The church encouraged such visions, since the ghosts' requests meant more money in its coffers.

"I believe in a Spirit World," I said, "where unusual things can happen."

"We went to Little Kit's Coty a few nights ago in a taxi to try to conjure ghosts there," said Big Head. "It's a formation of stones older than Stonehenge."

"Did you have any luck?" I said, intrigued to see modern-day Englishmen still believing in the mystery of stones.

"I felt something pretty spooky all around me," said Red Top. "But didn't see anything."

"I saw one," said Big Head. "But nobody believes me."

"I believe you," said Red Top. "I just didn't see it myself."

Big Head looked a bit lonely.

"Maybe sometimes only certain people can see what's there," I said.

Big Head perked up. "Have you ever experienced ghosts or spirits?"

I was not in the habit of telling others about my spiritual life and beliefs. Just as with the pipe last night, that was usually kept to myself. But it now dawned upon me that while I had been listening to others' stories all along my route, I had not—except for with Anders and Kai—followed the medieval pilgrim's tradition of telling stories.

"I have had a few things happen over the years," I said, thinking that many people had their own similar and archetypal experiences. "One happened when I was on another pilgrimage."

"What?" said Big Head.

"Yes, tell us," said Red Top.

Our walk up the long hill slowed to a crawl as I revealed why I had walked the Trail of Tears. The first week into the walk, a Doberman attacked me, and I feared for my life till the owner secured the dog. Two months later, on the last day of my walk, I feared being attacked again when a huge black dog with long teeth raced from the woods toward me. But he began to wag his tail. Then he insisted on walking just a few feet ahead of me as if to lead the way, though I tried several times to make him go home—wherever that was. He kept looking into my eyes as though he peered right into my soul. We walked more than twenty miles into the night for me to finally reach home after hiking nine hundred miles. I named him Crow Dog. In the days that followed, however, I began to feel guilty that his rightful owner was sick with worry. So I put an announcement on the radio that I had found a beautiful black lab. A man came only an hour later and swore that Crow Dog was his, though my new friend hid behind me.

"He's been gone over a month," said the man, "but I know it's him by the collar. I made it special for him."

It was suspect that the man had not put the dog's name on the collar, but I tried to believe him. When I put Crow Dog in the man's car, he gave that look from the trail as if to say, "I am yours and you are mine. Don't you understand?"

Crow Dog gave a single mournful howl as the man drove them away. I became depressed and phoned a Native American friend to tell her what had happened. She was consoling. After a three-day fast, I entered a sweat lodge to cleanse myself of any evil spirits encountered on my Cherokee pilgrimage. I asked the Spirit World to send me a sign in Nature or in a vision that my journey had been fully blessed, that I had accomplished all I sought to do. But I received no vision or sign from Nature.

The next day I visited my Indian friend to return some camping gear I had borrowed. After she answered my knock on her door, she said someone wanted to see me. She led me into her living room, and there was Crow Dog.

"He came here the day after you phoned," she said.

The man who had taken him lived miles from my friend, and there were thousands of other homes in the area he could have chosen. But I didn't question why he was here as he jumped up to place his paws on my chest.

"Wild," said Big Head.

"Your sign from the Spirit World," said Red Top.

"That was ten years ago," I said. "Crow Dog died a few months ago."

They now looked as sad as they had looked awed only moments earlier. But I told them that Crow Dog was still with me. I reached into my pocket and pulled my medicine bag forward.

"The first year he and I were together," I said, "I cut some hair from his back and put it in here."

Just as with the pipe, their eyes ached to hold the medicine bag. Their fingers explored it just as medieval Christians once handled sacred relics.

"I've done my share of mind-altering substances," said Red Top, "but the high I feel right now is a new one on me."

"Yeah," said Big Head. "Something's going on. Something really strange is going on. I've never felt just like this before either."

Something always goes on when people truly connect with matters of the spirit, and I felt that even more as we reached the top of the hill to behold a breathtaking valley that seemed to stretch as far as the eye could see. Somewhere down there was the monastery and new people to meet, more stories to hear. But before parting with Big Head and Red Top, I dug into my pack and gathered some tobacco to give them.

"Save it till the time is right," I said.

"How will we know that?" said Big Head.

"You'll know," I said, hoping that I was right.

A hundred yards down into the valley, I turned to see the teens still standing where I had left them. We stared for some time before Red Top raised his hand and Big Head gave a howl, just as surely as if it were Crow Dog, back from the grave.

The boys turned away to walk back toward town, and I liked that because I got to watch them vanish one step at a time, which we too seldom get to do with those we let into our hearts.

Walking on, however, I was surprised to find myself haunted by something that had been said last night at the campfire gathering.

"Why is it so fashionable in America," said Sir Pretty, "for people to kill each other? Is it that you don't like each other or that you don't like yourselves?"

I couldn't deny that we are a violent society. Nor could

I pretend, since this question had been presented more than once on the pilgrimage, that it didn't disturb and perplex the British, their mirror staring me right in the face.

It seemed that my soul had recalled Sir Pretty's question while in this elevated state to show my mind something important. The increasing sense of peace and freedom I was experiencing on my pilgrimage evolved from more than meeting fascinating people, exploring beautiful countryside, and examining medieval history and literature. It evolved because I had almost zero anxiety of encountering any violence. Sure, there were crimes committed in England—Pilgrims' Way itself was linked to murder—but they were scarce compared to those in my own country, and handguns, as common as maggots in the United States, were almost as rare as elephants here. Even the British police didn't carry them. Yes, this was a startling revelation. I was basically a confident and secure person, but in the United States I had been living in some subtle fear. It was hammered into my mind and heart day and night by newspapers, radios, televisions, and movies. And as my third eye opened wider, I now grasped how that fear lives hidden in most of my countrymen, to come out, not usually in guns or overt violence, but in their aggressive attitudes. Work more hours. Make more money. Climb the ladder. Instant Internet. Coolest cell phone. Talk louder. Faster. Get the last word. Pass the next car. Purchase the bigger house. Check the stock, high or low. Yes, we are a society stressed to the limit, fearing our failures and lack of material goods, which we believe are our ultimate personal and cultural weapons.

But we are all powerless against our shrewdest foe—death itself. Are we scared to the bone to slow down enough to reveal what is really inside us; is that just too personal?

Medieval men and women were just as afraid as we are but couldn't hide it with as many complexities in their pre-technological age. Hell was as real to them as our six o'clock news is to us. Their skin would peel from their bodies like boiled beets as they burned eternally if they didn't do as the clergy preached.

Such unsettling thoughts compelled me. I pulled a box of matches from my pack, struck one, and put the flame to my finger ... till I could no longer endure the pain. It hurt like hell, and, my God, for the first time on this journey, I experienced more than just a fragile connection to my British ancestors: I felt compassion. At times they lived in absolute, inescapable *terror*. No small wonder that so many took pilgrimages to Canterbury with the hope that it would help them avoid eternal roasting, as if the Creator were a cosmic sadist.

When a footpath led into a grove of trees, I knelt and stuck my finger into the moist soil till the pain eased ... a little. After a self-lecture on playing with matches, I pushed on toward the monastery. Perhaps the monks there could skip washing my feet and just offer some ice for my stinging flesh.

The word *monk* comes from the Greek *monos*, which means a man by himself, and it was alone in a desert, cave, forest, or wattle hut that hermits or anchorites lived. They survived on the basest elements—nuts, berries, and other fruits—while praying, with the hope that their ascetic life would lift them above earthly delights to God and assure them a place in heaven.

These spiritual loners, however, soon inspired others who chose to live near them and follow their examples. As these monasteries grew in numbers, rules evolved to guide the monks. In the fifth century the monk Cassian visited monasteries in the East, where monasticism began, and established a rule based on what he found there. "We must seek solitude," he wrote, "and submit to fastings, vigils, toils, bodily nakedness, reading and other virtues," as a means of purifying the heart. The monk Columban's rule read: "Let not a man seek his bed until he is already asleep on his feet." "Perfection is this," urged Saint Bernadino: "On seeing a leper, you feel such compassion for him that you would rather bear his sufferings yourself, than that he should."[1]

A monk's life, however, wasn't entirely sacrifice and suffering. One monk during the seventh century draws a lighter picture with his cat, Pangur Ban, in this poem:

> I and Pangur Ban my cat
> 'Tis a like task we are at,
> Hunting mice is his delight,
> Hunting words I sit all night.
> 'Tis a merry thing to see,
> At our tasks how glad are we
> When at home we sit and find,
> Entertainment to our mind.
>
> 'Gainst the wall he sets his eye,
> Full and fierce and sharp and sly,
> 'Gainst the wall of knowledge, I
> All my little wisdom try.
>
> So in peace our task we ply:
> Pangur Ban my cat, and I
> In our arts we find our bliss,
> I have mine and he has his.[2]

Most monasteries based their lifestyles upon Saint Benedict's Rule (A.D. 526), which Benedict compiled from the monk Cassian, the Lives of the Desert Fathers, Saint Augustine, and "Rule of the Master," written by an unknown monk. Saint Benedict envisioned an abbot as a fatherlike figure over the monks, whom they loved rather than feared. While the abbot ruled the monastery, important matters were to be discussed among the monks: "The brothers shall give their advice in all humility and deference. They shall not presume to discuss their views heatedly." But the abbot had the final word: "Once he has decided let all obey him."[3]

Saint Benedict's Rule determined the monks' daily routine. Following prime at sunrise, the monks bathed in basins before breaking their fasts. Terce and mass came next, followed by a meeting in the chapter house to discuss the day's business and air differences among them. From here they worked in the orchard and garden, tended to animals and birds, copied manuscripts, and instructed novices.

When the monasteries grew, monks were assigned more official positions. The cellarer bought food and drink, and some monasteries allotted each monk a gallon of ale daily. The guestmaster oversaw the guesthouse, and the novice-master managed the school for aspiring monks. The librarian decided who should copy which manuscript.

High mass followed the fourth service of the day, sext. During dinner a monk read from the refectory pulpit. Five hours' work followed nones, and then the monks got a short rest before vespers. The monks washed again before supper, and bedtime followed the service of compline. When the bell rang at midnight, they awoke to sing matins and lauds before crawling back onto their pallets. The dawn's bell awoke them for prime to start the cycle anew.

Not all monks in the West relished devout asceticism, rooted in the East. One Gallic monk argued: "Let a Cyrenean endure it if he will. Necessity and Nature have accustomed him to eat nothing, but we Gauls cannot live in the manner of angels."[4]

It was, however, asceticism—and the belief that it brought the monks closer to God and heaven—that inspired many in secular society to donate their riches to them. In 910 the aging Duke William of Aquitaine, haunted by a murder he committed when he was young, drew up a charter to found an abbey at Cluny:

It is evident that Devine providence counsels the rich to use well those goods they possess in transitory, if they wish for eternal recompense.... Wherefore, I, William, by the grace of God, count and duke ... wishing to make provision for my salvation have found it right ... to dispose for the good of my soul of some of the temporal possessions which have been bestowed upon me.... I will provide at my expense for men living together under monastic vows, with this hope, that if I cannot despise all the things of this world, at least by sustaining those who despise the world, those whom I believe to be righteous in the eyes of God, I may myself receive the reward of the righteous.[5]

The charter further states how the abbey should be organized with respect to houses, cottages, land, vines, fields, meadows, forests, water, mills, and crops. Then it lists all of William's kin by name for whom the monks must pray regularly.

I give, on condition that a Regular Monastery be established at Cluny, in honour of the apostles, Peter and Paul, that the monks should live under St. Benedict's Rule, that the house shall unceasingly be full of vows and prayers, that men shall seek there with a lively desire ... the sweetness of the converse with Heaven.[6]

Wealth slowly corrupted monasteries. Monks abandoned the tonsure, began wearing beards, hair down to the shoulders, jewels, and wide sleeves to reveal fur or silk linings. They entertained themselves with jesters, dogs, and falcons. Some traveled abroad, attended by servants. Others became notorious as seducers of women. They sold furs, girdles, and small dogs to wives and wenches "to get love of them."

Even the Abbey of Cluny, which Duke William had helped

build so the "monks should live under St. Benedict's Rule,"
had succumbed to decadence. Saint Bernard criticized its
worldliness:

> What is the object of all this? . . . [T]he church walls are
> resplendent, but the poor are absent, . . . the curious find
> entertainment there, no doubt, but the wretched find
> within them no comfort for their misery. What has all
> this imagery to do with monks? What with those who
> profess poverty and spirituality of mind? As for the im-
> mense height of the churches, their immoderate length,
> their superfluous breadth, their costly marbles and strange
> designs, while they hinder the devotion of the worship-
> per, they remind me of Jewish ritual. This is all done for
> the glory of God it is said. But as a monk I demand "Tell
> me, O Professors of Poverty, what does gold in a holy
> place?" . . . In fact, such an endless variety of forms appear
> everywhere, that more time is spent in admiring these
> oddities than in meditating on love of God. Before God,
> if they blush not before its wrongfulness, why do they not
> recoil from the expense?[7]

Several movements tried to rehabilitate monastic life. In
1084 Saint Bruno led the monastic foundation at Chartreux,
where each monk kept his own house. There he studied,
prayed, cooked, ate, and slept alone. A wall surrounded the
houses, which faced a courtyard, and the monks gathered only
for mass or feasts. The Benedictine Rule of silence was obeyed,
and at least for Saint Bruno, this lifestyle worked beautifully, as
he described in a letter to a friend:

> I live the life of a hermit, far from the haunts of men
> on the borders of Calabria, with my brethren in religion,
> some of them learned men. . . . What words can describe

the delights of this place—the mildness and wholesomeness of the air ... the hills rising gently round, the shady valleys with their grateful abundance of rivers, streams and fountains, the well-watered gardens and useful growth of trees? Why should I linger over these? The delights of the thoughtful man are more profitable than these, for they are of God. ... For only those who have experienced the solitude and silence of a hermitage know what profit and holy joy it confers on those who love to dwell there.[8]

Unlike monks bound to monasteries, the friars were free to roam the land. In 1223 the pope granted the request of Saint Francis of Assisi to live in such a manner, walking barefoot among the poor as he taught the words of Christ. He and his followers were so admired by some knights and noble ladies that they dressed in the Franciscan habit when they became ill. They thought that if they died and were buried in it, they would avoid hell. To help assure this, they made large contributions to the Franciscans.

As early as 1226, however, Saint Francis became troubled that his followers were being seduced by the world. Many wanted to build churches and friaries and settle down to enjoy their growing wealth. Others were wearing leather boots, dining with the rich, and having exotic sex. Saint Francis pleaded with the friars:

I, little Brother Francis, desire to follow the life of poverty of Jesus Christ, persevering to the end. And I beg and exhort you, always to follow His most holy life of poverty. Take care never to depart from it upon the teaching of anyone whatsoever.[9]

Chaucer poked fun in the *Tales* at his worldly Friar, Hubert, who was "wanton and merry." He knew the taverns better than he knew the almshouses and slept with as many women as he could. When they became pregnant, he would help them get married but not without a fee. He was a polished manipulator in every house he entered:

> There was no man nowhere so virtuous;
> He was the beste begger in the hous.
> For though a widow hadde not a shoe,
> So plesant was his *In principio* [first words of the
> Gospel according to Saint John]
> Yet wold he have a ferthing ere he went.

A century after the death of Saint Francis, most of his followers had succumbed to worldly temptations. But a few refused to give in and became known as the "Spirituals." In 1318 four of them were burned as heretics in Marseilles because they insisted that the Rule of Saint Francis was identical to the teachings of Christ.

As my footpath led deeper into the woods, it became easier to appreciate the letter of Saint Bruno describing his pastoral monastery: "What words can describe the delights of this place ... the hills rising gently round, the shady valleys with their grateful abundance." Though certainly no saint myself, I did feel something sacred there among the trees and understood how people could choose to live in a community in Nature, especially if they had their own dwellings. The Benedictine Rule of silence, however, did not whet my appetite for even heaven's golden confetti. Though I had occasionally met people who I wished would not speak quite so loudly or would shut their mouths altogether (thank you very much), I couldn't imagine not hearing the words of my fellow man on a regular basis. Without the stories people tell that reveal themselves and how I am connected to them, I would feel the loss as much as that of

an amputated hand. After all, I realized there along Pilgrims'
Way, I grip my life by the human voice as much as my fingers
lift food to nourish me. At times I had become spellbound by
the voice of a total stranger on the phone or in person simply
because it was filled with honest and vulnerable emotion, surely
one of the most vital strings on that instrument we sometimes
call the soul. Indeed, the tallest mountains and deepest valleys
can't whisper, "I love you."

It did seem, however, that the trees all around me began to
speak as the wind gusted and eight or ten leaves drifted earth-
ward. One twirled only a few feet away, and I raced to catch it.
When my fingers met it at shoulder level, I felt all that mattered in the whole world was right there in my hand. Then I
studied my prize with all its tiny veins, caught between Nature's
artistic creation and the knowledge that this summer leaf
would never turn its autumn colors with those left on the tree.

Saint Augustine wrote of such moments:

> Where in all the variety of created things is there any-
> thing that is not wonderful, even if our familiarity with
> them has reduced our amazement? How many com-
> mon things are trodden underfoot when, if we stopped to
> pick them up, we might be astonished. Take, for example,
> the seeds that grow into plants: does anyone really under-
> stand . . . the secret power, which makes them evolve from
> such small beginnings into such great things?[10]

On the same oak tree that dropped the leaf grew a trunk
knot. Such a growth in the Middle Ages was a treasured find.
The tree developed the knot to protect itself after a wasp had
gnawed through the bark to lay its eggs there. The knot filled
with a prized clear acid, which was used as ink (*encaustum*, from
the Latin *caustere*, "to bite") because the oak fluid bit into the
parchment, made of skin from a calf or a lamb. The crushed

oak knots were thickened with gum arabic after being soaked in rainwater or vinegar. Iron salts were added to color the ink. The "Julius Work Calendar," complete with illustrations, was created this way in 1020 by a monk in the Canterbury Cathedral manuscript studio.

Today's oak offered more than the beautiful fallen leaf and a look at medieval ink making. A dead limb about six feet long and just big enough around to make a strong walking stick protruded from it. It seemed to be waiting on me some ten feet from the ground. When I climbed to the limb, I tried to break it. But it wasn't as willing to depart the tree as the leaf had been. I began to cut it with my pocketknife, and the shavings fell like snowflakes.

When the limb was freed, my new staff dropped to the ground with a discreet thud before leaning onto a bush, as though it gave a helping hand to cushion its descent into the world below.

I eased down the tree and lifted the staff, getting a feel for my new companion. It was strong and weighed just enough for me to appreciate the muscles in my hand and arm that would have to move it forward with each step. Medieval pilgrims received their blessed staffs from the parish priest's altar. I thought no less of mine coming from the tree, an altar in its own right since my Native American blood considered the surrounding woods a church as well.

Somewhere in the head of the staff, I wanted to believe, was a figure of some kind—a bird, an animal, or a person—waiting to be carved. But at the moment it did not call out to me. But then again the staff and I were yet strangers. Perhaps it would tell me its own story after I had held it for a while, treating it like a needed companion.

The sound of the staff hitting the footpath as I moved on toward the monastery added music to my pilgrimage, a *tap-tap-tap* that led the way. If I had had a bell, I would've fastened it to the top of the staff as medieval pilgrims sometimes did to jingle-jangle along the trail. It felt reassuring, too, that a third leg was always handy for a climb up a hill, over a log or a creek, or against an attacking dog. At one point it simply amused me to balance one end in my palm like a snake standing on the tip of its tail. Its head, held against the sky, bit the sun as its shadow fell across the earth like black skin it had just shed.

The farther I hiked, the more I felt an intimacy with the new staff, as though my very hand had longed for something and I hadn't been aware of the need till it was filled. By the time the path led into Aylesford, my fingers around the staff seemed a perfect fit, my new glove gifted by a dying leaf.

Aylesford looked like a fairy-tale village with a treed hill to its north and the river Medway to its south. Roses bloomed around sixteenth-century houses, and small gardens grew cabbages, lettuce, tomatoes, and corn. A boy around five or six years old played in the dirt with a toy truck carrying plastic sheep and cows. He stopped mooing and pretending to change gears in the truck when he spotted me on the sidewalk.

"Who are you?" he said.

I told him my name and that I was going to the monastery. I had come all the way from America.

"The monastery is down there," he pointed to the west. "You don't look like the other monks. Do you walk everywhere you go?"

"Just sometimes," I said.

"Where is America?"

"Across the ocean," I said. "Have you ever talked to the monks?"

"No," he said. "They scare me."

"Why?"

"They dress funny."

"I like your sheep and cows," I said, walking on and thinking that medieval children would've been taught to view monks as special people who could help them get into heaven. Some would've been encouraged to become monks themselves.

"I'm taking my animals to the market," he called after me. "I'm going to buy an airplane."

This kid was definitely not monastic material. Nor were those drinking in the pub just up the street when I popped in for ale and grub.

"Mind you down at the monastery," said a man in his sixties who had had his share of booze that afternoon. "They got some nuns, and they're hot under more than the collar."

"Know them pretty well, do you?" I said. He moved to sit at my table, though I hadn't invited him.

"Not those particular sisters," he said. "But I wasn't always old and fat."

Three men at the bar chuckled, but he looked so lonely that I felt sorry for him. There was also something in his green eyes that made me want to know more. I gave him that look that said so.

"I was once handsome," he continued, "and found my own salvation in the fairer sex. The best I ever knew were those who had once been nuns. Not just one or two, mind you. I knew three. They craved the flesh as much as Christ craved the spirit. Maybe all those years without a man just made them starved. I don't know. But they were hell to hold, God bless 'em, and when they got excited, they'd moan as if the Devil himself were being christened."

Hearing his sexual history, and especially with others around, made me a bit uncomfortable, but I was also intrigued. No, it was more than that. Thoughts of making love to a woman who had dedicated her life to matters of the spirit but also wasn't afraid of her body made for a rare and seductive combination. It seemed to me that God was as much a part of erotica and all its joys as were the things in Nature I found to be so magical.

"Did you fall in love with any of the ex-nuns," I said, "or was it all just sex?"

"I'm softhearted," he said. "Of course, I fell in love. I fell in love with all of them."

"What made them leave the convents?" I said.

"It all boiled down to the same thing," he said. "They felt trapped having to confess to a priest. You know, thoughts they had and things they did alone that wasn't proper to the church."

I wanted more details but wasn't comfortable asking. He must've seen the interest in my eyes anyway.

"One of them had fallen in love with Judas," he said. "At night she would lie awake thinking about him. Said he needed more love than most. That's when she'd wrap herself all around me."

"Were you not tempted to marry or stay with any of them?" I said.

"No," he said. "I was foolish and thought I'd stay young forever, that there would always be another one looking for me. Now women don't have much to do with me. Sometimes I don't have much to do with myself."

His story, as true to human nature as those told by Chaucer's pilgrims, made me wish I could talk to the ex-nuns he had once loved.

"Have you considered trying to locate them now?" I said.

He gave a look that I will remember till the day I die.

"It's hard to make a river flow backward," he said.

His eyes transfixed me, reminding me how my own life was speeding past. I bought him another pint of ale, which had no trouble flowing as he wanted, and finished my meal to hike on toward the monastery on the outskirts of the village.

Birds chirped in the trees at the entrance to The Friars as if I were about to enter paradise. Once I stepped foot on the grounds, I thought I might've done just that. A lake rippled with ducks and swans, surrounded by a manicured lawn with flowers blooming red, yellow, and white before stone buildings with great arched doors and hallways. The world's troubles seemed left behind. A single white feather from a duck or swan floated in the breeze some ten feet above the ground. In the midst of the tranquillity, I almost suspected that the monks had learned how to hear such a delicate thing hitting the earth.

Eager to rid myself of my pack so I could freely explore the grounds, I headed for what appeared to be the monastery office. A RECEPTION sign soon appeared, but where were the monks? Not a living soul stirred.

Getting closer to the office, I beheld big, bold letters on the door, YES YOU CAN, which I assumed was an affirmative pledge of welcome to pilgrims like myself. Though they were only three simple words, they were just right after a day's walk. The monks here were not only thoughtful, they were kind. But my romantic heart soon sank into secular mud when I realized that YES YOU CAN wasn't a Norman Vincent Peale banner after all. It was a slogan for Visa, letting one and all know that plastic electronic money could get them a night in the monastery, something that had been free in the Middle Ages.

The cynicism that threatened to stink the air like burned hair, however, quickly vanished when I entered the office to behold Brother Anthony. He was in his twenties, tall, thin, and smiling inside his brown habit, which looked like a cape big enough to throw over a horse. His glasses were huge as well, looking more like windshields than bifocals. I didn't know if it was God, but he beamed as though he were certainly in touch with something powerful and mysterious. I hoped he hadn't just consumed a gallon of ale, as some medieval monks did daily.

"You must be tired," said Brother Anthony. "Just fill out this form and you'll be free to go to your room. Breakfast is served between seven and nine in the morning."

"Are there other pilgrims here?" I said.

"Oh, yes," he said. "We have rooms for a hundred people,

and there's several now that have come all the way from Amsterdam. The leader of that group is also an Indian."

"An American Indian from Amsterdam?"

"I think his name is Crazy Horse. Sitting Bull? Oh, I'm so bad with names."

I guessed that monks living the way they did had developed an unusual sense of humor. Who would dare take the name of a great chief?

"Did I say something funny?" said Brother Anthony. "The other brothers laugh at me a good bit, I'm afraid. I'm the youngest of the lot."

I wasn't sure what a night in the monastery would bring, but it was already proving to be vastly different than one in the Middle Ages. Brother Anthony hadn't even glanced at my feet—so much for having them washed—and the Benedictine Rule of silence was as dead as a doornail.

When medieval monks did obey the Benedictine Rule of silence, they communicated through sign language. "Monasteriales Indicia," located in the mid-eleventh-century British Library manuscript *Cotton Tiberius* A.III, lists 127 signs. It's not certain if the manuscript was written in Christ Church, Canterbury, the cathedral, but it was found there and is the chief medieval source of monastic sign language in England, which varied somewhat from the one used on the Continent. If hands became mouths, fingers became tongues:

> Church: make two hands pretend to ring a bell, place your index finger to your mouth and raise it up. Abbot: place your two fingers to your head and pull your hair. Rectangular book: stretch your left hand and move it about before putting your right hand over the left arm to designate the length of the book. Girdle: put your hands in front of you below the navel and stroke to your hips. Wine: pretend that your two fingers are undoing the tap of a

cask. Candlestick: blow on your index finger with your hand half closed as if holding a candle. Bible: move your hand about, hold up your thumb and put your hand flat against your cheek. Rod: move your fist as if you're about to hit someone. Cloth or napkin: put your two hands over your lap and spread them as if to smooth out a cloth. Knife: pretend to slice with one finger over another. Leeks: pretend that your finger bores into your hand and put your hand to your nose as if smelling something. Pepper: knock one index finger against the other. Beans: place your index finger forward on the first joint of your thumb. Butter: stroke the side of your hand with three fingers. Salt: shake your hand with three fingers together. Beer: grind your hand on the other. Bedcover: move your clothes and lay your hand to your cheek. Pillow: stroke the sign of a feather inside your left hand with your index finger and lay it to your ear. Water: pretend to wash your hands. Soap: rub your hands together. Shirt: move your sleeve with your hand. Underpants: stroke your hands up your thigh. Monk whose sign you do not know: take hold of your own hood.

No medieval documents tell us just how inventive or humorous monks might've become with sign language, aided by facial contortions, twisted tongues, and bulging eyes. But we do know, from the biographer of Saint Odo, that at least one of them became outraged. The monk Adolfus was washing his shoes, a ritual before washing the feet according to Saint Benedict's Rule, when an "unreformed" brother observed, "Tell me where St. Benedict orders monks to wash their shoes?"[11]

Adolfus made the sign for him to follow the rule of silence. "Who are you that come to preach the Rule to your betters? You pounce like a hawk on property, and refuse to talk. God did not make me a serpent to hiss as you do, nor an ox that I should bellow. No, he made me a man with a tongue in my head—to talk with."[12]

Brother Anthony gave me keys and directions to the room, and I slipped yet again into my pack to head that way, with my staff *tap-tap-tapping* over the cobblestoned courtyard like some slow but determined bird pecking at a door. I climbed the stairs of the Guest House to the second floor, took a right, and followed the narrow, shadowy hallway to my room. It was small, but the most inviting room I had had thus far on the journey. The bed had been made with care, and there wasn't a speck of dust anywhere. A small wooden cross adorned the wall above the head of the bed, and a window overlooked trees and a meadow. The bathroom was down the hallway, but that didn't bother me. The room offered a lavatory. Washing my face, I took a drink from my hands and began to feel somewhat refreshed. Then, for the oddest moment, I thought my staff had a spirit of its own. I heard *tap-tap-tap* only feet away. It proved to be a woodpecker in the tree by the window. I *tap-tap-tapped* the staff against the wooden floor. The baffled bird looked my way and turned its head as though expecting to find friend or foe. It seemed to look me right in the eye before leaping from the tree, its wings a blur as it vanished to who knows where. Yes, I decided, I like it here in this little monastery room, just high enough to be among the birds.

The sun was setting when I departed my room with the staff, and the sky was a pale gold, as though just over the horizon some enormous fire were dying, fighting its demise all the way. Its magnificence became overshadowed when a man turned the corner of the Guest House. He was in his thirties, tall and slender with a face as noble as I had ever seen in all my years on the road. His skin was olive-brown, and his shoulder-length hair was a classic raven-black. His eyes were just as dark, and his nose was strong and chiseled. Was this the Indian with a great chief's name? If so, he was not a full-blood, for his features were not altogether Native American. His lips were too thin. Still, he had a presence as demanding as a chief.

"Some sunset, huh?" I said.

He eyed the horizon and nodded, as if he had his own rule of silence.

"I just arrived," I said. "Have you been here long?"

He turned to the sunset again, as though it had far more important things to say than I did.

"Two hours," he said.

His accent was British, but it seemed to be his second language.

"I'm walking from London to Canterbury," I said.

For the first time, his eyes flickered with interest, that first fragile beam of a bridge between strangers.

"I live in the woods back in America," I said. "It feels good to be here because I feel a similar peace."

His guarded eyes softened just enough for me to see somebody in there wanting out.

"I live in London," he said. "I came here to get away from all the noise there. It gets trapped in my head, and I can't think straight."

"I know the feeling," I said. "I've spent time in Hong Kong, Paris, Madrid, Rome, and others, but after a while you pay the price. I always return to the woods."

The last rays of sunset faded as dusk approached.

"People in London forget what life is about," he said, after introducing himself as Peter. "It's all just money to them. I'm more concerned with what's in here." Like a monk using sign language, his hand—palm up—slowly floated from his guts up to his heart.

"Yeah," I said. "The inner world means something to me as well."

"Without it," he said, "we are only walking dust."

He was freeing himself before my very eyes, and that, in turn, helped free me with him.

"There is something about you," he said, as if groping to complete his thought.

"What do you mean?"

"I don't usually talk to people when I come here," he said, as if I should read between the lines.

"I'm glad you're talking to me," I said. "Did you grow up in London?"

"No." His body shifted a bit to the right.

Fearing that he might try to hide again, I offered him my staff to hold, as if it might add another beam to our yet shaky bridge.

"I cut it from an oak today," I said. "What do you think?"

"It's a good walking stick," he said, as he pushed it against the ground.

"I collect them," I said, "every time I walk a new trail. Each one is different. Just like the journey. I want to carve something in the head of this one, but I haven't yet seen what it is."

He was back again, as his body shifted to face me.

"You can see things in wood?" he said.

"Sometimes."

"What other trails have you walked?"

When I finished telling him about my life on the road and how it led me to walk Pilgrims' Way, he seemed to take a giant step toward me as well as toward some very private part of himself.

"I had a journey by foot," he said, as if conjuring all his courage. "It was across a desert."

We sat on the monastery lawn as he told his story. He was born in Iran and arrested when he was a teenager because he protested again the government. One of the guards bound his squatting body with a rope, stuffed his mouth with rocks, and told him if he dropped a single one, he would be shot on the spot. He could hardly breathe and went without food and water all day while the guard spit on him. From time to time he squeezed Peter's cheeks and dared him to give up. It wasn't till the next guard came on duty that he could finally spit the stones from his mouth.

When he was released from prison, he swore he would leave Iran or die trying. Under cover of night, he and three friends sneaked across the border on foot. They thought they were safe till gunshots rang out.

"I could see the light from the firing of the bullets," said Peter. "I was horrified and started running. My friends yelled as they were hit. I stumbled and fell. Ran and fell again, smashing both my knees. One of my friends called my name, begged me to help. But it was dark, and I couldn't see. I was just too afraid anyway. I didn't want to die. I ran until I could run no more, thinking they would find me and kill me just as they had my friends."

The moon was out, and light from the Guest House shined on us just enough to see that he was trembling. It seemed more than ironic that I would meet him here, someone born in that part of the world where monasticism was rooted and where spices as well as the plague traveled the trade routes to medieval England.

"I wandered in the Afghanistan desert for two days before a group of smugglers on camels took me under their wing," he said. "It was only by the grace of God that I survived. I bought a counterfeit passport and made my way to London ten years ago." He took a deep breath. "I hadn't talked to anyone about this in over seven years."

His story moved me more than any of those told by Chaucer's pilgrims, but I was almost afraid that he had revealed too much. His voice was cracking. I wanted to say something to reassure him, but words just then seemed as wooden as my staff.

"Have you ever tried this?" I said.

I rose from the ground and placed the tip of the staff in my palm to balance it, as I had done earlier in the day along the trail.

"I see it as a snake standing on its tail," I said. "Want to try?"

He hesitated.

"Your story humbled me," I said. "I have never had to endure anything as harsh as that. I'm sorry you had to go through it."

He took the staff. A moment later it stood in his palm. It didn't matter if he viewed it as a stick or a snake. Either way, it reached upward, allowing two men with diverse backgrounds to climb a little closer to the kingdom of brotherhood.

Aylesford Priory, or "The Friars," was founded in 1242, when the first Carmelites arrived from the Holy Land. Richard de Grey, a crusader, gave them land at his manor. A General Chapter of the Order was held when the bishop of Rochester officially recognized the foundation in 1247, changing the lifestyle of the Carmelites from hermits to mendicants. During that same period, Saint Simon Stock, prior general of the order, had a vision of Our Lady. She promised to protect those wearing the Carmelite habit.

When the monastery was dissolved in 1538, The Friars became the property of Sir Thomas Wyatt of Allington Castle. In the 1670s Sir John Banks turned the monastery into an elegant Caroline mansion. The Carmelites bought back their ancient home in 1949, and it soon became a monastery again, opening its doors to pilgrims from around the world. Behind the altar in the Relic Chapel, the reliquary housed the skull of Saint Simon Stock.

I awoke shortly after sunrise in my little monastic room to recall an owl hooting in the night. It was a witch, said my Cherokee ancestors, and the only way to protect themselves from it was to place a broom across the door of their cabins. Otherwise, the witch would take their souls so deep into the forest that they would never find their way back to the light.

I took the cross—no bigger than my hand—from the wall over my bed. Someone had carved it with love and care. Like the broom, it promised to keep its believers in the light.

My oak staff, leaning in the corner, was a testament to both Christian and Cherokee religions. At times I saw it as a rattle-snake, sacred to my Indian heritage because it once saved the earth from the sun. To medieval and modern believers, how-ever, the serpent was evil because it had convinced Eve to sin, eating from the Tree of Knowledge. For a short stick, it sure stirred deep waters.

Sunlight shone golden on the monastery as I left the Guest House with my staff to explore the grounds, which I had planned to do yesterday when I became entranced with Peter's story of survival in the desert. Ghostly fog floated over the Medway, snaking around the border of the monastery. Two or three frogs croaked along the bank, and not another human stirred. When a white swan in the lake flapped its wings, I understood how some could've seen an angel dancing on wa-ter. The ripples it made seemed to travel right into the earth and up my feet, for certainly something lifted my spirits that morning.

Someone had stirred earlier than myself after all, because a foot-long candle burned before Our Lady, standing in constant vigil for those who came to lay their burdens down. Like the swan, Our Lady's face invited peace. Five other candles, unlit, cast a somber note. Striking a match, I placed it to a wick. Two flames flickering side by side didn't seem as lonely as one.

A stone bowl shaped like a boat was marked HOLY WATER, but the black bug in it argued that. It swam for its life, going in circles. Round and round just as humans so often do with trou-bling thoughts. Easing my index finger into the water, I brushed against the lost-at-sea. It crawled aboard, and I blew drying breath on it before it flew away, baptized more than enough for the day.

Entering The Rosary Way, I felt welcomed to a hidden garden. White roses grew along a rectangular stone wall, and every fifteen or twenty feet stood a rock column, depicting the life of Christ in a series of mosaic art pieces. The birth scene brought memories of childhood Christmases, with the three wise men on their camels, presents under the tree decorated with angels, a star on top, and Santa Claus on his way.

But innocence faded as I walked on to see Christ struggling to carry his own Cross. The pain in his face was too universal to ignore, and when the scene of his crucifixion came, blood dripping down his cheeks, it caught me off guard, sucking away some of my breath. Then something archetypal arose deep within as I approached the resurrection. Some part of my soul yet wanted to believe in the supernatural that came in the form of a human being.

No, it didn't even have to be someone supernatural. I just wanted with all my heart to believe there was someone who always told the truth, offered a helping hand, and stayed an inch or two above greed, anger, deceit, and vanity—though he or she might grope with them daily just like the rest of us.

Then I saw what the top of the staff had been hiding from me, or what I had kept concealed from it. I would carve one side with the face of Christ and the other side with the face of Sequoya. Both had reached out to others from the depths of their souls. Both moved me with their humanity, their convictions, their persistence, and their suffering. Yes, and I would carve the end of the staff with the buttons of a rattlesnake. Like beauty in the eye of the beholder, the staff would carry varied and interrelated meanings. It would be a walking stick of stories, a bridge of cultures, *tap-tap-tapping* toward Canterbury.

As the fog rose from the river along the stone wall in the rose garden, I sat on a bench beneath a tree and fished my knife from my pocket. First, I had to whittle smooth the top of the staff where I had cut it from the oak. Then I could begin work on the two faces. The serpent's tail would come last. But I had only begun when Peter appeared in the garden.

"You're up early," I said.

"So are you."

His eyes said that something was on his mind. I feared he still felt vulnerable from revealing so much last night. I told him how I had decided to carve the staff and a little about Sequoya, how his wife had burned all his notes—several years' worth—when he was trying to develop the Cherokee alphabet.

"Why did she do that?" he said.

"She thought he was wasting his time," I said. "Even his friends began to consider him an outcast."

"And Christ was an outcast as well," he said, studying the part of the staff where I planned to carve the faces. His eyes were still uneasy.

"Are you OK with what you told me yesterday?" I finally had to just ask.

He looked away, down to the ground where some of the wood shavings had fallen. When his gaze met mine, his eyes groped.

"The night before I left London to come here," he said, "I dreamed I met someone on a journey who listened to my story. That's why I stared at you the way I did yesterday."

I was as intrigued as he seemed to be.

"You think it was a premonition?" I said, realizing that he might simply have reached a point in his life at which he needed to tell anyone who cared to listen, and I just happened along at the right time.

"I don't usually remember my dreams," he said. "Now I must return to London this morning, back to a routine I've come to dislike. But I return knowing that destiny is with me, talking through my dreams. I had started to lose faith in it."

His eyes moistened, and I wasn't sure what to do. Finally I reached out to shake his hand.

"I'm glad we met," I said, knowing in my heart that our meeting was not just a coincidence.

But instead of taking my hand, he leaned forward. Then he did something I had never experienced with a man. He kissed my left cheek and then my right, just as surely as if we were old friends.

When he disappeared from the garden, I recalled something from the Bible about Christ's having the ability to appear as many different people. I now understood more fully the concept of trying to see him in all those we encounter. Certainly there must be divine presence anytime people touch in the name of the spirit, call the Creator whatever you will.

When a crane dropped from the sky and into the fog to land by the river, I stopped carving the staff and sneaked that way to observe the bird. But before I got very close to the water, a man loomed from the fog with a cigarette, puffing away as if he had just found a new thrill. In his thirties and wearing jeans and a T-shirt, he looked like a rock musician on tour who had stopped at the monastery to catch his breath before blasting on to the next concert site.

"Good morning," I said.

"Oh, hi," he said, as if just now realizing anyone else was around.

"I got here yesterday," I said. "Have you spent many nights here?"

He seemed to add them up, and I expected him to answer "four or five times" at the most.

"About seven thousand," he said.

My thoughts did a somersault before—

"You're a monk?" I said.

"Brother Lawrence," he said, chuckling at my expression.

I liked Brother Lawrence instantly and guessed, by the way

he puffed the cigarette, that he was pleased that the Bible didn't say "No Smoking." I told him why I was there.

"Over there," he pointed to a building, "is where the pilgrims stayed when they walked to Canterbury. They also traveled by boat right here on the river."

The Medway suddenly took on new meaning, its swirling surface once a path for those who sought healing or redemption at Becket's shrine. Medieval pilgrims who walked barefoot, however, must've looked twice at Christians sailing past without fear of stones to stub their toes, thorns to pierce their feet.

"Why did you become a monk?" I said.

Though I cherished people at times as much as food and water, I couldn't fathom living with a group day in and day out. Solitude was one of my strongest allies. It had never let me down, had never judged my thoughts or actions.

"For the fellowship," he said, puffing again on his cigarette. The smoke drifted into the fog over the river, and the crane lifted its wings and long, delicate legs to rise toward the treetops. For a moment, as the bird aligned itself with Brother Lawrence's back, it appeared to fly right from his head, as if he were a magician doing a phenomenal trick. Saint Augustine would've said that it was no illusion at all. It was just another example of how God worked with Nature to show man the beauty and wonder he had created. Those who doubted it sadly cheated themselves.

"I've met a lot of people on this walk who said they don't believe in God," I said, hoping he would offer wisdom from his twenty years as a monk.

"God's not in fashion for some right now," he said. "But that doesn't change their need for him. When the time comes for them to do some serious housecleaning, they'll rediscover what they buried in the closet."

"The monastery grounds are beautiful," I said, "but what do you do for excitement?"

"We have a television in the common room," he said. "There's news and documentaries. I like movies, too."

I envisioned Brother Lawrence watching spiritual films like *Gandhi*.

"What's your favorite?" I said.

"That's an easy one." He took the last drag off the cigarette, which was about to burn his fingers. "*Bullit*, with Steve McQueen."

"Yeah?"

"Oh, yeah," he said. "You've seen it? Well, then, you remember all those chase scenes in San Francisco." His right hand motioned the cars racing up and down the steep hills. But I also remembered the shotgun sticking from the thug's car window, blasting at Steve McQueen as his tires squealed like a stuck pig. "Talk about action, that movie's packed." He eyed his watch. "I lost track of time. Got to get into my habit." He dashed away but turned back. "You might want to see this in a few minutes. In the chapel we have a nun taking her vows to become part of the order. First time in seven hundred years of our monastery."

As quick as Steve McQueen himself, Brother Lawrence raced into the monastery. It amused me that a modern monk could be both religious and worldly.

Chaucer's Monk in the *Tales* was far more secular than holy. An outrider for his monastery, he oversaw outlying property. His horses were decorated with fancy saddles and bridles. He loved to eat roasted swan—hmmm, that one in The Friars' lake did look pretty plump—and hunt with his dogs, though the church forbade it. Fat and bald-headed, he wore clothes trimmed with fur.

> A MONK there was, a fair for the maistrye [excellent above
>   others]
> An outrider, that loved venerye [hunting];
> A manly man, to been an abbot able.

Full many a daintee [valuable] horse had he in the stable,
And whan he rode men might his bridle heere
Ginglen in a whistling wind as clere
And eek as loud as doth the chapel belle.

Heading for the chapel's historic event with the nun, I noticed a woman in her early thirties gathering feathers from the grass around the lake. She held five or six, and one eight or ten inches long stuck out from her curly black hair. She beamed as if she had just encountered a UFO or the Holy Ghost. It seemed that at any moment she might spread the feathers in each hand and start running across the monastery ground as she tried to join the crane that had lifted into the sky only a minute earlier. When we made eye contact, I was compelled to hear her voice to see if it was as inviting as her face.

"Nice feathers," I called out.

"Oui, you like?" came her sweet French accent as she held up the feathers.

"I like," I said, and turned my hat to show its feathers.

"Oh, you have, too," she said, coming my way. "Are you here with a group as well?"

"I'm alone," I said, and we exchanged names. She was Claire. "What is your group?"

"We come to . . ." Claire groped to find the words in English. "We come to meet ancient trees. To hear what they say."

"What do they say?" I said, becoming more curious about her and her group by the second.

"They say . . ." Her hands, like a medieval monk following the rule of silence, tried to show what the trees spoke. "They say it here," she placed her hand over her chest. "Not here," she pointed to her ears.

"I want to talk to you some more," I said, as she eyed my oak staff. "But right now I must enter the chapel to see a nun take her vows."

"Take what?" she said.

"Make promises to God," I said. "Do you understand?"

"No," she said. "Promises are difficult. We meet here later. When?"

We agreed to meet in an hour, and I hurried into the chapel, where some forty or fifty people had already gathered. A woman handed me a program for today's rare event, which contained a photo of the nun when she was a teenager in her habit. On the back of the photo was written:

I say to the Lord "You are my God my happiness lies
in you alone." Ps15
                    Please pray for
ELIZABETH RUTH OBBARD
Consecrated to God as a Carmelite solitary
                       On
                 June 24th 1999
Feast of St John the Baptist
          Aylesford, Kent

Jesus, when I meet with such sweet love from you
how can my heart fail to go out to you
how can my trust in you have any limits?
                       St Therese

Kings and nobles founded early medieval convents, and the first nuns came from aristocratic families, which had the money to get their daughters accepted into the nunneries. While canon law and monastic rule forbade direct payment to the church, the girls could be required to have dowries of cash, rents, land, clothes, and furniture. A serf's daughter, no matter how much she professed to love God, didn't stand a chance at becoming part of a convent—except as a servant. The head of the convent, an abbess, was often of royal blood, as in the case of Cecilia, the daughter of William the Conqueror. She directed the convent her mother founded at Holy Trinity, Caen. The royal abbesses of Quedlinburg and Gandersheim were powerful enough to strike their own coins. Those at royal nunneries in Saxony in the tenth and eleventh centuries could order knights to war and preside over their own courts.

The convent provided an alternative lifestyle to women who couldn't find a husband or never wanted one in the first place. It also served as a retreat for female intellectuals as well as for those who truly dedicated their lives to worship and prayer. The kin of those who financed the convents found them to be handy inns when they traveled and convenient boardinghouses if they became ill. They were sometimes schools and social clubs for their daughters.

Thirteenth-century England had more than 600 Augustinian and Benedictine houses for men, who numbered fourteen thousand. But only 140 houses provided for three thousand nuns. The church viewed nuns as unequal with monks, and they could not hear their own confessions or hold mass. The double monastery, pioneered in England in the seventh century, housed monks and nuns on the same grounds and made it easy for the males to "offer" their services.

Convents, a term that can properly be used interchangeably with *monasteries*, were surrounded by stone walls and contained fishponds, orchards, gardens, and outbuildings for the bakery, brewery, granary, stables, dovecote, and mill. The main buildings were the church; cloister; infirmary; refectory with adjoining kitchen; dorter, where the nuns slept; chapter house, where they held their meetings; and abbess's housing. Shallow troughs with pipes and taps, called lavers, were placed just outside the refectory for washing. From 1226 to 1257 Abbess Euphemia at Wherwell, England, "with material piety and careful forethought built, for the use of both sick and sound, a new and large infirmary away from the main buildings, and in conjunction with a dormitory with the necessary offices. Beneath the infirmary she constructed a watercourse, through which a stream flowed with the sufficient force to carry off all refuse that might corrupt the air."[1]

Beneath the abbess came officials known as obedientiaries, who were usually picked from older members of the convent. The prioress, subprioress, and treasuress managed the executive level, while a chantress oversaw the church services. The sacrist provided for sacred vessels and altar cloths and also employed candlemakers and furnished them with wicks, tallow, and wax. The fratress kept the lavers clean and made certain that the convent stayed stocked with dishes, cloths, tables, and chairs, which she could also repair. An almoness managed almsgiving, and a chambress was responsible for clothes and bedding. The cellaress bought food and distributed it to the kitcheness, who supervised the cooking. The infirmaress cared for the sick.

The routine in a Benedictine convent was similar to that of monks, with the nuns' time divided among work, study, and prayer. The daily meetings in the chapter house allowed them to discuss all aspects of their business, and they used the convent's seal to formalize approved documents. But the chapter house also gave them the opportunity to confess their wrongs or accuse others. Their penance was often delivered with a rod.

A German bishop, Johann Busch, visited the convent of Dorstadt, where a ten-year-old nun was chosen to punish a mature nun with the rod because she had strong arms. The bishop, upon cautioning the nun that the child should be instructed to stop, was told, "When I do that, she hits me all the more. And I dare not say anything to her on account of the prioress' presence, but I think to myself, I must bear these blows on account of my sins." She added, "Before her profession I

used to teach her and often beat her with a rod; now she pays
me back."[2]

Nuns were forbidden to eat meat except in the infirmary,
but abuse was common. An abbess of royal blood took her
meals in private quarters, and servants cooked anything her
heart desired. She could invite her favorite nuns to dine with
her, creating jealousies and animosities that no rod would beat
from flesh or soul. It was also against the rules for the sisters
to own personal property. But some possessed jewels, clothes,
chickens—they bickered about the eggs—dogs, and cats. In 1257
the nuns of Montivilliers, near Rouen, pleaded with Archbishop
Eudes Rigaud to allow them to keep keys to their chests containing personal items. He refused, but they disobeyed him, because in 1262 he again demanded that they forfeit the keys or
endure harsh punishment, "for . . . when the abbess asked them
for their keys certain of them would not give the keys up for
two or three days, until they had gone through their things and
taken away those which they did not want the abbess to see."[3]
The archbishop was equally upset that the nuns at Holy Trinity,
Caen, were keeping larks and other songbirds caged and making faces as they sang at the feast of the Holy Innocents.

While the nuns tested Archbishop Eudes Rigaud's patience
and authority, he did not go to the extremes of the medieval
Premonstratensians. They expelled all women from their double monasteries. Abbot Conrad of Marchtal wrote:

> We and our whole community of canons, recognizing
> that the wickedness of women is greater than all the
> wickedness of the world, and that there is no anger like
> that of women, and that the poison of asps and dragons is
> more curable and less dangerous to men than the famili-
> arity of women, have unanimously decreed for the safety
> of our souls, no less than for that of our bodies and goods,
> that we will on no account receive any more sisters to the

increase of our perdition, but will avoid them like poison-
ous animals.[4]

In theory medieval nuns committed themselves not only to
poverty and communal life but also to claustration. But they
often found excuses to go to town to buy things that were not
produced at the convent, such as soap, nails, pots, salt, spices,
and parchment. The nunnery was also forced to interact with
the secular world, since it sometimes took in students, guests,
and boarders and acted as a manorial lord to sell or lease land
and impose fines and fees.

The most accomplished medieval nun was Hildegard of Bin-
gen, whose mystical and intellectual powers were recognized at
an early age. The youngest of a noble family of ten, she was offered to the abbey of Disibodenberg in the Rhineland before
she turned eight. She wrote *Physica*, which classified the natural
elements of the world and included fish, birds, animals, plants,
stones, and metals. *Causae et Curae* addressed physiological matters, blending science, symbolic applications, and common sense.
She also composed songs and a liturgical drama, *The Order of
Virtues*. She corresponded with Thomas Becket as well as with
popes and kings. When Emperor Frederick Barbarossa sought
her advice, she wrote: "I see you in a mystical vision, surrounded
by many storms and struggles.... Take care that the Highest
King does not strike you down because of the blindness which
prevents you from governing justly. See that God does not
withdraw His grace from you."[5]

When Hildegard turned thirty-eight in 1136, she became the
abbess of Disibodenberg and began to write about the many
visions she had experienced the past ten years:

A great flash of light from heaven pierced my brain and
made my heart and whole breast glow without burning
them, as the sun warms the object that it envelops with its

rays. In that instant my mind was imbued with the meaning of the sacred books, the Psalter, the Gospel, and the
other books of the Old and New Testament.[6]

In today's world Hildegard's claim of sudden enlightenment
would most likely get her branded as a drug user or a mental
case. But in 1147 Pope Eugenius himself, after reading chapters
from her book entitled *Scivias* (*Scito vias Domini, Know the Ways of
the Lord*), embraced her:

> We are filled with admiration, my daughter ... for the
> new miracles that God has shown you in our time, filling
> you with his spirit so that you see, understand, and com-
> municate many secret things. Reliable persons who have
> seen and heard you vouch to us these facts. Guard and
> keep this grace that is in you.[7]

It took ten years for Hildegard to write *Know the Ways of the
Lord*, her principal work, and out of fear she first resisted the
project when a vision led her to it:

> God punished me for some time by laying me on a bed of
> sickness so that the blood was dried in my veins, the mois-
> ture in my flesh, and the marrow in my bones, as though
> the spirit were about to depart from the body.
>   In this affliction I lay thirty days while my body burned
> as with fever.... And throughout those days I watched a
> procession of angels innumerable who fought with Mi-
> chael and against the dragon and won victory.... And one
> of them called out to me, "Eagle! Eagle! Why sleepest
> thou? ... Arise! for it is dawn, and eat and drink." ... In-
> stantly my body and my senses came back into the world;
> and seeing this, my daughters who were weeping around

me lifted me from the ground and placed me on my bed, and thus I began to get back my strength.[8]

Hildegard's mystical visions continued throughout her life:

From my infancy up to the present time, when I am more than seventy years of age, I have always seen this light in my spirit. . . . The light which I see . . . is more brilliant than the sun, and I name it the cloud of living light. And as the sun, moon, and stars are reflected in the water, so the scripture and sermons, and virtues, and works of men shine in it before me. . . . But sometimes I see within this light another light which I call the Living Light itself. . . . And when I look upon it every sadness and pain is erased from my memory, so that I am once more as a simple maid and not as an old woman.[9]

Another mystical medieval nun was Mechtild of Magdeburg, who wrote songs as well as prose that blended the spiritual with the erotic:

My body is in long torment, my soul in high delight, for she has seen and embraced her Beloved. Through him, alas for her! she suffers in torment. As He draws her to Himself, she gives herself to Him. She cannot hold back and so He takes her to Himself. Gladly would she speak but dares not. She is engulfed in the glorious Trinity in high union. He gives her a brief respite that she may long for Him. . . . He looks at her and draws her to Him with a greeting the body may not know.[10]

The most famous romantic story of a medieval nun centered on Héloïse, who was a prioress at Argenteuil and later an abbess of the Paraclete. She was seventeen and living in Paris with her uncle, Canon Fulbert of Notre Dame, when she met Peter Abelard. A suave teacher in his thirties and chaste, he seduced her. She gave birth to a son. This along with a secret marriage enraged Fulbert, and he arranged to have Peter castrated. The mutilated teacher then took refuge in a monastery and insisted that Héloïse become a nun to join him. She agreed, notes one of her letters, because she loved him, not God, that much. Legend says that on her deathbed she asked the other nuns to place her body in the tomb with Peter, who had been dead twenty years. The nuns granted her last wish and claimed that Peter's arms reached out to embrace her corpse when they opened the tomb.

Medieval women who wanted a life dedicated to work and prayer without being under the clergy's thumb could become Beguines. They kept vows of chastity but could leave the sisterhood anytime they chose and marry. This unofficial order free of male monasticism, however, brought the wrath of a church council at Vienne in 1312:

> Since these women promise no obedience to anyone and do not renounce their property or profess an approved Rule, they are certainly not "religious," although they wear a habit and are associated with such orders as they find congenial.... We have therefore decided and decreed with the approval of the Council that their way of life is to be permanently forbidden and altogether excluded from the Church of God.[11]

Other spiritual women chose to live as anchoresses in cells connected to convents, monasteries, churches, castles, or even the Tower of London. Ritual accompanied the enclosure and began with a mass. Holy water was then sprinkled throughout the cell, and the recluse reclined on a bier, where earth was scattered over her. The ceremony was completed when the priest instructed, "Let them block up the entrance to the house."

The cells usually consisted of two rooms, and the door had a hole where the woman received food and water. She spent her time in prayer and offered guidance to those who gathered just outside her door. Some, however, were unable to truly leave the world behind; they gossiped and conducted businesses through the door's hole.

Margery Kempe, author of the first autobiography in English, the *Book*, chose yet another spiritual path. When she convinced her husband—they had fourteen children—to let her "live chaste" and separate, she dressed in white and began a pilgrimage to the Holy Land. Other pilgrims, however, tried to avoid her because she would often break into great fits of crying and shouting when she experienced mystical visions. She was once imprisoned at York, where the York minster asked, "Woman, what dost thou here in this country? Hast thou a husband? Hast thou any letter of record [of permission from her husband]?" The archbishop accused her of being a heretic: "I am evil informed of thee. I hear it said thou art a right wicked woman." Margery had a mind of her own and answered, "I also hear it said that ye are a wicked man. If ye be as wicked as men say, ye shall never come to Heaven, unless ye amend whilst ye be here." The archbishop was so flustered that he paid a servant five shillings to "lead her fast out of this country."[12]

Contrary to Chaucer's female pilgrims en route to Canterbury, medieval women rarely took pilgrimages, and Margery's *Book* was a rare look at a woman's view of the spiritual life on the road. She writes of her mental breakdown after the birth of her first child and how apparitions of hell tortured her till a vision of Christ restored her sanity, though others argued that she was more an unfit mother and an escapist than a dedicated Christian.

*   *   *

Brother Lawrence rushed into the Friars' Chapel via a back door only seconds after I had found a seat. He looked like a monk now in his habit and stood out from the others because only three of them wore robes of white. But I still couldn't separate him from Steve McQueen in *Bullit* as the car chase scenes in San Francisco raced through my mind. Pondering the faces of the other monks, I questioned if one chose *The Full Monty* or *Saturday Night Fever* as his favorite movie.

The secular world paled, however, when mass began and Sister Elizabeth stood to face the celebrant. "Are you resolved to persevere faithfully in following Jesus Christ as a Carmelite solitary," he said, "so that your whole life may be a faithful witness to God's love and a convincing sign of the kingdom of heaven?"

"I am," said Sister Elizabeth.

The printed program now informed us to say, "Thanks be to God."

The nun then offered herself to God with words, which included: "In chastity I choose the Lord as the first Love of my heart and my body. In poverty I take Him as my only joy and riches. In obedience I wish to embrace the will of the Father as it unfolds in my life."

Sister Elizabeth next knelt while the celebrant extended his hands over her and said the prayer of consecration. Afterward she received the insignia of that consecration.

"Receive this ring," said the celebrant, "the seal of the Spirit, and wear it as a sign of fidelity to the Lord who has chosen you as His own. Receive the book of the Liturgy of the Hours, the prayer of the Church. May the praise of our heavenly Father be always on your lips. Pray without ceasing for the salvation of the whole world."

When the nun now stood, she took me by surprise. She extended her arms toward Christ on the cross above the altar as if he were truly alive and would embrace her as she sang: "The kingdom of the world, and all earthly adornment, I have held as nought for love of my Lord Jesus Christ; whom I have seen, whom I have loved, in whom I have put my trust, in whom I take my delight."

Her words didn't move me as much as her voice. It disarmed me because she seemed so full of sorrow and joy at the same time, as if the human condition lived in her tongue and lips and had been waiting for years to release itself in this particular song. She inched closer to Christ with each new word, and her extended arms trembled. Her fingers longed to touch his face, his lips, his wounds. I had never seen more longing in a human face. Everyone looked as spellbound as I, and Christ seemed to gaze the nun right in the eye. Somehow she was making a universal sound, that one we all know when we are alone and in touch with the deepest parts of ourselves. Her voice was so haunting that the hairs on my arms stood as a chill ran up my spine and followed me even after her singing had stopped and I had left the chapel. I wanted the feeling to last as long as possible because it was feeding some part of my spirit that was hungry, giving it new strength to go on against the many holes in life's roads. It didn't matter in the least that I was not Catholic like Sister Elizabeth and that her voice had brought me this rare little feast. Only a prideful fool would turn down free and much-needed food because he did not prepare it himself. Then for the first time I understood how Christ had fed a multitude with only a loaf of bread and two fish. In Sister Elizabeth's voice, he was still breaking bread.

My thoughts and feelings, however, became a combination of the sacred and the secular when I spotted Claire at our meeting place. Sitting on the grass, she put another feather into her curly black hair. Though her arms were not outstretched to embrace God as the nun had just done, they certainly drew my close attention all the same. She wore a short-sleeved blouse, and her skin was brown, her arms muscular and defined, as if she exercised regularly. Her face yet glowed as it did an hour ago.

"Did the nun promise?" said Claire, when I joined her.

"Yes, she sang to Christ upon the cross," I said, still lifted and haunted by her voice.

"He could hear her all the way up in Heaven?" she said. I shrugged. "Maybe the monastery will make a music video of the nun."

Just as the nun's voice had moved me so, now Claire's eyes took me somewhere special as well, as she rocked her shoulders and waved her arms as if she were in that video herself. It was difficult to know, however, if her play meant to celebrate or mock.

"Do you like nuns?" I said.

"No," she said. "I went to a Catholic school. The nuns were mean to us. They slapped our palms with . . . what you call it?" Her hands drew something in midair, and I told her the word. "Oui, a ruler. They hit hard. I would cry. At night in bed I would worry. I did not like to be hurt."

"Are you a Catholic now?" I said.

"No. My religion does not have a name. God is in the duck on the water. He is in the flowers and the trees."

"He's in the beauty of Nature?" I said, thinking that we might have a lot in common but that Nature was also filled with tornadoes and hurricanes.

"Oui, in the beauty," she said, in that sweet French accent I thought I could listen to all day long even if it just counted to a million. But a second later I guessed I had been wrong. "You Americans are only 4 percent of the world, but you use 25 percent of all energy. How can you be so thoughtful?"

She meant "thoughtless," but that was hardly the time for an English lesson. On the contrary, I was the one getting lectured, as if I were millions of people disguised as one. She didn't seem

to see me at all but the "ugly American." My first impulse was
to defend myself and my country, when—

"You call yourself a Christian nation," she added. "It is on
your money, 'In God we trust.' But how much do you do to help
the poor of the world when you have so much?"

A medieval English pilgrim, who often had never traveled
fifty miles from where he was born, walking to Canterbury did
not have to deal with someone like Claire. Armed with statis-
tics, information, insights, and opinions from books, the Internet, television, and newspapers, she had a global awareness as
well as a liberated spirit to speak her modern mind.

"You're right," I finally said. "For a Christian nation we sometimes sure don't act like it."

"And you still murder people for crimes," she added. "No one
does that in Europe anymore. It's barbaric. What would Christ
think of your country if he came back today?"

She made probing points, and I was more sympathetic to
them than she could perceive in her troubled state. It was
as though the cruelty of the world had picked up a giant ruler
to slap more than her palms. I wanted to hold her, to take away
her pain.

"Claire," I took a deep breath as I eased my fingers onto her
forearm. "Can you try to see *me*, a human being, instead of an
American, sitting on the ground here with you?"

I first feared that anger might overpower her because I had
been too forward. But as people so often do when gently reminded that they're on a high horse, she came back to earth, bit
her lip, and said, "I just get so bothered sometimes and want to
blame someone. I know it is not you or all your countrymen."

Her voice softened a little more with each word to become
as tender as an apology. "Did I tell you that I like trees?" I said,
and she studied me as if remembering, at last, that I, instead of
a national persona, was there.

"Oui," she placed her hand over her chest, just as she had

when we first met, "they talk to you here. I talk to them, too. I sing to the trees." She extended her arms toward a willow by the lake, just as the nun had done toward Christ when she sang. Once again, the hairs stood on my arms, and a chill ran up my spine. It was as though the monastery grounds were charged with some archetypal spiritual force, moving the women to reach up and out to their own form of deity as they sang.

"My grandfather was Cherokee," I said. "When I was a child, he once took me into the woods and dug a hole a foot deep. He had me take off my shoes and socks and stand in the hole while he covered them with dirt."

"This is fantastic," she said. "So you could be a tree?"

"No," I said. "So I could understand more clearly that I was a boy and should be happy that I could walk freely and a tree could not. I have always valued that freedom. I love to walk."

"This is a strange story," she said. "You're funny. You take my mind off bad things now. Things I come here to forget."

"What's this group you're with?" I said, thinking that if they were all from France, they had come some distance on their pilgrimage, just as many did in the Middle Ages when they traveled to Canterbury.

"You want to meet my friends?" she said.

I nodded. She eyed her watch.

"I meet them in ten minutes in there," she pointed to the breakfast room. "I will see you, too."

She took a white swan feather from her hair, stuck it in my hatband, and dashed off toward the Guest House. When she entered the building, I removed my hat to discover that she had placed the gift in the very spot from which I had removed the "good-luck" feather to give to the boy on the bicycle on my first day's walk. It was as though the blue jay had come back to me as a swan, after perching for a while upon a French heart.

I entered the breakfast room to find Sister Elizabeth seated at a table while others stood in line to get plates of eggs, potatoes, ham, tomatoes, and toast. She looked different up close. She seemed older, with crow's-feet just beginning, but her complexion was more radiant, her eyes brighter.

"I was moved by your song," I said, in line to get breakfast. "Well, actually your voice. It really came from your soul."

She looked down.

"You liked the service?" she said.

"I had never seen anything like it," I nodded. "It was truly history in the making. What led you to become a nun?" She hesitated.

"I knew a sister when I was a little girl," she said. "She inspired me. My younger brother had just died, and ..." She seemed relieved that the breakfast line moved forward to take me away, as if I were asking questions too personal on such a special day. "The details of my life are in my new autobiography. It's on sale at the monastery bookstore."

She now looked me in the eye with a whole new twinkle, and I no longer perceived the nun singing to Christ. I saw a saleswoman holding up a YES YOU CAN! sign. But I didn't blame her any more than Edward III faulted the nun Isabella of Lancaster when, in 1335, he paid one hundred marks for her book of romances. Chaucer's nun in the *Tales*, a Prioress named Madame Eglantine, was not a purist either. Though she made certain no crumbs fell from her mouth and would cry to see a mouse caught in a trap, she also traveled with small hounds— forbidden by the church—and wore a most worldly gold brooch with the inscription "amor vincit omnia [love conquers all]." The sly Chaucer was poking fun at her "amor vincit omnia" because the expression could refer to sacred love or carnal desires.

She was so charitable and so pitous
She wolde weep if that she saw a mouse
Caught in a trap, if it were deed or bledde.

Of small houndes had she that she fedde
With rosted flesh, or milk and wastel breed;
But sore wept she if one of hem were deed,
Or if men smote it with a yerde smerte [with a stick
    sharply].
And all was conscience and tender herte.

When my plate was filled, I chose a table with an elderly lady. She had auburn hair but no eyebrows except for the black ones painted there. Her lips were bright red, and she wore a delicate gold necklace with rubies and diamonds.

"Oh, I'm so happy someone is sitting with me," she said, with a musical Irish accent. "I'm always afraid I'll end up as alone as an old abandoned house."

"Can't imagine that," I said.

"Oh, darling, you must have a bit of the Irish in you. Tell me your name at once before you run away."

She seemed to be around eighty years old, but her beauty had not faded. Indeed, she was one of those rare persons who had aged with such grace that it was difficult not to stare at the accomplishment, though the painted eyebrows added carnival flair.

"My name is Maggie," she said. "My husband always sat with me before, but he died three months ago. A lovely man, a doctor. That's why I've come to the monastery. To try to find some direction. I can't make up my mind whether to stay at our home in London or return to Dublin to die. Oh, not that I want to do it anytime soon, but you know as well as me the train is coming, darling. And there's no slowing it down. The brakeman is as drunk as a young man at his wedding. Are you Catholic, dear?" I shook my head. "That's a crying shame. You have the eyes of a good Catholic. Warm and strong, and you've suffered your share. Oh, but I see a wee bit of the Devil's brother dancing there as well, don't I, darling? Never mind, we all have our fires to contain."

In all my many years on the road, I had never met as many fascinating people in such a short period of time as I found there at the monastery. I couldn't say which I liked the most, but this Irish gem was near the top of the list. She made me hope that I could be as full of life as she when I reached her age, should I be lucky enough to live that long.

"I like how you talk, Maggie," I said.

She grabbed my hand. "Oh, darling," she said. "You remember my name. Say it again."

"Maggie." She then gripped my fingers with both her hands.

"One more time for a widow." Her painted eyebrows arched so high that they seemed to perform a trick.

"Maggie," I repeated.

"Oh, yes, I am not forgotten just yet. Guess where these hands have been?" she said, with a hint of pride and the enthusiasm of a Chaucer pilgrim about to spin a tale. "No, you couldn't guess it if the moon sat on your pretty head. I'll give you a hint. They've held the hands of two of the world's most famous people: John F. Kennedy and the pope himself. Just as tightly as I'm holding yours right now. It's true. May God strike me down like a squashed rabbit if it's not. The pope, bless him, was easy to get to because I was in the right line. But President Kennedy was a slippery catch. It was in Dublin, darling, and the place was so packed that air itself was getting the life squeezed right out of it. There I was, tiny me, no taller than a weed, with everybody's elbows banging my ears. But I had two American flags, and you know what I did? I did right the opposite of all those around me. They waved their flags up and down, but I waved mine sideways with the force of a gale. Darling, I was a woman on a mission, and I didn't stop waving those Stars and Stripes till the president himself made his way through the sea of

Irishmen to pick me from the crowd. When he did, I dropped
the flags and grabbed both his handsome hands. He wasn't just
a man. He was a legend, and right then and there I became part
of it in my own small way. Now that legend holds your hands.
We're links in a chain of history, tragic as it turned out to be for
him and his poor family and the rest of us who cared."

I placed my hand atop hers and gave a quick squeeze. "You're
a real fireball," I said. "You must inspire a lot of younger
women."

"Oh, they're too busy to notice an old rag like me," she almost blushed, which made her all the more endearing. "But I
understand. When I was their age, I couldn't see the train coming either. Better that they don't, really." She looked disappointed when I moved my hand from atop hers. "Isn't touch
such a heavenly thing? Sometimes I just can't help myself. Last
week, on a street in London, I saw one of those monks from
Tibet. I asked him if I could touch his shaved head. He bowed
while I did it. It was smooth as a pear, darling. I was with my
neighbor, and she thought I was out of place, but I don't want
to die letting little things pass me by. Now if I could just decide
on whether to stay in England or go back to Ireland."

Her eyes searched me.

"Why don't you go to Ireland for a visit and see how it feels?"
I said.

"I just did that," she said. "That's why I'm so torn. I have one
foot in Dublin and another one in London. I don't do the split
as well as I used to." Her eyes widened at something behind me.

I turned to discover Claire waving and pointing to a table
near her. A two-foot-high silver rod stuck from it with a sign
atop it saying GERONIMO.

"My friends eat here," she said. "You come?"

There was either a convention of Indians at the monastery
or this Geronimo was the name that Brother Anthony had
tried to remember when he mumbled "Crazy Horse" and "Sit-

ting Bull" upon my arrival. I excused myself from Maggie and
walked to Claire as six others, three men and three women, entered and began sitting around her table.

"Who is Geronimo?" I said.

"That's me," said the tall one, who was around thirty-five years
old. He wore a leather hat, silver bracelet, brown cowboy-style
vest, and a ponytail. His accent was Dutch, and he didn't look Indian. But that was common for Natives whose ancestors had
intermarried with other nationalities. I introduced myself and
told him of my tribal affiliation, expecting him to do the same.

"He is our teacher," said Claire. "He knows Indian spirituality. Today we go to new trees over a thousand years old."

The others nodded and smiled, as if they had just undergone
some great religious experience. My intrigue grew.

"What did you say your tribe is?" I asked.

"I like what Black Elk had to say," said Geronimo.

Black Elk, an Oglala Sioux, was perhaps the most famous of
Indian holy men and had grown up in South Dakota. He fought
at Little Big Horn against General Custer and converted to
Catholicism after having a vision of all races coming together.
He became internationally famous when his biography, *Black Elk
Speaks,* hit a nerve with readers. But while he carried a prayer
book by day, which gave him freedom to move about the reservation, he conducted secret Native American teachings at
night.

"I see," I said, thinking that Geronimo's heritage was unique.
"You're Sioux and Dutch?" In 1730 a delegation of Cherokee
sailed to London to be the guest of the king and queen. Perhaps
some Sioux had gone to Holland on a similar mission to pass on
their genes to Geronimo.

"No," he said. "I have no Indian blood. I'm Dutch."

Geronimo's teaching Native American spirituality when he
had no claim to such heritage disturbed me. It was as questionable as Chaucer's corrupt Pardoner, who had just returned

from Rome with a bagful of pardons to sell at a great profit to the uninformed. The look on my face must've revealed far more than I realized, for a man around forty in the group said, "We are under much stress from our jobs. Coming here with Geronimo helps us relax. We go back to the rat race not so crazy as before."

"I live in a seventh-story apartment in Amsterdam," said Geronimo. "I cannot see a single tree from my window. My country has cut down all the old ones. That's why we must come to England. I would bring more people each time, but I can only get seven in my van. I wish I could bring my whole country. So many people are hurting for what the trees offer."

Even if Geronimo was a little less than pure, he now touched my heart. He seemed to ache as much as the others around the table to connect with something meaningful. Besides, who was I to judge him, just as surely as royal-blooded abbesses judged that the daughters of serfs were unfit to become nuns, servants of God? If I did judge him, not really knowing what wisdom he might possess, I would've been as blind as Claire, who first held me personally responsible for the woes of America. Maybe humans, after all, are really just like that black bug found swimming in the holy water that morning. We are just trying to find our way to a little higher ground before Maggie's inescapable train takes us away.

9

A hooting owl woke me in the monastery Guest House, as it had done the night before. Its call was part of a dream, in which mammoth trees surrounded me. A campfire flickered as I crafted a spearhead by chipping one stone with another. The stones were black flint gathered in wheat fields along Pilgrims' Way. Each time the stones collided, a spark flew, growing bigger as it shot above the treetops like a shooting star. Then a Native American and an Englishman appeared. They, too, were making spearheads, cosmic sparks flying. I had never seen them before, and yet as we spoke telepathically, we knew one another like brothers. As our sparks flew faster, they merged into a shaft of golden light as big around as a horse, which shone from our hands up into the Milky Way. In perfect unison we moaned in awe at the sight of this paradise, where all sorrow, longing, and anxiety were banished forever. Our spirits were not only free, they were empowered with primal and eternal forces—the secrets of the universe—as if the golden light that came from our hands and artifacts were part of the same "Living Light" about which the medieval nun Hildegard wrote in her mystical visions.

Coming more awake, I tried to hold the feeling of the dream as tightly as a man embraces the woman he loves when they must part for more time than either thinks they can bear. I did not want to awake at all but live in the arms of this vision from that moment forward.

Ever since childhood my most magical dream had been to find ancient stone artifacts, and in "real" life I do collect Native American relics. But this was the first time that I ever dreamed of making stone spearheads in an ancient world, and to have done so with these two particular dream companions led me to believe that my soul was connecting me to the collective unconscious, a deeper reunion between my dual heritages.

Medieval dreams aroused, amused, perplexed, and frightened, and Chaucer gives us a taste of that in the *Tales* when Chauntecleer has a nightmare of being chased by a fox. While the modern world may turn to Freud or Jung for dream analysis, medieval folks consulted priests. They helped identify their dream visitors. Some priests kept a "dream book," which listed objects in alphabetical order and explained their meanings. This was sometimes frustrating, however, because dream books varied from priest to priest. One said that the appearance of the dove meant peace, while another claimed it meant damnation. An orchard could suggest anguish or happiness. Gossip over who was right or wrong, just like human nature, was as constant then as now.

Dreams were considered a doorway to the supernatural. The daughter of a knight named Sewal in the 1170s repeatedly dreamed that she was attacked by black dog devils. She was convinced that her dream was real, and her parents took her to Saint Leonard de Noblat, near Limoges, and then to Canterbury seeking a cure. A fifteen-year-old boy from the Cluniac priory of Pontefract was also taken to Canterbury after dreaming that demons were trying to strangle him. But it wasn't just the young who traveled to shrines seeking cures from nightmares. Stephen of Hoyland, a knight of some standing in his

community, was haunted by the same dream for thirty years before a visit to Canterbury gave him peace of mind. In a stained-
glass window of the cathedral, he is pictured awake at night in
bed with two devils around him.

A vision in the Middle Ages carried more credibility than a
dream unless the person had the same dream two or three times.
One woman reported having the identical dream six times.
Seeing saints in a dream also strengthened its merit. In one case
the Virgin Mary spoke to a Hereford canon in French, and in
another the deceased Becket talked to a dreaming Irishman in
his native Gaelic.

Medieval dreams helped authenticate relics, as in the case
of Moses' rod, discovered at Sens in the eleventh century. Some
thought it sinful to ignore dreams, but this created problems
with the relics of John the Baptist. In the fifth century his
head was discovered in Constantinople, only to be "discovered"
again in the same city in the eleventh century. Each head,
belonging to different churches, was alleged to be genuine
because of revelations in dreams. A third dream led to yet another head of John the Baptist, at Saint-Jean-d'Angély, in central France.

As with most matters in the medieval world, the higher one's
status, the more believable one's story became. When a serf reported a dream, he had only his family or the village priest to
believe him. In one recorded episode, even parents didn't offer
support. They simply laughed when their blind Gloucester
daughter said a "night vision" of the Blessed Virgin Mary instructed her to take a pilgrimage to Saint Wulfstan's tomb. To
avoid suspicion, people began to claim that their dreams were
visions as clear as day.

As I packed that morning to leave the monastery, I was
getting some objective distance on my remarkable dream in
the night, and I chose this world over that without hesitation

because there was so much I yet longed to experience on earth
in flesh and blood. But that awareness didn't diminish the wonder of the light shaft that reached from hands to stars. It even
seemed to linger in the sunlight when I left the Guest House
with the staff in my hand and the pack on my back. Everywhere
I turned, its golden rays played and danced as if it felt some joy
to drive away the night. It reflected off the lake, where the
swans and ducks swam with an intensity I had not perceived
yesterday. It shone through leaves of trees to make them glow
in a way I had not noticed till now. Had I been blind? Had the
dream cleared my eyes with healing energy here at the monastery? If everything looked newer and fresher simply because I
was back in my element about to hit the trail again, that was
perfectly fine. Not all gift horses have to be looked in the mouth.
All that really mattered was that I felt a new bond with the
sun—without which the earth could grow nothing and our
proud tongues would shrivel like jerky.

Though I would not have admitted it to a monk at The Friars, the sunlight that morning, shining on the statue of Our
Lady, even softened her stone face into a sensual stare. My
fingertips couldn't resist brushing her cheek after lighting a
candle for the remainder of my journey to Canterbury, which
was passing far too quickly now.

The flame danced till wax began to melt. I let it drip over
my fingers. When it cooled and was pulled away, impressions
of my fingerprints made me think of those I had met at the
monastery. Brother Lawrence in a hot rod on the streets of San
Francisco, Peter running for his life in the Iranian night, Sister
Elizabeth singing to Christ, Claire having her palm hit by a nun's
ruler, Maggie swinging American flags at President Kennedy,
and Geronimo sitting alone at his seventh-floor window in
Amsterdam as he searched for trees that were long gone. Their
stories were melted wax stuck to me in places that would not
peel away.

Beeswax was sacred in the Middle Ages in more ways than one. As early as the sixth century, a piece of thread or string was used to measure the sick, and that became the wick of a candle for a shrine. The ritual was so popular that those in accidents often demanded to be measured before a doctor was consulted. When a girl at Ifield fell into a well and was pulled to safety just in the bubbling nick of time, her immediate words were "Measure me to Saint Thomas." A candle the length of her body was then made and taken to Becket's shrine. When one plague victim survived, he said, "Have me measured . . . whence a wax candle may be made to King Henry's honour."[1] An individual could measure himself as well and make a candle.

Threads were even used to measure land, a house, a ship, or a whole herd of sick cattle. When this was done, the lengthy thread—"500 arm-lengths" in one case—was folded back and forth or twisted and then sealed with wax to form the wick. When people were measured, it was crucial that the lengths, and sometimes even widths, be exact. If the thread or string broke at the proper place while measuring, it was considered a good omen. Medieval lives hung by a thread.

Wax was also used to make images of parts of the body that had been cured or objects that had been part of a miracle. These images were then left at shrines. Some were of people and life-size, though most were miniature. People could make their own images or buy them. Pilgrims who traveled to the tomb of Louis of Toulouse near Marseilles, for example, could purchase wax teeth and eyes. These images, which were then fastened to dangle from the shrines, ranged from hearts, heads, breasts, arms, hands, and legs to birds, cats, dogs, anchors, wagons, and a tiny wax man hanging from a gallows of wax. Silver and gilt images were also left at shrines.

On Tuesday, August 29, 1307, when papal commissioners traveled to Hereford to examine the remains of Thomas de

Cantelupe (buried in 1282) for canonization, they found his shrine adorned with 41 wax ships; 170 silver ships; 436 wax images of men; 1,200 wax images of body parts; 77 figures of horses, animals, and birds; 450 gold rings; 70 silver rings; 108 walking sticks for cripples; as well as iron chains left by prisoners, anchors of ships, lances, spears, swords, and knives.

Some items gifted to shrines were eerie, like the bone dislodged from a human throat, a boy's burned scalp, and stones, flushed from the urinary tract, set in silver. Other pilgrims, however, became so attached to the objects involved in their miracles that they couldn't part with them, like the man who denied the Canterbury monks the cherry stone he sneezed forth.

Pilgrims took bent pennies, thin silver disks, to the saints' shrines as well. A coin was usually bent while someone held it over the sick. Occasionally the bent coin was tied to the patient. Coin bending was most often done when someone feared for his life, as when he was on a long journey by foot or caught in a stormy sea. Childbirth and battles could evoke the ritual as well. As a person bent the coin, with either his teeth or his fingers, he made his vow and called out to the saint of his choice, Becket being the favorite in England. A blind horse was said to have been cured when a coin was bent, and a fire was claimed to have been turned back when a man named Geoffrey raised a coin to the threatening flames as if it were a silver cross held up to a vampire. Once a year during the reign of King Edward I, pennies were bent for his hawks and royal chargers.

More than a single coin could be vowed. One woman had a vision in which she was told to convert two farthings and one halfpenny into a lone coin, as if the saints were picky about their money in heaven. In 1307 the commission investigating Cantelupe's canonization branded coin-bending "the English custom." It lives on today with those who carry "lucky coins."

The wax peeled from my fingertips at the flaming candle of Our Lady didn't amount to the size of a pea, but it was a boulder of memory for my stay at the monastery. It fit into my pack with other items gathered along the way: the cigarette rolled by Albert, the sketch drawn by Kai, the rose petals from the retired hairstylist, seeds from the apple gifted by Rex, and a poker card from Big Head and Red Top. They rested in the same bag as the one that carried the tiny urn, now almost three-fourths full with ancestral earth collected each day.

Departing the monastery grounds, I took a deep breath, as if the magical air there might follow me on to Canterbury. It seemed to do just that when a crane dropped from the sky to land along the river Medway. Discovering a path to the water, I sneaked up on the long-legged bird. It looked just like the one I'd seen yesterday morning, when I met Brother Lawrence puffing away on his cigarette. It stood knee-deep in the river as its sharp five-inch bill readied to spear a fish and was as still as the stone statue of Our Lady. The bird was a testament to patience, reminding me not to walk so fast that day as to overlook details along Pilgrims' Way.

Some of the medieval pilgrims who journeyed to Canterbury were forced to learn patience through their means of travel, which extended beyond foot, boat, horse, and wagon. Those who could not use their legs depended on wooden hand trestles. Blistered and bleeding hands pulled them toward Becket's shrine as their lower limbs dragged behind like reluctant baggage. If they were lucky, someone helped them up hills, but as often as not they had to fend for themselves, creatures crawling. The lame who were a little more fortunate sat on a wheeled platform and pushed themselves, though they were vulnerable to tumbling over when their crude transports struck holes and stones in the road.

Some paid a penny to ride in litters from one town to another, the wooden structures squeaking along the way as the riders prayed to arrive safely in one piece. The homely wheelbarrow also served the disabled. In 1300 one pilgrim was assisted like this all the way from London to Hereford. The farmyard cart carried the lame, too, and in other cases they were placed across the back of a horse "like a sack."

The crane's bill dove in the water as fast as lightning to catch a minnow. Swallowing the slippery meal, it lifted its wings and wobbled into flight across the river and over the treetops. Passing the sun, it was consumed by golden rays before reappearing over a distant hill.

The splendor of the morning sun brightened even more as I began to carve the faces of Christ and Sequoya. Waves of golden light shot through tree limbs as the wind swished them back and forth, casting shadows onto the water, where they refused to float away with the current's parade of twigs and leaves. Shavings from the staff were cast into the water, just to see how long it would take before they sailed out of sight. This "a-ganging" with the pilgrims' river became pronounced every time the shavings hit a rock and scattered in its foam for each to go its separate way, as people too often do after hitting a rough spot.

At one point I simply leaned back on the grassy bank and closed my eyes to feel the breeze and mist from the water, which seemed to baptize me—not into any church but deeper into the earth I walked. Funny, too, that the golden light from the sun even felt different today now that I had stopped depending on sight to show me what mattered. With eyes closed sound also hit finer notes. Tree branches brushing against one another made a primitive song like someone rattling bones, while the sound of the rushing water played a tune to soothe fears about their being one's own bones.

When I opened my eyes, the bright light blinded me for a few seconds, and then I beheld a fishing lure dangling from a tree. The artificial lure was a red and yellow bug, swinging like a wax image tied to a shrine. Though no saint was buried here, there was little doubt—in my mind, anyway—that this watery and serene spot could cure aches and pains.

The faces in the staff were barely begun. But that was enough for the moment, because I wanted my new company on the pilgrimage to come alive slowly, for us to get to know each other a step at a time.

Following the river path, I found the sidewalk leading into town. Before a cottage's front door sat two glass containers for milk with a note on a chalkboard the size of a book saying, "Only one today, please." It seemed so innocent that I half expected to smell cookies baking.

It was not the aroma of mouthwatering pastry, however, that awoke my taste buds when I asked a woman coming from a grocery store for directions to Pilgrims' Way, heading for Sittingbourne.

"You take this street here," she said, "and cross the river there. American, are you?" I told her my mission. "I always wanted to go to America," she continued. "But I got married when I was young. That knocked the bottom out of that. When we divorced, I moved to Rome for a while. I married an Italian who hardly spoke a word of English. We found ways around that." Her discreet grin was playful if not out-and-out suggestive.

She was about forty years old, and her blue eyes gleamed with intelligence and that kind of passion that a man is drawn to like an ocean wave that's bigger than all the others and he can't stand the thought of not seeing it crest and foam upon the beach. She relished that the passion was recognized as well, for she looked away just long enough for me to await the return of her gaze, which softened a bit once she was assured that I wanted to see more.

"I'm married to an Englishman again now," she said, after introducing herself as Nancy, "and have lived in this godforsaken town for five years. You can't sneeze without ruffling your neighbor's laundry line."

"So you weren't born here?"

"I'm from London," she said, and eyed me as though to make certain that I truly cared. I did care, for with each passing second, some sadness, like a longing note in a bottle, was bobbing up and down in that huge wave of passion.

"I like to learn about people," I said, "what they think and feel."

"My word," she said, giving a closer look. "You might actually mean it."

Her face was becoming more real now, and the subtle wrinkles that were just beginning seemed to relax, as if they were no longer afraid to come out of hiding. She wore no makeup except for faint red lipstick, and her radiant complexion didn't need it. She may have bought her snazzy dress when she lived in Italy, because it appeared to be silk and fit her as if she liked what her body said. Her black leather shoes also looked Italian, and her manicured toenails were painted pearly. A thin silver anklet adorned her right leg. Her circular earrings were golden.

"I'll walk you across the bridge," she said, "and show you where to go from there."

"You don't have to work today?" I said, thinking she was kind to go out of her way.

"I work when I want," she said. "I'm a painter." She motioned that she loved to work with her fingers. "It helps keep the monkeys in the trees. And off my back." Her voice was softening, and the hint of sadness that flickered earlier was more pronounced now.

"What do you paint?"

She searched my eyes.

"Mostly people," she said.

"I met another painter back in Gravesend," I said. "He was from Sweden, and . . ."

She tried to grin, but her eyes were disappointed, as if I had committed a tiny sin by speaking of another artist.

"Why do you like to paint?" I said, and her eyes again filled with light and passion. But she was slow to answer, as if coming to a decision.

"It's the only way I know to address some of my feelings," she said. "My husband is a good man, but he doesn't understand my needs. I'm not sure it's his fault. He just never learned some things about emotions, and now I'm afraid it's too late. Men seem to learn it or they don't. We've grown rather distant, and he doesn't realize it."

She stopped walking and leaned on the railing of the bridge. I did the same, as we pretended to watch the water flowing toward the bend around the monastery. When she looked at me again, her soul seemed as naked as we all sometimes see our own in the frightening honesty of late-night mirrors.

"I paint people to keep me company," Nancy said.

She had some of the most sensuous lips I had ever seen, and they now parted just enough for the slightest sigh to escape. When she closed her lips, they quivered, as if she were alarmed by the confession to herself, let alone to a stranger walking to Canterbury. Still, when we made eye contact, she seemed a bit purged, and that high wave of passion rushed again toward the shore.

It was her soulful story that moved me, but neither was I blind to the inviting way her silk-covered body arched over the railing, her breasts testing the top button. And the golden light that was so magical since my dream now cast a shadow behind her ear like a shade where a man could cool from life's harshest heat.

"We're almost to your road," she said, as she backed from the railing and started once again across the bridge, that same golden light now shining through the silk dress onto the beauty of her swinging hips.

"You didn't really have to go out of your way," I said.

"Oh, but I did," she smiled for only the second time. When

we crossed the bridge, we turned left for two blocks where the street intersected another one. "Here's your turnoff."

She studied me as if gathering courage. "That's my house there," she finally added. An iron gate led to a two-story stone house, surrounded by yellow roses, and a red convertible was parked in the driveway. It was easy to picture her driving fast down country roads as she threw caution to the wind. "Want to come in for a cup of coffee?" The breeze was cool coming off the river, and the taste of coffee suddenly rose to a new height. "My husband is in London and won't be home till tonight." Now for the first time her sadness seemed to make a pact with her desires. This gave her eyes a new strength without pretending that she wasn't lonely and didn't ache for someone to hear her most private sounds as well as her universal stories.

Love, sex, and marriage were as difficult in the Middle Ages as they are in the modern world, and Chaucer offers us insight into that through the Wife of Bath. Though Nancy had been married three times, the Wife of Bath had had five husbands. She was most knowledgeable about all aspects of "amor" and carnal desires.

A good WIFE was there of biside BATHE,
But she was somedeel deef, and that was scathe [too bad].
Of cloth-making she hadde swich an haunt [skill],
She passed hem of Ypres and of Gaunt [Flemish wool].
In all the parish wife ne was there noon
That to the offring before hir shold goon [mark of prestige]
And if there did, certain so worth [annoyed] was she
That she was out of alle charitee.
Hir coverchiefs full fine were of ground [of fine texture]
I dorste swere they weyeden ten pound

That on a Sunday weren upon hir heed!
Hir hosen weren of fine scarlet red,
Full strait y-teyd [tightly tied], and shoes full moist
    and newe.
Bold was hir face, and fair, and red of hewe.
She was a worthy woman all hir live.
Husbands at chirche door she hadde five.

Saying no to a cup of coffee can be a challenge. I eased my hand onto Nancy's arm. It was warm, and the delicate hairs there made it all the more difficult to be frank.

"Thanks," I said. "But I better push on."

Her eyes didn't hide the disappointment.

"Very well," she said, "but if you change your mind . . ."

A block away, I yet heard the roar of that mighty wave that she carried in her flesh and soul. But more than that, I still saw her honest and sad eyes. They weren't that different from my own and those of countless others at different times in our lives. My walk slowed, and I turned to study her house, holding her there all alone in that silk dress, save for her friends on canvas. If my left foot was compassion, my right one was man's oldest desire.

The lustful Wife of Bath may be the most important character in the *Tales.* The church believed that more than one marriage was sinful, and yet she had had five husbands. Most medieval literature portrayed women as frail and evil, stemming from Eve's sin in the Garden of Eden. But Chaucer gives the complex Wife of Bath a strong point of view. She refuses to deny her carnal appetite, but she is also well versed in the Bible. The first female character in literature to stand up for women's rights, she addresses the timeless questions of love, sex, marriage, truth, and honor.

The "Wife of Bath's Tale" opens with a knight returning to

King Arthur's court when he discovers a young woman alone and rapes her.

> And so bifell that this King Arthour
> Had in his house a lusty bacheler
> That on a day came riding fro river,
> And happed that, alone as he was born,
> He saw a maide walking him biforn;
> Of whiche maid anon, maugree hir heed,
> By very force he raft hir maidenheed.

The countryside is furious about the violent act, and King Arthur sentences the knight to death. The queen, however, shows mercy and asks the king to allow her to pass judgment. She informs the knight that he can escape death if in one year he can answer a pressing question: "What is the thing that women most desire?"

As the knight travels through the kingdom, he asks women along the way what they most desire.

> Some saiden women loven best richesse;
> Some said honour, some saide jolinesse,
> Some rich array, some saiden lust abedde,
> And ofte time to be widow and wedde,
> Some saide that our herte is most esed
> Whan that we been y-flattered and y-plesed.

But the knight never receives an answer that he thinks will save his life. En route back to King Arthur's court, he beholds twenty-four maidens dancing and singing. When they magically vanish into thin air, he sees only an old woman, who is the ugliest human being he has ever encountered.

Where as he saw upon a daunce go
Of ladies four and twenty and yet mo;
Toward the whiche daunce he drow full yerne [eagerly],
In hope that some wisdome shold he lerne.
But certainly, ere he came fully there,
Vanished was this daunce, he niste where!
No creature saw he that bare lif,
Save on the green he saw sitting a wif:
A fouler wight there no man devise!

The old woman claims to have the answer he needs, if he
will promise to do what she wants for saving his life. The
knight agrees, and they journey to the king and queen, where
the knight announces that most women desire sovereignty over
their husbands. The women of the court can't deny the answer,
and his life is spared.

For her reward the old woman now asks the knight to marry
her. Though tortured by the thought, he agrees. On their wedding night, he ignores her, confessing that she repulses him. She
reminds him that beauty is only skin deep and that virtue is
what makes a person noble and gentle. She suggests that he remember the teachings of Christ and also see her ugliness as an
asset. If she were young and pretty, he would worry about other
men trying to steal her away. She asks if he now doesn't prefer a
true and humble wife though she has no outward beauty at all.

"The choice is yours," he says.

"And I have won the mastery?" she says. "Since I'm to choose
and rule as I think fit?"

"Yes, wife," he says.

"Kiss me," she says, and turns into a young, beautiful woman.

And whan the knight saw ver) all this,
That she so fair and so yong thereto,

For joy he hent hir in his armes two,
His herte bathed in a bath of bliss!
A thousand time a-row he gan hir kisse.
And she obeyed him in every thing
That mighte do him plesance or liking.

Though Chaucer's couple living happily and magically ever after might be too much to swallow for many modern readers, the "Wife of Bath's Tale" is balanced with the realism in the "Wife of Bath's Prologue." She admits that she married her first three husbands for money and that they died trying to please her sexually. Her fourth husband made her jealous because he flirted with other women, and her fifth died just when she had him trained to do as she wanted. If she was a loser at marriage, she was certainly a winner at life, in that she made no apology for who she was as she continued on down life's road toward Canterbury yet ready for more fun and games, with the painful wisdom that, unlike the old hag in her tale, she would never be young again.

The third and last time I turned to look at Nancy's house, only its roof was visible, and there sat a magpie, black and white as a zebra, with its long tail dangling in the breeze. For a moment I thought I smelled paint, the kind used to put people on canvas.

Before me Pilgrims' Way meandered among houses as it headed into the lush countryside, where two women on bicycles approached. Their long hair bounced when their front tires hit holes in the road.

"Excuse me," I called out. They stopped, and each had a stuffed bear strapped to her back. Bear baiting was a highly popular "sport" in medieval England. "Sorry to stop you and your zoo, but I'm on a kind of mission and hoped you might help."

"Our *zoo*, as you put it," said the one who introduced herself as Sarah, "is our business."

"We design and make the bears," said the other, named Carole.

The pride in their work made me take a closer look at the playful-looking companions.

"Really?" I said. "You made these guys?"

"We started five years ago in our home," said Sarah. "Now we can barely keep up with the orders. What's this mission you're on?"

"Wait a second," I said. "What inspired you to make bears?"

"Beats making burgers," said Carole.

"We're still children at heart," Sarah added. "A lot of people are, and it gives us pleasure to add a little something to their lives. We sell mostly to stores, but we have one client who has thirty different bears we've made. She sends us photographs of them with her sipping tea."

"You might think she's as mad as a hatter," said Carole. "But she's successful in London. She just likes to get her mind off all the fuss. Our little bears do that for her."

"I like to work with my hands as well," I said. "I started carving these faces in my staff a couple of days ago."

"You're a pilgrim?" said Sarah.

"At the moment, dear lady," I said, "I'm a humble knight." After explaining why I was en route to Canterbury, I told them about the knight's mission in the "Wife of Bath's Tale." "I'd like to hear what women in *today's* England desire most from men."

"That is a tasty question," said Sarah. "Wish my husband had asked it before we divorced."

"Mine as well," said Carole.

"The truth be told," said Sarah, "I guess I've always desired the impossible."

*Women grooming. (B.M. MS.
Luttrell Psalter. f.63)*

"Which is?" I said.

She seemed embarrassed.

"I've always wanted a man to see beyond my body and face," Sarah said. "I've wanted him to see what's in my heart."

"I'm more pragmatic," said Carole. "I've always wanted just what's opposite to me. I want to feel a man's hardness next to my softness." She motioned embracing a man. "Of course, before I let that happen, a lot must pass between us to build trust. I hope you understand that I'm not just talking about sex here? That's only part of it. How can I explain? Well, maybe like this. If I am a lake and a man is a dam, we push against each other, the soft against the hard. It can create a lot of electricity, if you have a turbine to turn with all that built-up energy. Yet what is one without the other?"

"Guess I'll always just be a little stream," said Sarah. "But at least I'll be free. Isn't that right, Mr. Berries?" She stroked the head of the stuffed bear strapped to her back.

"Any other questions, Sir Knight?" said Carole.

Both women intrigued me so much that I had plenty of questions. But as happens far too often on a journey, they were going in one direction and I was going in another.

"You've already been a big help," I said, and shook the hand of the bear on Sarah's back. "Nice to meet you, Mr. Berries."

As the women rode on, Sarah reached behind her to make Mr. Berries's arm wave good-bye. "Cheerio," she called out.

This was the first *cheerio* I had ever heard except in movies, and it seemed to fill the air like the finest notes of a birdsong. Walking on, I repeated it—"cheerio, cheerio"—as though it might vanish forever if my lips didn't feel it pass through them.

The delightful encounter with Sarah and Carole gave me increased confidence to ask other women along the way what they most desired from men. Respect and love, agreed two women in a grocery store. But one woman, hanging out clothes, offered a bluntly different response.

"Who do you think you are to go around asking such a question?" she said. "Consider yourself fortunate that my husband isn't home."

"I apologize," I said. "I meant no harm."

"And I suppose the rain doesn't mean to wet the ground?" she snapped.

An elderly woman, picking up trash from the sidewalk in front of her house, said she only desired that her husband not snore so loudly.

"That's the advantage of getting old," she said. "You don't want or need as much as you used to. His snoring doesn't even bother me like it once did." Her eyes twinkled as if she were still very much in love. "I've laid awake more than once thinking that the night will come when he won't snore at all, and I'll be alone. That puts a new link in the chain."

"You're blessed to love someone that much," I said.

"Oh, yes," she said. "I'm rich in that bank."

When it came time for lunch, I hit the jackpot with my knight's question in a pub named The Dirty Habit, its stone foundation remaining from the eleventh century. Once occupied by ale-making monks, the building served as a rest for pilgrims walking to Canterbury. Here they could have a drink or two and change their dirty habits. Today six female friends had gathered for their weekly wine tasting and were in just the mood to share their Bacchus-inspired wisdom.

"I desire a man on a string," said the one with red hair. "When I need him, I can give a little jerk and he'll come running."

"That's cruel," said the woman beside her. "That's what men expect of us."

"Exactly," said the redhead, "so why not have the same fun?"

"But what do you desire from him once you've jerked your string?" I said.

Her eyes filled with inviting mischief.

"First he can draw me a bubble bath," she said, sipping her Chardonnay as two of the women half-giggled. "Then he can undress me, pick me up, and lower me into the bubbles. Next he must light three or four candles, close the curtains, and turn off the lights. I'll watch him undress one piece at a time. And before he can join me, he must rub my neck and shoulders as he tells me why he thinks he deserves to be in my company."

"Really," said the woman drinking red wine, "this is wicked."

"Oh, yes," said a third woman. "Do continue."

"Very well," said the redhead. "He must sit at the other end of the bath and nibble on my toes. I trust he will be skilled with his tongue . . . and tell me the sweetest things on earth."

"Even if they are lies?" said a fourth woman.

"There are no lies in such a bath," said the redhead. "There are only truths as fragile as bubbles. I expect them to break, and it doesn't bother me in the least as long as I can enjoy them while they last." She seemed to relish telling her fantasy as much as Chaucer's pilgrims enjoyed spinning their tales.

"So you desire sensual pleasures above all?" I said, recalling that Chaucer's Knight found that to be true for some he encountered on his journey.

Woman feeding chickens. (B.M. MS Luttrell Psalter. f.166v.)

"It wouldn't hurt if he had money and some blue blood as well," she said.

A woman who hadn't spoken turned to me. "Aren't you looking for more serious answers?" she said.

"I'm very serious," said the redhead, pouring herself more Chardonnay.

"I have no agenda," I said. "What do *you* desire most?"

"I wouldn't turn down that bubble bath myself," she said. "But I've always desired to find a man who could keep me stimulated intellectually. Naturally I want love and loyalty, but I want him to be constantly learning and excited about it. I want him to tell me about how this new knowledge adds to his life and see it put to use. If he reads about a captivating place, I expect him to take me with him so we can share the experience. If he has a thought of inventing something, I want him to try it . . . even if he fails. I want him to tell me his secrets. Not all of them. I would respect his privacy. I certainly wouldn't tell him everything that squirms in my mind. I teach French and Spanish, and I think it would be fun if he spoke these languages as well. We could talk in the one that best suited our emotions at the time. I would like for him to surprise me a couple of times each week."

"My ex-husband certainly surprised me," said the woman with freckles on her nose. "I came home early and found him in bed with two women and a toy I don't care to discuss."

"Oh, I remember that like yesterday," said the woman drinking red wine. "You cried for a week."

"I burned the sheets," said the freckled woman.

"And not him?" said another.

"To a crisp," she answered. "In the courts."

"He could put a box of chocolates on my pillow to surprise me," the teacher continued. "Phone me at work to say he's found a new restaurant and we're going there tonight. Tell me he's learned to dance the tango. You know, things like that. I get bored easily and need a lot of stimulation."

"I've never heard you talk like this before," said a sixth woman, who had stopped drinking wine and turned to bottled water.

"No one had asked me such a question before," she said. "That Chaucer was a real busybody."

"I'm the easiest of the lot," said another woman. "I just wish my husband would learn to listen. If he did, that would be enough surprises to last me a lifetime."

"My husband listens," said the woman drinking the bottled water. "I'm just not always happy with what he says afterward."

"I'll still take mine on a string," said the redhead, as she mimed using a yo-yo.

Outside The Dirty Habit, Pilgrims' Way overlooked wheat fields and woods on a hill. Along the edge of the woods, a man *cantered* on a white horse with black spots, the term coming from the time when pilgrims once rode horses to *Canterbury*.

Houses were scarce, and if I didn't look a mile to my left beyond the wheat fields to the A2 highway zooming with cars, trucks, and buses, it was easy to imagine that I walked in medieval England. Butterflies and honeybees darted from flower to flower in an abandoned garden, where a single stalk of corn stood six feet tall. Atop it sat a sparrow, swaying back and forth in the breeze. The delicate bird's medieval ancestors were cooked in pies and eaten in the belief that they made the eater sharp-witted. In 1850 eight pairs of English sparrows were brought to Brooklyn to try to rid the area of caterpillars called inchworms. Those first few pairs were responsible for the millions of "house sparrows" now spread throughout the United States.

It was the hottest day on the journey, and I removed my hat to let the air cool my head. Sweat dripped down my cheeks, creating two tiny marks in the soil at my feet, as if someone had shed tears en route to Becket's shrine.

My journey was going so well that my own tears seemed as far away as the moon, and I gathered a handful of wheat from a waving plant to place in the pack with my other little gifts from along the way. The grains were hot in my palm and glistened in the golden light that yet made everything it touched seem magical since last night's dream. Squeezing the hot grains in my fist, I promised to remember this moment when winter's howling winds and blowing snows would make me lower my head and stick my hands into my pockets.

An hour later, however, I wished for a little of that winter cold now, because the day had grown so hot that my clothes were becoming wet with sweat. Even my socks were moist, and each step caused my jeans to rub raw my inner thighs. They burned like cuts sprinkled with salt. When a footpath appeared in a pasture and led into the woods, I rejoiced to walk in the shade beneath the umbrella of leaves.

My cool reprieve was short-lived, because the path soon came to a fence with a sign that read KEEP OUT, as if some feudal lord had suddenly turned on his serfs and I was one of them. Rather than backtrack across the pasture to the narrow road, I decided to intersect it by making my own trail through the woods down a steep hill. The thick undergrowth

fought me, and I accidentally stepped into a stump hole covered with leaves, where I fell and tumbled before landing
against a tree, as my staff flew from my hand. Saint Augustine would've said that this was no accident at all, but the
hand of God in Nature. He had struck me down as surely as
he had made the tree rot to create the hole into which I had
stepped.

It had been more than twenty years since I had fallen, and
the earth I so cherished now seemed to turn against me as if we
were ancient foes. My head had hit the tree. Blood dripped
from the corner of my mouth where my lip had been busted.

Coming to my feet, however, I was relieved to discover that
I had not broken any bones. At least, I didn't think I had. My
back, on the other hand, was hurting like hell. Some of the blood
had dripped onto my shirt, and I must've looked like someone
who had been in a fight.

Before I reached the base of the wooded hill to intersect Pilgrims' Way, the grade became so steep that I was forced to sit
and slide, as if the same earth that had slammed against me now
demanded that I crawl. This was not the kind of "a-ganging" I
had wanted with the English countryside.

Reaching the road, I brushed off my clothes. But the earth
had already spoken, and my jeans and shirt were as dirty as
those of a medieval pilgrim, begging his way from town to
town. My upper vertebra was broken, chipped, or knocked out
of line, because the pain was growing worse by the minute.
The sun's golden light, which had been so welcome earlier, was
now a curse as I hiked toward Sittingbourne, because its heat
only made things worse. It had been one thing to put a match's
flame to my finger for a few seconds to empathize with those
walking to Canterbury in the Middle Ages, but this pain in my
back was becoming almost unbearable. And I was not one to
crack easily. Ever since I was fourteen, I had pushed myself to
many limits of pain in lifting weights. I had even thrived on it

at times as a ritual to burn away my private sins and redeem myself. But none of those times could compare to what I felt now. I was no longer a free man on an extraordinary journey. I was a prisoner within my own body. I wanted to pull the demon from my back, its teeth sunk into the flesh around my backbone. It was chewing on it like a rat, slowly grinding away. If this was a dose of what medieval pilgrims experienced as they hiked barefoot to Canterbury in search of healing, I now felt more of a connection to my British ancestors than I had bargained for. It was as if their spirits had grabbed me in the woods to shake some real sense into me about their plights, their medieval world. It was one thing to have fun in The Dirty Habit with beautiful, tipsy women who shared their lives in response to a question from a knight, but it was something else to walk alone again down a road where there was no laughter, no inviting eyes, no tender voices—only constant, nagging pain so severe that it began to make me sick to my stomach. I grew up in the woods and live in the woods, so how could I have been so damned careless as to have stepped in a stump hole anyway?

The sun was setting when I finally reached the Sittingbourne city limits. But it was another two miles before I found a pub with rooms and a VACANCY sign. When I entered to inquire, the barmaid disapproved before I ever opened my mouth. Her eyes swept over my dirty, sweaty, and bloody clothes as if I were a walking insult.

"It's been a long day," I said. "I'm hiking to Canterbury and took a fall in the woods. You do have a room?" Thoughts of a shower and a clean bed gave me hope that I could put some of the pain to rest.

She took a cigarette from her mouth as she shook her head.

"But your sign," I pointed to the window. "It says—"

"I forgot to turn it over," she said. "We're full."

She knew her lie was as obvious as her eyes and even seemed

to find joy in it. Placing the cigarette back in her mouth, she discarded me by drawing herself a pint of ale. My lips parted, but . . .

Stepping outside, I leaned on my staff, the pain in my back sucking away all the wonder of the past several days. The rare golden light had vanished just like last night's dream as darkness fell. Now I was just another stranger in town, every person from the Middle Ages to the modern world who had ever felt misjudged because of his clothes. My soul, propped up on a stick, filled with a kind of loneliness that comes when something dies.

CHAPTER

10

S tanding outside the pub, I wasn't sure where to turn in the growing darkness. The pain bent me forward a few inches as I hiked down the street. Viewed from a distance, I must've looked like an old man on his last legs. A medieval doctor would've sworn that one of my four bodily fluids—blood, phlegm, red choler or bile, and black bile—was lacking. These were thought to correlate to the elements of fire, water, air, and earth and flowed in the body in varying degrees to produce different emotions and physical conditions. When blood predominated, it made people joyful. Red choler made them thin. Black choler made them serious, and phlegm made them slow and sleepy.

"Can you recommend a B and B?" I asked a man walking his dog. He pointed to the pub I had just left.

"They're full," I said.

"Might try the other end of town," he said. "I think there's one there."

When I reached the end of the street, no B and B was in sight. Laughter erupting from a café made my misery worse. I stuck my head through the doorway.

"Is there a B and B nearby?" I asked.

"You're almost there," said a man playing darts. "Just up the hill."

Hiking up the hill, I feared that the B and B might be full. Thoughts of sleeping on the ground in my tent disgusted me. I wanted to take a bath, wash away my fall from grace in the woods, and put on clean clothes. I could at least find a little dignity in that.

It seemed to take forever to climb the hill, and I still saw no B and B. The pain grew worse. When the B and B sign finally appeared in front of a two-story house and said VACANCY, my steps quickened.

After knocking on the door, I was greeted by a man in his thirties. He looked me up and down in the porch light, and I could almost hear him repeating the words of the barmaid: "We're full."

But I was wrong.

"Come in," he said. "Come right on in." His simple words were as sweet as they come.

"You have a room?" I said.

He eyed my sweaty and dirty clothes again.

"That we do," he said. "And it has a very nice shower."

Without asking for my name or passport, he led me upstairs to a cozy and elegant room and said I could pay him in the morning.

"You look a little tired," he said. "I hope you rest well."

The room was as inviting as a friend. I took a shower and went to bed, but the pain didn't ease. No matter which sleeping position I tried, my back was in the way. Taking three aspirins didn't help. It was like trying to push a bull with a toothpick. An hour later I got out of bed and did something I had not done in years. I *knelt* and asked the Higher Power to help me.

Once I was back in bed, the pain grew worse yet. I considered going to the hospital but decided to try to make it through the night. Hours later I finally fell asleep, my dreams filled with

pilgrims on hand trestles pulling themselves toward Canterbury and medieval men and women measuring their bodies
with threads.

Near dawn—a rooster crowed—my sleep became peaceful
for about an hour before I climbed out of bed to find the pain
starting again. The day itself was a burden, and I dreaded each
approaching hour. If this was how some people lived, I understood how they eventually had no desire to go on, how anger
and disillusionment robbed them of life's beauty. I empathized
with their plight, their envy of and bitterness toward those
who were healthy and enthusiastic.

I was no longer myself. Thoughts of slipping back into my
pack were torturous. The pain was turning me into a beggar,
and I turned the shower on HOT to let the water pound my
back. It didn't matter that it burned the skin. Anything that took
my mind off the pain for even a few seconds was welcomed.

Questioning whether I would ever be pain-free again, I
feared that my pilgrimage had come to a grinding halt. If only I
could go back in time, I found myself thinking. If only I could
go back to the second before I stepped into the stump hole. It
was then, as I started to step from the shower, that an inner
voice spoke: "Place your hands on your lower back and bend
backward."

Obeying the voice, my hands eased down my back to just
above the hips. Somehow they seemed to know just where to
stop, as if they were in touch with something my conscious
mind was not.

Then, as I bent backward, my back popped five or six times,
and the pain eased. No, it didn't just decrease. It was gone—
totally gone.

Coming from the shower, I slowly twisted to my left and
then to my right to make certain. Yes, the pain had vanished. A
thousand pounds was off my back. I was free again, just as if
something or someone had released me from chains.

The transformation left me spellbound. I had had problems with my back for several years, and it had often required trips to a chiropractor to have the spine manipulated back into the correct position. But nothing like this extraordinary healing had ever happened by my own hands. I could hardly believe it, and yet it was as real as my flesh and blood. Had some part of me deep within the psyche that had recorded the chiropractor's manipulations thrown a lifesaver, or had I just experienced what medieval men and women would've called a miracle? Did the Higher Power speak through that inner voice to guide me?

Splitting hairs at the moment didn't matter. All that counted was the result. Without the pain, I now felt a kind of rebirth. The day was no longer a dreaded burden but an opportunity. My rare journey that minutes ago seemed to be ending had instead taken a giant step, crossing over into the realm of an odyssey.

After getting dressed, I took my pack downstairs. The owner eyed me as if he had never seen me before.

"That rest did you some good," he said.

"More than you'll ever know," I said, paying him for the night.

"Breakfast is in there." He pointed to a room with four tables where a lone man used a laptop as he ate a bowl of cereal with bananas.

"On a hike?" he said, as I sat at a nearby table.

"I'm on the way to Canterbury," I said. "Started in London almost a week ago."

"I'm in communications," he said, closing his laptop. "I sell mobile phones. Wouldn't mind taking a long hike myself. Seems that I never have any time alone anymore. Hurry here, hurry there. That's the name of the game. Are you having a good walk?"

Still spellbound by my healing, I found myself telling him

about it. That proved foolish, however, because he began to gawk as if I were Chaucer's Pardoner pushing bogus wares.

"You have a mobile phone?" he said, as if changing the subject denied the existence of phenomena like what I had just revealed.

"No," I said, thinking that the last thing I wanted to hear on my walk in the countryside was a phone ringing.

"You ought to have one," he continued. "Look at this jewel."

He removed a phone from his belt and handed it to me, an act of which medieval folks never dreamed. He was secure there, his daily reality of phones as solid to him as the one I had come to know on the pilgrimage. It saddened as much as it amused me that some in the modern world had lost faith in the power of the body-mind-spirit connection, that they were more intrigued with sales figures than with the wonder of their own beings.

By the time I finished breakfast and slipped back into my pack, however, I didn't care in the least whether the salesman believed my popping-back story. I didn't have to connect with him to feel whole or have the healing validated.

Yesterday's golden light returned as I hit today's trail, and even the embryonic faces of Christ and Sequoya seemed more alive, as if their tiny wooden eyes shone with some discreet gleam. To have good health that morning made me feel blessed, and my belief in prayer was as strong as my back was straight as my staff *tap-tap-tapped* toward Canterbury.

When the elderly man first appeared, he looked like a skeleton wearing a dark blue coat and a beret. Slumped in a wooden chair, he pruned red roses. His cheeks were sunken, and his jawbones protruded as he chewed a cookie, the crumbs falling to his feet, where a bag marked "Chocolate Chip Cookies" sat. His frailty didn't disturb me, however, as much as it drew me closer, as if my recent pain had deepened my empathy for another's wounds.

"You've really got a green thumb," I said.

The rose garden surrounded a restaurant named One for the Road, and the well-dressed gentleman eyed me as though he weren't accustomed to strangers' saying hello. A cookie crumb rested on his thin lip.

"I like roses," he said, in a tone as gentle as his body was frail.

I told him my name and what I was doing.

"Mind if I rest here for a few minutes?" I said.

"No," he said. "Want a cookie?" He lifted the bag, and I took a cookie. "I never get enough of them," he continued. "When I was a boy, I would dream about chocolate chips. I had six brothers, and when mother made deserts, I never got all I wanted. Now I eat to my old heart's content."

He didn't appear to have a single tooth and broke tiny pieces from his cookie, placing each one in his mouth.

"If you let them melt on your tongue," he said, "you can taste them better than just chewing them up right away."

"I'll try that," I said, placing a piece of cookie in my mouth.

"Well?" he said, after telling me his name was Jim.

"You're right," I said. "You can feel the chocolate drip down your throat."

"That's it," Jim said. "That's it."

His childlike mannerisms led me to feel protective of him, though against what, I wasn't certain. I only knew for sure that I wished more people enjoyed such simple things as letting chocolate melt on their tongues and sharing the experience with a total stranger.

Jim had worked for the railroad for thirty years. His brother became an engineer, but Jim never progressed beyond caring for the tracks.

"A train needs tracks," he said, placing another piece of cookie on his tongue. "That's what my brother always told me. He died when I turned seventy. How old do you think I am?"

"Seventy-five?" I said, thinking that he was at least eighty.

"I'll be ninety-three next month," he beamed. "I'm not afraid to die. You can live too long. See too many of your friends go first. Then you have no one to remember things with."

His thoughts about death were as universal and timeless as the tales told by Chaucer's pilgrims, and I asked if he could recall any stories passed down from his ancestors about those who walked to Becket's shrine.

"My great-uncle William," Jim said. "He walked all the way to Canterbury from York. That's what mother always said. He was from her side of the family. Had a big growth right here," he touched his sunken cheek. "And women would have nothing to do with him. Mother said a worm with two heads lived in the growth. When I was just a lad, he scared me so much I could not eat at the same table. I thought that worm would crawl from his face and get me."

"He walked to Canterbury seeking a cure?" I asked.

He nodded. "It was a cyst. Years later some doctor cut it out, but the place left an ugly scar. Uncle William never did marry, and when he talked to you, he placed his hand over the spot. He tried to look like he was resting his head, but you could tell he was hiding."

Medieval folks sometimes turned to a charm to try to rid themselves of cysts:

May you be consumed as coal upon the hearth. May you shrink as dung upon a wall. And may you dry up as water in a pail. May you become as small as a linseed grain, and much smaller than the hipbone on an itch-mite, and may you become so small that you become nothing.[1]

Charms, rooted in paganism of northern Europe, were recorded by monks and adapted as Christianity spread through these areas and into England. The "Jordan" charm was used as early as the ninth century. It originated from the story of Christ and Saint John when they neared the river Jordan and Christ told the waters to stop flowing. Thus, someone in a blessing could command that blood stop flowing from a wound just as Christ once stopped the Jordan. The charm could also become an adjuration against thieves, fire, animals, disease, and weapons to command that they stand still.

It was believed that pregnant women could protect themselves from miscarriage or troubled births by stepping over a grave three times and saying a charm: "This is my help against the evil late birth, this is my help against the grievous dismal birth, this is my help against the evil lame birth."[2]

Medieval exorcisms were longer than charms and were used by the clergy as well as by laypeople:

In the name of the Father, and of the Son, and of the Holy Spirit, amen. I conjure you, O elves and all sorts of demons, whether of the day or of the night, by the Father, and the Son, and the Holy Spirit, and the undivided Trinity, and by the intercession of the most blessed and glorious Mary ever Virgin, by the prayers of the prophets, by the merits of the patriarchs, by the supplication of the angels and archangels, by the intercession of the apostles, by the passion of the martyrs, by the faith of confessors, by the chastity of the virgins, by the intercession of all the saints, and by the Seven Sleepers, whose names are Malchus, Maximianus, Dionysius, John, Constantine, Seraphion, and Martimanus, and by the name of the Lord + A + G + L + A +, which is blessed unto all ages, that you should not harm nor do or inflict anything evil against this servant of God N., whether sleeping or waking. +

Christ conquers + Christ reigns + Christ commands +
May Christ bless us + defend us from all evil + Amen.[3]

Every time the exorcist found the cross in the text, he made
the sign of the cross over the possessed person. He would call
on God's saints to send the "elves" to eternal hellfire and ask Jesus to bless the afflicted so that the elves could no longer harm
him. Special attention was given to Heradiana, the "deaf-mute
mother of malignant elves," to make certain that she departed.
Sometimes it was thought necessary to also make the mark of
the cross on parchment and write down the opening of the
gospel according to John. The words were then scraped into a
bowl of holy water and drunk by the afflicted person.

Medieval culture also relied upon amulets to protect against
evil forces. Kept next to the body in a pouch or tied around
the neck, the amulets—much like medicine pouches of Native
Americans—consisted of plants and animal parts. A hare's
right foot or a dog's heart was meant to prevent dogs from
barking. A hare's foot, tied to the left arm, enabled a person to
travel without danger. Rosemary, placed at a door, frightened
away snakes. When the herb was carried, it made evil flee. A
spoon made of its wood overpowered poisons. When heliotrope was gathered under the sign of Virgo and wrapped in
laurel leaves with a wolf's tooth, it prevented anyone's speaking
badly of the bearer. If heliotrope was placed at a church's door,
it stopped adulteresses from leaving the building. Lion's fat
smeared on the body protected the wearer from snakebite, just
as anointing oneself with lion's blood guarded one against other
animals.

Saint Augustine himself recommended an amulet made
from "the herb of Solomon" when a mother told him that her
daughter and son were tortured by demons. He instructed her
to tie the herb around their necks, and the children were supposedly cured.

Talismans differed from amulets in that they had written words or letters inscribed on them. Even the respected medieval medical authority Bernard Gordon (who died around 1320) professed that epileptic attacks could be prevented by carrying the biblical magi's names written on a piece of parchment. The most common writing used on talismans was the SATOR-AREPO formula[4]:

SATOR
AREPO
TENET
OPERA
ROTAS

The square reads the same four ways and was thought to be an anagram for the opening words of the Lord's Prayer in Latin, presented as a cross, with a double A and O for Christ, the alpha and omega (Revelation 1:8)[5]:

```
          P
          A
      A T O
          E
          R
P A T E R N O S T E R
          O
          S
      A T O
          E
          R
```

The square's usage dates back to a first-century Christian house in Pompeii, and in medieval Europe it was most com-

monly inscribed on cloth to be carried on one's person to influ-
ence everyone one met.

The "Chocolate Chip Cookies" inscription on Jim's bag, which
rested at his feet, didn't appear to be a talisman. But magic was
certainly in the air all the same as he insisted that I take a couple of the cookies with me to push on down the trail.

"Don't forget to let them melt on your tongue," he said. "It's
the only way to taste the real flavor."

Though Jim was nearing his ninety-third birthday, I could
see in his eyes the boy who had once feared the two-headed
worm squirming in his great-uncle's cheek. It hurt a little
knowing that I would never see the child or the old man again.

"I'll remember," I said, holding up the cookies.

His toothless smile stayed in my mind long after I had eaten
the cookies. At times in my life, I had ached to go to my grave
knowing that I had made a difference on earth and that I had
accomplished something that would live on in history. But that
morning I aspired to something far more grand and noble,
wishing to live to be the age of Jim and happy just to have a
piece of chocolate melting in my mouth.

Time was moving much too fast no matter how slowly I
walked along Pilgrims' Way, which now led to the outskirts
of Sittingbourne. Even a clock outside a hardware store—its
walls lined with hoes, shovels, and rakes—seemed to rub it in
that Canterbury would come too soon and my journey would
end. The trek had rekindled my ability to live by my own time,
more in rhythm with Nature and the stories of strangers, and
thoughts of rejoining America's clocks weren't nearly as sweet
as chocolate.

Most of medieval society wasn't gauged by minutes or hours
either. The need for clocks in Europe, as previously in Asia,
evolved because of the demand for instruments to help track

stars and planets, since it was believed that astrology strongly influenced lives. One's birth time was used to determine his or her horoscope in conjunction with heavenly bodies, and decisions in romance, business, travel, and war were made accordingly. A surgeon needed to know which signs of the zodiac affected which parts of the body so he could operate at the right time under the appropriate constellation. Even the University of Bologna, famous for its medical studies, taught aspiring physicians how stars influenced human anatomy.

Many forms of fortune-telling were popular at medieval courts, but none was more popular than astrology. All the lords employed personal astrologers, and a chaplain to William the Conqueror (reigned 1066–1087) found astrology so compelling that he preferred to spend his nights studying stars rather than resting. The chronicler Matthew Paris reported that the emperor Frederick II (reigned 1215–1250) used astrologers to determine his children's horoscopes and the best time to consummate his marriage to the empress Isabella. Michael Scot advised Frederick not to have his blood let when the moon was in Gemini because he feared that the emperor would be cut twice instead of once. To test Scot's warning, the emperor went to a barber-surgeon at the proscribed time. The barber ignored Scot's advice and began to bleed the emperor, when he accidentally dropped his lancet on Frederick's foot, causing a serious wound. When an astrologer predicted the death of Henry VI, the king became so disturbed that he demanded a new horoscope to help him regain his composure.

Medieval astrology hinged on an understanding of astronomy and "heavenly laws" that today's science would find laughable. It was thought that both the sun and the moon were planets and that they traveled across the earth daily from east to west. Mercury, Venus, Mars, Jupiter, and Saturn were thought to do the same. Following the same path, but farther from earth, were twelve constellations that made up the zodiac: Li-

bra, Sagittarius, Scorpio, and the rest. Since everyone as educated as Chaucer believed that these "heavenly laws" were true,
they went unquestioned, and the zodiac was accepted as a symbol for the passage of time.

The astrolabe and the equatorium, both Islamic instruments,
calculated positions of planets and later aided blacksmiths in
understanding how to build the first mechanical clocks, which
were placed in towers. In 1309 Saint Eustorgio had one in Milan. Such clocks did not strike the hours and had no face or
hands. They simply sounded an alarm, telling the ringer when
to pull the bell rope. In 1335, in the tower of Milan's Visconti
palace chapel, a clock struck automatically for the first time in
history. "There is a wonderful clock with a very large clapper,"
wrote an observer, "which strikes a bell twenty-four times according to the twenty-four hours of the day and night, and thus
at the first hour of the night gives one sound, at the second two
strokes . . . and so distinguishes one hour from another which is
of the greatest use to men of every degree."[6]

When Jacopo di Dondi, the first known maker of mechanical clocks, created a clock for the Carrara palace at Padua in
1344, it showed the phases of the moon. His son, Giovanni, in
1364 built a clock for the castle of Pavia. Its seven dials depicted
astronomical motions as well as a calendar showing the holy
days. Of lesser concern was a small dial telling time.

The colossal clock constructed at Strasbourg in 1354 housed
an astrolabe with pointers, which showed the movement of the
sun, moon, and planets. Each noontime a magus bowed before
the clock's statue of the Virgin Mary while the carillon played a
tune. A cock atop the clock flapped its mechanical wings, crowed,
and opened its beak. Such musical clocks that were wonders to
some became bothers to others as they began to regiment their
days into employers' precise hours, driving a wedge between
the sun and people who had till then depended on its light to
gauge the length of the workday.

Household clocks did not appear until near Chaucer's death, shortly before 1400. Unlike the huge tower clocks made by blacksmiths, the home versions—made by goldsmiths and silversmiths—had faces, hour hands, and later minute hands. They were the first machines made entirely of metal. Previous machinery had been mostly wooden.

My wooden staff was a kind of clock on Pilgrims' Way. Like the Roman sundials once positioned along this route, its shadow on the ground changed as the day advanced. At times it disappeared into my own shadow as though we became one, and then we would both be swallowed by the shade of a tree as if we had never existed at all. Each time my shadow and that of the staff emerged, I felt a new joy in making a mark, however fleeting, on the ancient earth.

When an antique store appeared on my left, I was tempted to go inside just to see what I might find and take a break from the hot sun. But I walked on. That is, till I found myself turning to eye the store again. Like the fallen tree that so seemed to pull me toward it on my first day's walk, the store now did the same. It was as though my inner voice were again talking to me, but not through words—through feelings. It wanted me to enter the store for some reason.

Especially after the instant recovery in the shower that morning, I wasn't about to ignore my inner world. Opening the door to Jackson's Antiques, I was greeted by a man wearing glasses who was in his forties. His eyes were a bit wild, as if he had more energy than he always knew what to do with, and his beard and hair were turning gray. But what mystified me was in his hands, a naked, life-size baby made of wax, with red lips, blue eyes, and blond hair. For a split second the doll seemed to look me right in the eye.

"Serene, isn't he?" said the man, with the pride of a brand-new father.

"He looks alive," I said.

The man moved closer to me, and the doll's tiny fingers were outstretched, as if asking for something. Both arms had been broken just above the elbows and repaired with white gauze. Though no blood dripped from the breaks, the wax baby somehow had a soul peeking from those blue eyes. I felt sorry for him.

"How did the arms get broken?" I said.

"There are a lot of cruel people in the world," he said, "when it comes to the helpless."

The baby then appeared in two places at once, and I had become so taken with the man's caring nature toward it that it took me a moment to realize that I was simply seeing its reflection in a mirror on the wall.

"He's over a hundred years old," said the man. "Do you recognize him?"

He led me to a wooden box filled with golden wheat straw and a white blanket. The baby's cheeks were pale red, and the man lifted him closer to me.

"A replica of Jesus in the manger?" I guessed.

The man nodded. "He was made in a French convent, and I've had him stored away for years. I just got him out a few days ago because I had a feeling that the right person was coming for him. Want to hold him?"

The baby again seemed to look me right in the eye.

"Not really," I said, thinking that I might drop him.

"But you are on the way to Canterbury, right?" He studied my staff and pack. "You're a pilgrim?"

He extended the wax Jesus closer to me yet.

"You won't drop him," he said.

Then he placed the doll so close to my hands that I felt guilty not to take it. I had not held a doll since I played with my niece some years ago, and I had never touched a Jesus doll in my life. It reminded me of medieval wax images left at shrines, but its body was as warm as human skin. Whoever had created it must've longed to touch Christ as much as many people ache to be loved.

"Do you work here?" I said, placing the baby back in the box with the wheat.

"It's my store," he said, offering his hand. "My name is Grant. I can often tell the moment someone walks through the door what they're after. Things like furniture and this wax Jesus are not dead, you know. They have spirits, and those spirits reach out to certain people. I could tell as soon as I saw you that you're a spiritual person. This building draws people like you. It's built where a church once stood, and right here," he led me to the center of the floor, "just a few feet down is the tank of water where people were baptized. The building also has a ghost, and sometimes things move around."

A crash alarmed me when ten feet away a plate fell from its stand on a shelf. I expected to see a wire or string on the floor that Grant had pulled to play a trick on me. Such trickery as entertainment was prized in the Middle Ages, and Thomas Betson, a monk at Syon Abbey in Middlesex, kept a notebook giving instructions for this kind of "magic." He instructed readers how to take a woman's hair and attach it to a hollowed-out egg. The egg could then be moved about, and no one would see the thin hair. The egg could even be suspended in a house or pub, and "many people will think it is being held up by nothing at all." The hair could also be attached by wax to a coin, which could be pulled across a table, and "many people will think it is done by magical art."[7] The monk encouraged fellow pranksters and magicians to place a beetle inside an apple with a hole in its center so that when the beetle rocked, people would believe that the fruit rolled by itself.

But I discovered no string or wire used to make the plate fall, and Grant looked as astonished as I was. Thinking that he or I had stepped on a loose board that had triggered the plate's tumble, I moved my feet here and there to uncover only a couple of subtle squeaks.

"The ghost usually moves furniture," Grant said.

Still not satisfied, I examined the unbroken plate. It pictured a medieval cottage with a stream running nearby. Even the baby Jesus seemed to look on, wanting an explanation in a room where no wind could've caused the event because the door and windows were closed.

"Who is this ghost?" I finally said.

"It only moves things," said Grant. "It doesn't talk or leave messages in the dust, so I really don't know. Nor do I really want to learn. Sometimes it's more fascinating to live surrounded by a secret than to expose it. Take, for example, the fingers I found some years ago when I bought an estate down near Canterbury. I was going through all the drawers in various tables and chests when I uncovered them in a finely carved box. God only knows how old the relic was or which saint the fingers might've belonged to. But I could sense that they needed to stay in the chest of drawers where I found them, and I refused to sell the piece of furniture until the right person came along. Six months after I put it in the shop, a woman I had never seen before came in, and somehow I just knew she was the right one. Today she keeps the relic in the same box in the same drawer, and her life is never without a little intrigue and mystery."

Relics, rooted in the cult of saints, were more treasured than gold and silver in the Middle Ages because they symbolized the apex of earthly holiness: the saints, like Christ himself, had dedicated their lives to God, and their martyrdom set examples for others to follow in fighting evil—thus helping ensure their entry into heaven, away from the eternal flames of hell.

From the beginning, however, the cult of relics troubled some as being a form of paganism. The Gallic priest Vigilantius condemned the worship of all inanimate objects, such as bones of the saints, and particularly the bodies of Saint Peter and Saint Paul in Rome. Saint Jerome answered such criticism:

> We do not worship their relics any more than we do the sun or moon, the angels, archangels, or seraphims. We honour them in honour of He whose faith they witnessed. We honour the Master by means of the servants.[8]

Saint Augustine wrote that saints' relics were "temples of faith," and Saint Cyril of Jerusalem defended the holiness of a saint's body itself "on account of the virtuous soul that once inhabited it. For it is well known that such external objects as handkerchiefs and aprons have cured the sick after touching the martyr's body; how much more then will the body itself heal them."[9]

Thomas Aquinas—from whom we get the term "Dumb Ox" because that's what his intellectually inferior fellow monks nicknamed him—in the middle of the thirteenth century argued for the veneration of relics. They were pieces of the saints' lives, and "he who loves some one reveres the things that they leave behind them." The relics worked miracles at tombs, which was a sign from God himself. "We ought therefore to hold them in the deepest possible veneration as limbs of God, as children and friends of God, and as intercessors on our behalf."[10]

The earliest Christians and pilgrims did not venerate bodily relics but pieces of cloth and paper that came in contact with a saint or his shrine. These items, known as "brandea," were recorded by Gregory of Tours at the tomb of Saint Peter:

> He who wishes to pray before the tomb opens the barrier that surrounds it and puts his head through a small opening in the shrine. There he prays for all his needs and, as

long as his requests are just, his prayers will be granted.
Should he wish to bring back a relic from the tomb, he
carefully weighs a piece of cloth, which he then hangs inside the tomb. Then he prays ardently and, if his faith is
sufficient, the cloth, once removed from the tomb, will be
found to be so full of divine grace that it will be much
heavier than before. Thus will he know that his prayers
have been granted.[11]

No records have been discovered to prove that such cloths
became heavier, but it didn't matter to medieval believers, since
they weighed such matters with their faith. Fragments of tombs
and oil from the lamps that burned near them were collected as
holy relics. Even dust that had settled on the tomb or on the
ground around it was venerated. An inscription on a fourth-
century funerary table, now in the Louvre, promises that it once
held "dust from the land of our redemption." Dust from the
tomb of Saint Marcel was said to have saved the life of a friend
of Guibert of Nogent after he accidentally swallowed a toad.
Dust and other brandea were often carried in reliquaries, dangling from chains around the owners' necks. Gregory the Great
wore a crucifix that contained the filings from the chains
of Saint Peter and the gridiron of Saint Lawrence. When the
monks of Fleury presented the tooth of Saint Benedict to Saint
Hugh of Lincoln, he had it set into his ring.

The early church, in keeping with Roman municipal law,
forbade bodies to be moved even a few feet. But as the popu-
larity of relics grew into frenzy, the translation of bodies became common, and it was difficult to then know which relics
were truly those of saints. Multiplicity of the same relic added
to the confusion, as Guibert of Nogent noted:

Some say they have such and such a relic and others loudly
assert that they have it. The citizens of Constantinople

claim the head of John the Baptist while the monks of
St.-Jean d'Angély confidently believe that they have it.
Now what could be more absurd than to suppose that this
great saint had two heads? Let us therefore take this matter seriously and admit that one of them is wrong.[12]

Guibert, who died in 1125, was the abbot of Nogent-sous-
Coucy, near Laon. A detailed author, he wrote an autobiography and a treatise *On the Relics of the Saints*. His logic about the
two heads of John the Baptist, however, was easily refuted: The
appearance of a relic in more than one place is simply another
miracle. Everyone should rejoice that God has blessed us with
such wonders.

It was thought wise to fast and pray for three days before
opening the casket of a saint to move his body or even a finger
bone. Jocelyn of Brakeland, the biographer of Abbot Samson
of Bury, recorded that the abbot—required to translate the
body of Saint Edmund because the abbey was being rebuilt—
dressed in white and flagellated himself before opening the lid
to the casket. Then he cradled the saint's head, yet wrapped in a
winding sheet, and said, "Glorious martyr St. Edmund, ... con-
demn me not to perdition for this my boldness that I, a misera-
ble sinner, now touch thee. Thou knowest my devotion and my
good intent."[13]

The snowballing demand for relics came from two sources.
First, it was believed that relics were needed to consecrate
churches. Gregory the Great shipped to Augustine in England
"all things needed for the worship of the church, namely sacred
vessels, altar linen, ornaments, priestly vestments, and relics of
the holy apostles and martyrs."[14] The Second Council of Ni-
caea in 787 required that all new churches be consecrated with
relics and that any churches that were without them should get
some immediately. England, as well as France and Germany,

had few native martyrs and were forced to obtain most of their relics in Rome.

Relic collectors were the second reason saints' bodies and parts were in such demand. In 1171 the king of Jerusalem, Amaury, became upset when he visited the emperor Manuel Commenus and found the imperial chapels filled with reliquaries as well as silks and jewels. Henry I sent relic buyers to Constantinople, and Louis IX of France once owned the crown of thorns, a portion of the true Cross, a piece of the holy lance, and fragments of the purple cloak of Christ.

Relics were a chief source of national pride during the Middle Ages, and Walter Stuffield, bishop of Norwich, once gave a sermon declaring that England was superior to some nations because of its relic collection. The sermon was inspired in 1244 during the translation of a vase of Christ's blood to Westminster Abbey, when the bishop noted that Louis IX of France possessed a piece of the true Cross:

> But we must consider not the nature of matter but the causes thereof. Now it is true that the Cross is a very holy relic but it is holy only because it came into contact with the precious blood of Christ. The holiness of the Cross derives from the blood whereas the holiness of the blood in no way derives from the Cross. It therefore follows that England, which possesses the blood of Christ, rejoices in a greater treasure than France, which has no more than the Cross.[15]

Saint Augustine complained of wandering relic salesmen disguised as monks as early as the fifth century, and each new century's ever-increasing appetite for the "temples of faith" brought more bone-rattling merchants. Deusdona, a Roman deacon, in 820 sold relics ransacked from the Roman catacombs to Hilduin, abbot of St.-Medard of Soissons, and Einhard, the biographer of Charlemagne. In 1017 the bishop of Benevento traveled to England with the arm of Saint Bartholomew with the sole purpose of seeking a buyer for the relic, which proved to be Emma, Canute's queen. When Constantinople was sacked in 1204, the relic business soared to epidemic proportions, and the authenticity of saints' bones was lost forever.

Since relic salesmen could rarely prove where their goods came from, many of the more serious bone collectors chose to steal them. Charlemagne's friend Einhard, who founded the abbey of Seligenstadt, ordered his servant to open the tomb in the Roman catacombs to carry off the bodies of Marcellinus and Peter. The poorest pilgrims craved relics as much as the rich and famous and sometimes stole them with their bare teeth: in 385 armed guards surrounded the true Cross at Jerusalem to prevent the pilgrims from biting off splinters when they kissed it. Even the count of Anjou, Fulk Nerra, was said to have given the Cross such a sticky-fingered kiss when he visited Jerusalem in the eleventh century. Likewise, pilgrims at Bury St. Edmunds had to be constantly supervised because they tried to bite off pieces of the gilt at the shrine of the martyr king.

The medieval mind rationalized the thefts of relics as pious, and a prime example of this logic is seen in the translation of Saint Nicholas to Bari in 1087. His body had rested at Myra for several centuries when forty-seven men carrying crowbars asked to enter the monastery of Saint Nicholas to pray at the shrine. When they came from their prayerful knees, they then demanded that the monks—surely aware before this point that the visitors were not simply holy carpenters—lead them to the martyr's remains, just as the pope himself had instructed them to do. In keeping with the supposedly pious thefts of the Middle Ages, the forty-seven crowbar-toting men swore that miracles began the moment that they placed the saint's body in Bari.

The account of Saint Nicholas's translation was written by

Nicephorus, an Italian Greek, who believed the theft was proper based on the scriptural passage "bona est fraus quae nemini nocet" (there is no harm in deceit if no one is injured). When the citizens of Myra protested the robbery, the crowbar-toters argued: "We too are worshippers of Almighty God, so why distress yourselves? You have had the precious body of St. Nicholas for 775 years and St. Nicholas has now decided to bestow his favours on another place.... The city of Bari deserves him."[16] And if this weren't enough to satisfy protesters, the thieves took their defense a step further by saying that if Saint Nicholas didn't want to be moved, he would have miraculously stopped them. Also, they were convinced of the righteousness of their theft because they smelled a miraculous odor coming from the relics—a traditional medieval sign that a saint was pleased with his translation.

In some cases, however, saints' relics did intervene to prevent their removal. When the king of Navarre, García, decided in 1053 to relocate the body of Saint Millan, a minor Spanish saint of the sixth century, the coffin became so heavy on the road that the bearers could not carry it. The miracle compelled the king to build an oratory on the spot where it had occurred. Such miraculous events were common, claimed the author of the twelfth-century *Guide for Pilgrims to Santiago*. Saint James, Saint Martin of Tours, Saint Leonard, and Saint Gilles had refused to be moved—even by the attempts of the king of France.

Theft of relics became so severe that the Lateran Council in 1215 restricted their showing to the public except in a reliquary, and in 1255 a Bordeaux synod forbade even monks to remove the relics from their reliquaries to get a closer look. Monks guarded the relics of Saint Cuthbert around the clock, and four protectors bearing iron maces stood by the portrait of Christ in the Lateran basilica of Rome.

Fraud was as rampant as obsession when it came to medieval

relics, but popular belief in the authenticity of sacred objects prevented most doubters from speaking out. When a relic salesman at a public gathering professed to hold a little box containing a piece of the bread chewed by Christ at the Last Supper, he announced upon spotting Guibert of Nogent in the crowd: "There is a distinguished man, famous for his learning. He will confirm if I am telling the truth."[17] Feeling the pinch of public opinion, Guibert later recorded that he shamefully only bit his tongue and blushed as the fraudulent bread peddler pushed his wares down the throats of those starved for more than they dared to grasp.

When relics were taken from a church, its reactions could resemble moves in a chess game, with the church often countering the loss by claiming that the thieves had taken the wrong bodies and possessed only fraudulent bones. Since scientific examination was never used to determine the authenticity of a relic, the owners of the bones in question relied upon showmanship to validate their claims before a public that, already somewhat hysterical over such religious matters, could become outraged if confused. For example, in 1162 a rumor shook Paris that the head of Saint Geneviève, the city's patron saint, had vanished from its reliquary in the church dedicated to her. Before sunset that same day, an angered and disillusioned mob met at the church and demanded answers. Louis VII swore to flog and expel the canons of Saint Geneviève if the matter was not quickly resolved. The archbishop of Sens tried to soothe the mob by promising to conduct a detailed examination of the relics. A special stand was hurriedly erected for the king, his royal family, and ecclesiastical dignitaries so they could observe the archbishop opening the reliquary as the pushing and shoving mob watched from down below.

A wave of awe and relief spread across the crowd when the archbishop revealed the head of the saint to be intact, as if he had just made a mountain reappear from thin air. With such "proof" apparent, the prior then led the satisfied onlookers in a spontaneous rendering of the "Te Deum." When the bishop of Orleans yet questioned the genuineness of the head, the prior offered to carry it over a bed of burning coals as further proof. But the archbishop demanded that the bishop keep his mouth shut and listen to the singing instead, avoiding the smell of roasted feet.

The simplest way to test the authenticity of a relic was to throw it into a fire and see if it survived as a product of its own miracle. In 979 Egbert, bishop of Trier, broke a finger from the body of Christ and tossed it onto red-hot coals, where it lay unharmed as mass continued. The monks of Monte Cassino owned a fragment of the cloth that Christ had used to wash the disciples' feet and put it in a burning crucible, where "it changed to the colour of fire but as soon as it was removed from the coals it reverted to its original appearance."[18] When the citizens of Clermont-en-Beauvaisis questioned the authenticity of the arm of Saint Arnoul, they dropped it into flames. It leaped out as quickly as a frog. Four Canterbury monks, goes a legend, gifted King Edgar with bones of Saint Ouen and swore to validate their worth: "We can prove it in any manner you suggest by casting them in the fire, for example, and withdrawing them unharmed. And if no such miracle occurs then we will admit that the relics are false and that we are outrageous liars deserving of all penalties of the law."[19] In the end, however, the relics proved themselves genuine by healing a leper when he touched one of the bones.

Since the general public wanted to believe that all relics were genuine, the church tried to censor any reports to the contrary. After all, religion's success traveled on the wheels of faith, and if a single one broke, the entire Christian carriage couldn't roll. The writer Gilbert of Nogent, however, refused to bury his head in the sand despite being ignored by most of his contemporaries. Though he believed in the veneration of genuine relics, he doubted the authenticity of many. When the monks of Saint Medard advertised that they owned a baby tooth of Christ, Gilbert dismissed the claim by saying that he couldn't believe that anyone had saved such a childhood item, since Jesus did not particularly stand out as different from others till the middle of his ministry. The only true relic of Christ, argued Gilbert, was the Eucharist because it contained him altogether. Likewise, Gilbert believed the milk of the Virgin preserved in a crystal vase at Laon to be an imposture.

Gilbert's writings didn't change the minds of the populace, and stories such as that of the woman who kept the host hidden in her mouth for later use when it turned to flesh to seal her tongue to her palate were widespread. The *Pupilla Oculi*, an English manual for parish priests, cautioned against these very maladies.

The demand for the Lord's relics included his foreskin and the umbilical cord, which were displayed in the Lateran basilica in the eleventh century. The church maintained that an angel had taken them from Jerusalem and presented them to Charlemagne at Aachen before Charles the Bald brought them to Rome. A second foreskin, venerated in the Benedictine abbey of Coulombs, found its odd way to England in 1421 inside the baggage of Henry V's bride, Catherine of France, because she believed it would ensure her marriage bed.

After the eleventh century the venerated blood of Christ began to pop up almost anywhere a pilgrim turned. How did his blood spread so far? One version of the story went like this: The Jews had enticed a woman to steal a consecrated host one Easter Sunday, but on her way home, she became paranoid and hid the sacred bread in a tree trunk. It soon began to bleed, until the local clergy moved the bloodstained wood to a church at Aasche. Several other churches traced the origin of their phials of blood to the wooden statue of Christ at Beirut, which had started to bleed after Jews drove nails into it.

Thomas Aquinas declared it impossible that the blood from Christ's wounds had been preserved, but several churches, including the Norman abbey of the Trinity at Fecamp, boasted of owning it. When a vase of the blood was given to Henry III of England in 1247, Robert Grosseteste defended its genuineness by saying it was understandable and normal that the disciples had gathered and saved the blood of Christ all five times he had shed it.

No less astounding than the blood of Christ were his crib as well as locks of the Virgin's hair, samples of her milk, and fragments of her clothing, which could be viewed at the church of Santa Maria Maggiore in Rome.

Relics were also housed in statues of the saints. The statue-reliquary of Saint Foy more than once united and inspired the people in the valleys of the Auvergne. When disease threatened the community, the statue—mounted on a horse—was led through the land as young monks clashed cymbals and blew ivory horns, the crowds shouting in joy that new miracles were at hand.

No one shouted in joy as I started again down Pilgrims' Way after departing Jackson's Antiques, with its wax baby Jesus and plate-rattling ghost, but I certainly felt that miracles were at hand in simply being able to walk upright, yet rejoicing that my back was free of pain. Except for my first night on the trek, there hadn't been a trace of rain—rare for England—and today the sky was equally clear. This was especially good news because that night I had planned to camp out and wanted to see the moon and stars while cooking a meal from groceries I bought that morning in Sittingbourne.

"If you're looking for a place to pitch your tent," Grant told me back in the antique store, "you should aim for the Old Stone Church. Only the foundation remains, but it sets in the middle of a field surrounded by trees and is a good spot to

spend the night. The old church was built atop a Roman structure, and the pilgrims going to Canterbury spent the night
there. I've spent a little time there myself, and the place has . . .
Well, let's just say there's something about it."

The look in his eye intrigued me as much as his historical
commentary, and my curiosity about the Old Stone Church
grew with each mile I walked in its direction. When I first saw
it that afternoon some hundred yards to the left of the road, its
rock wall—one foot high in some places and five feet high in
others—aroused contradictory emotions. On the one hand it
was sad because, without a roof, it looked like a series of tombstones huddled together. On the other hand it stirred my soul
with mystery and humility. The countless pilgrims who had
once spent the night there, as I was about to do, were now dead
and gone and knew the Other World, while I was ignorant
of that realm. Yet I welcomed such ignorance. If I had one
strength, I had come to realize with greater clarity the past several days, it was my love of life. I wished I could live to be 150.
Better yet—not die at all.

Getting closer to the historical site—surrounded by flower-
ing Queen Anne's lace—I could see where the early Christians
had added white stones to the Romans' red foundation to create their church, and I wandered around the rectangular shape
to run my fingers over it, as if it might tell me something
through touch that my eyes and intellect could not discern.

While the stones did not reveal secrets, the foundation wall
led me to the east side of the structure, which was shaded by
towering trees and struck me as an ideal place to camp. The
wall, at its highest point here, would shelter me from the road,
busy with cars. Also, no one would be likely to see my campfire
and come to investigate.

When I slipped from my pack and began to pitch my tent, I
discovered that I was not the day's only visitor. Dog tracks led
to a hole in the ground twenty feet away, as if the dog had been

digging for a rabbit or some other frightened creature. Dirt was scattered as far away as five feet from the hole, which was about the same size as the one into which I had stepped in the woods. The moist earth smelled like a freshly plowed field, and some part of me wanted to place seeds in it—wanted to see things grow that were not there before.

Moving closer to the hole, however, I became thrilled to discover that the earth offered a rare artifact. The dog had uncovered part of a scallop shell, the type pilgrims sewed to their hats when they traveled to holy sites. At first I did not pick it up because I wanted, as I had done with American Indian artifacts, to let the memory of the discovery seep deeper into my psyche, that I might better recall it in the years to come. After all, I had not simply come upon a piece of history. I had possibly made contact with another pilgrim who had lived more than eight hundred years ago. Perhaps a medieval pilgrim slept here, and the shell I now saw had dropped from his hat or clothing. Perhaps he had buried it here at the Old Stone Church as a kind of prayer or had even lost it when he was robbed and beaten. Whatever the reason, I felt blessed that the dog had uncovered such a gift. Saint Augustine would've said it was no coincidence at all. The dog was meant to dig the hole, just as I was meant to find the relic. My Native American beliefs didn't argue that for a moment as I recalled the story of Crow Dog. Ever since my childhood, I had felt a mystical connection to birds and dogs.

When I finally lifted the Shell of the Unknown Pilgrim, as big around as a half-dollar, I blew the moist dirt from it before placing it in my hatband alongside the feathers and snake rattle. Like an answered prayer, a marriage had taken place between my English and Cherokee heritages.

That night my small campfire flickered as dinner cooked near my tent, its back side snug against the wall of the Old Stone Church. From time to time I lifted my hat from the ground to admire the shell, still amazed that the dog had uncovered it. I

half expected him to materialize in the moonlight just as won-
drously as the shell had appeared. I wanted him to lie by the
fire as I rubbed his neck and head. His not appearing, however,
actually gave me something else—a subtle and sweet archetypical longing to touch another living creature in the night and be
reassured that I was not alone in the world. This longing did
not sadden me. Rather, it made me thankful that I had not lost
such a simple but profound need.

As the flames danced, I inspected the hole where the shell
had been buried for hundreds of years. It was as if the very
earth that had tripped me in the woods reached out to make
amends. I could not think of a better and more appropriate
way to "a-gang" with the British countryside as my journey
neared its end.

The Milky Way, the "Way of Saint James," from which the
shell symbol originated, seemed brighter than usual that night.
Long after dinner I added little pieces of wood to the fire as
crickets chirped. They sang about the beauty and tranquillity
of the wheat field, the trees, the heavens, and the Old Stone
Church with the fire casting my shadow against the rock wall. It
was as though the silver ring I wore suddenly became the one
the knight offered in "The Squire's Tale." He who wore it could
understand the language of all living things.

Any traveler who has found a place that has won the heart knows the feeling of leaving such a treasured spot. That was true for me the next morning after camping at the Old Stone Church, where I awoke shortly after dawn to the sound of a dove cooing. It perched on a dead limb twenty feet over my tent as a light fog lifted from the surrounding wheat field.

No cars passed on the road, and the serene British countryside was as lush today as it had been in the Middle Ages. It wasn't until a train passed along the edge of the field that the modern world tapped on the door of my private little world, nestled against the ancient stone foundation. But when passengers on the train waved, I didn't mind the intrusion at all. Standing by my fire, I raised a cup of coffee to toast their commute into London. I suspected that they wished they could have a cup with me by the flames rather than race on to their confining offices.

After breakfast I welcomed the rising sun and continued carving the faces of Christ and Sequoya. From time to time, I searched the surrounding field for the dog that had dug the shell-bearing hole.

Medieval dogs were sometimes more than guards, hunters,

A dogcart. (B.M. MS. Roy. 10. E. IV. f.110v.)

and cherished pets. They were even used in the art of magic, when it came to the mandrake. The plant's root looks something like a human being, and the medieval mind thought it had a personality that accompanied its power. Fearing that the plant might take vengeance on anyone who pulled it from its home in the earth, those in Chaucer's world let a dog do the dirty work. A rope was tied around the plant and the animal's neck. Then a piece of meat was thrown several feet in front of the dog, so he would run for it and pull the mandrake from the ground. Anyone who has ever heard some dogs' eerie howls in the middle of the night might be tempted to believe that they are haunted by the past deeds of their ancestors.

The prized scallop shell looked a little different today. The soil left between its tiny ridges had dried, and the sunlight gave it a slightly yellow hue, as if brushed with pollen. Resting between the snake rattle and the feathers, it seemed to bond more than even my dual heritages as it connected creatures of the air, earth, and sea. At times in my life, I have felt part of all three.

Once my tent was repacked, I gathered a thimbleful of soil for my urn and started across the wheat field scattered with Queen Anne's lace. My fingers brushed the flowers to behold them swaying back and forth like hand-size islands dusted with snow. When I came upon two of the plants connected with a spiderweb covered with dew, I squatted before them to see the sunlight reflecting in the delicate strands. Leaning closer, I blew just hard enough to make the web vibrate, and the spider ran to the top as if a threatening storm approached. Little could he have known how doing harm to any living creature was the last thing on my mind.

When I came to a babbling stream, I pulled off my shoes and socks to stick my feet into the water. My sore feet welcomed the cool three-foot-wide creek while I wiggled my toes and threw pebbles upstream. The water swirled around a bend and disappeared among roots of a big oak, which stuck into the stream like black snakes swimming toward the other bank. Only a foot deep, the water seemed to baptize me as it flowed over my feet and I washed my face. Salvation sometimes comes in the simplest things, and all water is holy.

The field alongside the stream was thick with ripe English peas, and I had gathered a handful to eat. Like many people, I had seen times when nothing could beat the pleasure of chewing popcorn in the dark while an engaging movie took my mind off worries. But that morning no theater could've topped the stream's story, and I promised myself to remember this time whenever I started to take life too seriously. I threw a pea overhead and caught it in my mouth.

"When you leave the Old Stone Church," Grant had told me as I exited the antique store, "you'll soon climb a hill with a surprise at the top."

"What'd you mean?" I said.

"You'll see," he said. "Just keep your eyes open and look straight ahead."

Leaving the stream, I soon saw the hill and leaned on my staff as I climbed toward the top. Grant with his wax baby Jesus was such a curious personality that I wasn't sure what to expect. His dangling carrot urged me forward.

By the time I neared the summit, the sun was high, and I was sweating. When a breeze came, I removed my hat and wiped my brow. Even the wooden faces of Christ and Sequoya seemed to look toward the top of the hill. Taking a drink of water from my canteen, I started walking again with new vigor.

Anticipation in love or sex has its own overwhelming power, just as Chaucer's pilgrims' told in more than one of their tales, but so does the anticipation that comes with discovering something extraordinary on the distant landscape. At the top of the hill, it took several seconds before the horizon gave birth to shape and form that finally became a tower that reached right into the heavens. Then, in the distant haze like a mirage, the tower became part of an otherworldly structure that proved to be the Canterbury Cathedral. I had seen some of the world's highest snowcapped mountains, and once climbed a volcano to behold fireballs shooting from it into the night as glowing lava flowed, but Canterbury Cathedral, which was so steeped in tales of murder and miracles, at first seemed like something I could never truly touch. It would always be just a little farther down the trail, like something read about in an exotic adventure novel. But there it was awaiting me, just as the shell had been in the moist earth, and as with the finding of the relic, I stood staring at the cathedral, letting it wash over me with its undercurrents of history.

This was the very spot where most English medieval pilgrims viewed Canterbury Cathedral for the first time, and it would've been the tallest man-made structure most had ever seen. For those who were ill as well as those horrified of burning in hell, the promise of Becket's healing and forgiving shrine's being only miles down the road was a religious experience in itself. Some dropped to their knees and wept, while others, and especially those on crutches or those with bleeding hands from pulling themselves horizontally on wooden trestles as their limp legs dragged along the ground, were assured that at the very least some of their pain would be lessened from soon not having to struggle forward each day.

A cripple drags himself along. (B.M. Roy. MS 13.B.VIII. f.30v.)

Atop this monumental summit was also where Chaucer's festive pilgrims beheld the cathedral, and *The Canterbury Tales* came to an end with "The Parson's Tale." After stories of rape, love, revenge, deceit, greed, vanity, robbery, and murder, it was no accident that the author chose to conclude his medieval narrative on a religious and somewhat didactic note. The sun was setting when the Host urged the Parson to put the finishing touch on their storytelling:

> "Sir Preest," quod he, "artou a vicary [vicar],
> Or art a person [parson]? Say sooth, by thy fay!
> Be what thou be, ne breek thou not our play,
> For every man save thou hath told his tale.
> Unbuckle and shew us what is in thy male [bag]!
> Or trewely, me thinketh by thy cheere
> Thou sholdest knit up [wrap up] well a greet mattere.
> Tell us a fable anon, for cockes bones!"

The Parson answered that he was not good at rhyming, nor did he have a tale to amuse and entertain, such as the other pilgrims had told. Instead, he offered a sermon that would help them enter Heaven.

And therefore, if you list, I wol not glose [hedge],
I wol you tell a mirrye tale in prose
To knit up all this feest [feast of stories] and make an ende:
—And Jesu for his grace wit [inspiration] me sende
To shewe you the way, in this viage,
Of thilke parfit glorious pilgrimage
That highte Jerusalem Celestial [Heaven].

The Parson then revealed how God wanted each and every person to enter the celestial city and that there were several noble ways this could be accomplished. Penitence, the lamenting of sin and the will to sin no more, was a noble way. The roots of the penitence tree were contrition, and confession was its branches and leaves. Satisfaction was the fruit, and the seed was grace. The love of God was the heat in the seed.

Contrition, the Parson added, was the heart's sadness for sin. Pride was the first of seven deadly sins, and it took the varied forms of arrogance, impudence, boasting, hypocrisy, and joy at harming another. Humility was the remedy for pride.

The remedy for envy was to love God, your neighbor, and your enemy. Anger was cured by patience. Fortitude should replace sloth, and the remedy for avarice was mercy. The remedy for gluttony was abstinence, temperance, and sobriety. Lechery was expelled by chastity and continence. Regular confession made in good faith was necessary, and satisfaction came from physical pain, penance, fasting, and almsgiving. Anyone who followed the Parson's advice would reap the fruits of Heaven.

Following the Parson's words of wisdom, Chaucer added a "Retraction" to the *Tales:*

Here taketh the maker of this book his leve:
Now pray I to hem all that herken this litel tretise or rede, that if there be anything in it that liketh hem, that

thereof they thanken our Lord Jesu Christ, of whom pro-
ceedth all wit [wisdom] and all goodness. And if there be
anything that displese hem, I pray hem also that they ar-
rette [attribute] it to the default of mine unkonning [my
ignorance], and not to my will, that wolde full fain have
said better if I had the konning. For our Book saith [the
Bible says, 2 Timothy 3:16] "All that is written is written
for our doctrine"—and that is mine intent. Wherefore I
beseek you meekly, for the mercy of God, that ye pray for
me that Christ have mercy on me and foryive me my
guilts, and namely of my translacions and enditings of
worldy vanities, the which I revoke in my retraccions.

Chaucer goes on to list his major literary works, including
"the tales of Canterbury, thilke that sounen into [tend toward]
sin ... and many another book, if they were in my remembrance, and many a song and many a lecherous lay; that Christ
for his greet mercy foryive me the sin." The "Retraction" ends
when he begs that Christ and "his blissful Moder and all the
saints of heven" give him the grace to ponder his soul that "I
may been one of hem at the day of doom [judgment] that shall
be saved: Qui cum patre et Spiritu Sancto vivit et regnat Deus
per omnia saecula. Amen."

The date on Chaucer's tombstone, October 25, 1400, was
likely the correct day of his death. He drew a payment on his
exchequer annuity on June 5, 1400, but did not receive his next
payment, due in November. A new tenant leased his Westminster house in the fiscal year beginning September 28.

Chaucer was buried in London's Westminster Abbey, near
the entrance to Saint Benedict's chapel. Today's tomb, erected
in 1556, probably doesn't house his remains. In the seventeenth
century this part of the abbey, honoring Chaucer, became known
as the Poets' Corner and includes the graves of many English
authors. The simple stone that first marked Chaucer's remains

was moved when Dryden's grave was dug. Used to mend the pavement, the stone sank into obscurity.

The Great Fire of London, in 1666, destroyed materials that might've shed light on Chaucer's life. Henry VIII's librarian, John Leland, did have access to such materials, however, before they went up in flames and wrote that Chaucer "grew old and white-haired, and felt old age itself to be a sickness."[1] Leland also recorded that Chaucer's health sharply declined over the years and that he died while in London on business.

Chaucer was still employed by the court as late as May 4, 1398, because he was issued a safe-conduct on that date while traveling for the king's "arduous and urgent business," protecting him from enemies and lawsuits. No records have been found, however, to indicate the exact nature of that business.

Henry IV on his coronation day—October 13, 1399— renewed Chaucer's annuity of £20 and a barrel of wine from King Richard as well as adding 40 marks to the income. But Chaucer did not receive the money until February 1400. On the day before Christmas 1399, Chaucer signed a lease for a house in Westminster. A small home in the garden outside the Lady Chapel of the abbey, it was a serene setting surrounded by Benedictine monks, where Chaucer could write and ponder his soul, just as he said he hoped to do in the "Retraction." The abbey grounds may also have provided protection against Chaucer's creditors.

The protection offered by the abbey began during the time of Saint Edward the Confessor, and most of those who retreated there were murderers and thieves. Sanctioned by the state, the church prevented their arrest. They were required to confess their sins to the prior and wear a black robe with a yellow cross. Later they could renounce the kingdom and be taken to a ship. If no ship was available, they were expected to walk knee-deep daily in the sea as they cried, "Passage, for the love of

God and the king's sake!" So many criminals thrived in the area
of the abbey that a nearby street became known as Thieves
Street.

Whether Chaucer ever called upon the abbey for protection
against creditors is unknown—his pay in February 1400 was
retroactive for four months—but it's a safe bet that he often
prayed in the nearby church as he grayed, his sexual powers declined, and death approached. Like most medieval people, he
was horrified at thoughts of going to hell and wanted to do all
in his power to avoid it, just as his "Retraction" states, as if it
were a letter to God himself as well as to his readers.

Chaucer had been frightened by images of death when he
was a child and observed victims of the Black Death dropping
dead on the streets below his window. One of the gravest such
images in the Middle Ages was Death as a figure with a spear
stalking the land, one that Chaucer wrote about in "The Pardoner's Tale" and that quite possibly haunted him in his last
months on earth. Three rioters were drinking in a pub when
bells on the street indicated that a coffin was passing. When
they inquired who had died, a servant answered that it was a
friend of theirs who had been stabbed in the back:

> And suddenly he was y-slain tonight [last night],
> For-drunk. As he sat on his bench upright,
> There came a privee theef [thief] men clepeth [call] Death
> That in this countree all the people sleeth,
> And with his spear he smoot his heart a-two,
> And went his way withouten wordes mo.
> He hath a thousand slain this pestilence [plague].

The towering Canterbury Cathedral in the great hazy distance vanished as I descended the hill, the Old Stone Church
now far behind me, save for its unburied shell snug in my hatband. Medieval pilgrims whose very footsteps I followed would

have at this point in the journey said a special prayer of thanks to Saint Christopher, the saint of travelers, who had carried the infant Jesus on his shoulders. Many wore a medallion of the saint of their choice, chosen for life, on their hats. Craft guilds as well as individuals had patron saints. Archers and crossbowmen prayed to Saint Sebastian, martyr of the arrows. Bakers relied upon Saint Honore. His banner showed an oven shovel argent and three loaves gules. Saint Nicholas, who saved three children from the sea, protected sailors. Unmarried girls believed in Saint Catherine, who was said to have been beautiful. Charitable brotherhoods selected Saint Martin, because he gave half his cloak to the poor man.

A mixture of sadness and joy tugged at my heart as I approached Habletown, bordering Canterbury, and began to leave the countryside behind. While medieval pilgrims relied upon their saints, I had come to depend upon the English landscape as a kind of companion who was strong and always there. Trusting its rolling hills, stone walls, wheat fields, trees, birds, flowers, and streams, I cherished its worth as much as I believed in the dignity of mankind. Walking through the countryside for hours a day, I had come to feel clothed by the massive fair-weather sky. When I would close my eyes to go to sleep at night, I would still see its unending blueness over lush greens as if my spirit yet hiked on into a realm that only it—not the conscious mind—could comprehend. The landscape and the sky had joined forces to lift my inner world to another level, one that I did not want to lose in the journey's ending paradox: arrival is a victory born of departure from the path that gave it.

Still, I was excited to near Becket's shrine to join the history of thousands of medieval pilgrims who had journeyed there long before me. They were representative of my British ancestors, and to complete the trek would take me closer to the roots of that archetypical tree. Any conflict I had had between my Native American heritage and my English blood in the beginning of the pilgrimage had been reconciled by the heartfelt connections made with people along the way. Some of them were just as loving and unique as Indians I had let into my heart.

Before totally departing the countryside, however, I slipped from my pack one last time beneath an oak and sat to carve the design of snake rattles into the last seven inches of my staff, a number sacred to the Cherokee. But the staff didn't seem finished until a tiny cross was carved two inches above the rattles.

After writing in my journal, I lifted the pack once again and headed into Habletown, where I entered a pub to refill my canteen with water. Only a single customer, a man in his twenties with a red mustache, was there with the bartender, who stuck his hand into a bag of potato chips.

"Hot day for a hike," said the bartender, who filled my canteen with water. "Want some ice?"

I shook my head. "Just water's fine," I said. "Today's my last day on the trail. I left London a week ago."

"You walked all the way from London?" said the customer, as he and the bartender glanced at each other with conspiratorial eyes.

"I'm on a pilgrimage," I said.

"Pilgrimage?" said the bartender.

They studied my carved staff.

"Just down the street here is where Henry II began walking barefoot to Canterbury," I said.

"Without shoes?" said the customer.

"It was part of his penance for Becket's murder," I added. They apparently knew nothing of their own local history.

When the bartender handed me the canteen, I took a drink and placed it back into my pack. Both men gawked, as if I were from another world.

Exiting the pub, I heard them snicker before I was fully out the door. Being laughed at is one thing. Everything under the

sun deserves the test of humor. But their snickering made me
uncomfortable because it had a sinister bite to it, a darkness
oozing from the human soul.

My spirits were too high to let such a fluke drag me down—I
had met my share of less than enlightened folks long before my
trip to England—but I questioned if the encounter was a fore-
shadowing of what I might find in Canterbury. After all, any
place steeped in a history of miracles and murder was bound to
entice the extremes of human nature: a belief in the sacred
begged the opposite, a ridicule of anything suggesting it.

My staff *tap-tap-tapped* along the route Henry II walked barefoot into Canterbury. His secretary, Peter of Blois, chronicled
his service under the king in *Epistola:*

> If the king has promised to spend the day anywhere, es-
> pecially if a herald has publicly proclaimed that such is his
> royal will, you may be sure that he will start off early in
> the morning and by his sudden change of mind will throw
> everybody's plans into confusion. You may see men run-
> ning about as if they were mad, urging on the pack-
> horses, driving chariots one into another, and everything
> in a state of confusion. The tumult is such as to give you a
> vivid picture of the infernal regions. But if the king de-
> clares his intention of going to a certain place early the
> next morning, he will undoubtedly change his mind, and
> you may be sure that he will sleep to midday. You will
> see the packhorses waiting under their loads, the chariots
> standing ready, the couriers falling asleep, the purveyors
> uneasy and everybody grumbling. . . .
>
> You may ask me to send you an accurate descrip-
> tion of the appearance and character of the king of En-
> gland. That surpasses my powers, for the genius of Vergil
> would hardly be equal to it. That which I know, how-

ever, I will ungrudgingly share with you. Concerning
David we read that it was said of him, as evidence for his
beauty that he was ruddy. You may know then that our
king is still ruddy, except as old age and whitening hair
have changed his color a little. He is of medium stature
so that among small men he does not seem large, nor yet
among large men does he seem small. His head is spheri-
cal, as if the abode of great wisdom and the special sanctuary of lofty intelligence. The size of his head is in
proportion to the neck and whole body. His eyes are full,
guileless and dovelike when he is at peace, gleaming like
fire when his temper is aroused, and in bursts of passion
they flash like lightning. As to his hair he is in no danger
of baldness, but his head has been closely shaved. He has
a broad, square, lion-like face. His feet are arched and he
has legs of a horseman. His broad chest and muscular
arms show him to be a strong, bold, active man. His
hands show by their coarseness that he is careless and
pays little attention to his person, for he never wears
gloves except when he goes hawking. . . . If he has once
loved any one, he rarely ceases to love him, while one for
whom he has once taken a dislike he seldom admits to
his favor. He always has his weapons in his hands when
not engaged in consultation or at his books. When his
cares and anxieties allow him to breathe he occupies
himself with reading, or in a circle of clerks tries to solve
some knotty question.[2]

It's unfortunate that the king did not chronicle what he
thought and felt as he walked barefoot into Canterbury, but it's
a safe bet that in paying penance in this manner, he experienced
a mixture of sorrow and humiliation as medieval Englishmen crowded to see him lowered, at least for a while, to the

demeanor of a pilgrim desperate for salvation. He and Becket had once been as close as brothers, and William Fitzstephen— friend and biographer of Becket—documented a revealing story:

> The chancellor [Becket] therefore because of his virtue, his noble spirit, and his eminent merits, was in great favor with the king, the clergy, the army and the people. After business was done with, the king and the chancellor used to play together like two little boys, whether in the palace, in the church, in public, or in riding. One day they rode together in the streets of London. A strong wind was blowing, and the king saw a poor old man approaching in thin worn clothes.
>
> "Do you see that man?" said the king.
>
> "Yes," said Becket.
>
> "How poor, how weak he is," said the king, "and how very thinly clad. Would it not be a great charity to give him a warm cloak?"
>
> "Most certainly," said Becket, "and your majesty ought to have the spirit to do it."
>
> In the meantime the poor man came up to them, and the king stopped and Becket with him. The king quietly addressed the beggar and asked him if he would like to have a good cloak. The beggar, not knowing who they were, supposed they were not in earnest but joking.
>
> The king said to Becket: "You are the one to show this great charity," and laying his hands upon him he tried to pull off a fine new cloak made of thick scarlet cloth which Becket wore, while Becket on the other hand tried to prevent him. Thereupon there was a great commotion and struggle. The courtiers who were following then ran up in astonishment to learn the reason for the unexpected contest. There no one would tell them, for both the king and

Becket were fully occupied with their hands, and seemed to be in danger of falling off their horses. At length Becket reluctantly allowed the king to conquer, to draw off his cloak and give it to the beggar.[3]

As I walked on, the cathedral loomed on the horizon to a height of 235 feet in the Bell Harry Tower, where swallows circled. Towering over Canterbury, the cathedral yet seemed unreal, like something in a dream. The awe it instilled in me now that it was so close was like the first time I saw the ocean when I was a child. Its great waves crashing upon the shore made me feel so small and big in the same breath. It, like the cathedral, was of almost overpowering beauty, and yet it housed mysteries that scared me. Unknown creatures crawled along its dark depths. When I finally stepped into the water, foaming over my feet, the undertow pulled me, thrilling as it threatened to take me closer to those creatures.

The Canterbury Cathedral was now an equally paradoxical sea. Its creatures were the self-righteousness and hypocrisies of orthodox religion, while its archetypical power of bringing people closer to God—however they chose to worship him—was the beauty of its shimmering if turbulent waves.

The cathedral was still a ten-minute walk ahead when, a couple of blocks north of the river Stour, flowing along Canterbury's stone wall, a sign captivated me: it hung in front of a restaurant named The Bishop's Finger and pictured the cleric dressed in all his glory as his finger pointed accusingly into the air. Tired, hot, hungry, and thirsty, I entered the restaurant.

"Hey, some walking stick you got there," said the bartender, who introduced himself as Neil. "Theatrical. Can I see it?"

Handing him the staff, I took a seat and eyed the daily specials on a chalkboard. Among the food and drinks listed were "Holy Madness" and "Heaven's Gate."

"What's in those drinks?" I asked.

A bishop gives the tonsure. (B.M. Addl. MS. 38120. f.8.)

"Divine alcohol," said Neil, who was a college student. "Want to leave your earthly troubles behind?"

"Not just at the moment," I said, and explained my mission to Canterbury.

"I've got an interest in spiritual matters right now myself," said Neil. "I just accepted a part in a play in which Jesus is portrayed as gay." He raised the top of the staff closer to his eyes. "Who's this opposite Christ?"

As I was telling him about Sequoya, someone tapped on the window, and at first I thought I was imagining things. Four men dressed as nuns had painted their faces blue and grinned as if they were on their way to Mardi Gras.

"What's with them?" I asked.

"Oh, just having a little fun with the tourists," said Neil, returning their waves as they disappeared down the street.

"So you're here to see the cathedral?" said the other bartender, Sean, who had been listening all along and was in his twenties.

"Thought I would," I said. "It'll complete my journey."

"Waste of space," he said, "if you ask me."

"The cathedral is a waste of space?" I said.

"A stupid waste of space," Sean nodded. "If it was up to me, they'd convert the whole church into apartments."

"Why's that?" I said.

"Get real," he said. "This is the twenty-first century. People need shelter more than they need religion."

Somewhere between the blue nuns, the gay Jesus, and the proposed Canterbury Cathedral Condos, it sank in that I had just arrived at the crossroads of the sacred and the secular. After I ate lunch, Neil helped me locate a nearby B and B through the Yellow Pages. As I was walking out the door, the four blue nuns came in.

"Those are some wild costumes," I said, wondering just how long it took them to paint their faces blue.

"Bless you, my child, but these are not costumes," said the taller nun. "This is the latest fashion at the convent."

"I like the feathers," said the shorter nun, eyeing my hat. "Ever tickled a nun with one?"

"Could be a good habit to get into," said a third nun.

Two of the nuns groaned, and another almost giggled as they continued on into The Bishop's Finger, and I headed up the street, till pausing a few steps later. Looking through the very window where I had first seen the decadent sisters when they tapped on the window, I now beheld them before the chalkboard listing the daily specials. They appeared torn between "Holy Madness" and "Heaven's Gate." The one who had invited me to tickle with a feather turned to the window and winked. Having lived in New Orleans as well as San Francisco, I was accustomed to seeing men in fun-loving and outlandish costumes, but on the last leg of my pilgrimage, their carnival attire struck me as bizarre. For that matter, however, who doesn't wear costumes? Some are just unnoticed because they are conventional clothing. We're only truly real when we're naked with our thoughts, bodies, and souls.

The B and B was a brisk fifteen-minute walk from The

Bishop's Finger. Knocking on the door, I was met by a woman in her fifties, who wore a red robe.

"I called about the room," I said, removing my hat.

"Yes, of course," she said, pulling the robe modestly tighter around her chest. "Come in. Sorry to have met you like this, but I thought I'd be dressed before you got here. There's been a death in the family, and I must hurry to the services."

She appeared to be on the verge of tears, and I debated whether to inquire about her grief, death being no less crushing now than it had been in the Middle Ages.

"Was this a sudden loss?" I asked, after entering the three-story house.

"My aunt," she said. "She hadn't felt well the past week, but . . ." Pulling the robe yet tighter around her, she introduced herself as Gloria. "I'll show you the room. It isn't very big, I'm afraid, but it has a view of the garden, and the bed is comfortable. You're an American?"

I told her a little about my pilgrimage as we climbed three narrow flights of stairs, squeaking all the way. Gloria was an unusually attractive woman, with brown eyes and a radiant complexion, which somehow made her sadness all the more striking. A beauty mark highlighted the corner of her mouth.

"This is it," she said, upon opening the door to a room with a slanted ceiling, its wooden beams exposed. "There's the garden." She pulled back white-lace curtains, and down below in the backyard, flowers bloomed as if they had been given special care.

"It's just right," I said, and set my staff in the corner of the room by a table with a picture of Pope John Paul II resting atop it.

"You're Catholic?" I said.

"I don't go to mass as often as I should," she said, her tone apologetic as her eyes moistened again. She eyed her watch. "My aunt gave me the watch when I turned forty," she said.

Eyeing the watch again, she added, "I must rush." She handed me two keys on a silver ring, pointed out the bathroom across the hall, and started down the squeaking stairs. "I almost forgot," she called out from the second floor. "What time do you want breakfast?"

"Whatever is good for you," I said.

We agreed on eight A.M., and she vanished with the squeaks, the smell of her perfume lingering in the hallway. Its fragrance didn't suggest her sensuality, however, as much as it did flowers at a funeral. If the blue nuns had made me blink, Gloria's grief had opened my eyes a little wider to the human condition.

After taking a shower, I returned to my room, where the picture of Pope John Paul II now reflected sunlight from the garden-view window. It struck the framed glass for golden rays to radiate from his shoulders, as if the hands of the divine rested there.

Lifting the picture, I studied his face. It was gentle for someone with so much power—a power that many considered outdated and barbaric when it came to birth control and sexual desires—and it was an ironic disappointment to millions around the world that their prayers for the pope to be cured of his Parkinson's disease had not been answered. His visiting and forgiving the jailed man who had shot him was a testimony to his faith. He practiced what he preached. Not all medieval popes were as Christlike as he was, however.

At the end of the ninth century in Rome, chaos churned the city as various factions, claiming to be descendants of Charlemagne, quarreled over who should be in power. In March 896, at the "Synod borrenda," the current victorious faction was headed by Pope Stephen VII. He oversaw a trial for the late Pope Formosus, who had been leader of the opposing faction. Dead for eight months, Formosus's corpse was taken from his tomb and adorned in its sacerdotal robes before being propped up in his throne in the council chamber.

The counsel who had been provided for the corpse didn't dare make a peep as Pope Stephen paraded before the shriveled body to shout insults at it. Though Pope Stephen pretended to put Formosus on trial for accepting the bishopric of Rome while he was yet bishop of another diocese, the true crime of Formosus was another matter. A member of the rival faction, he had crowned an illegitimate descendant of Charlemagne as emperor after having done the same for a member of Pope Stephen's party.

The majority of Romans didn't care which puppet emperor wore the crown, and this mock trial was simply a means by which the corpse and the faction it had represented could be humiliated. After Pope Stephen condemned Formosus, the propped-up and shriveled remains were stripped as the three fingers of benediction were chopped off. Then the mutilated corpse was dragged through the palace and tossed to a riotous mob in the streets, which kicked it and spit on it as they threw it into the Tiber River. It wasn't until merciful fishermen pulled the corpse from the water that the former pope received a proper burial.

Alone in the B and B after Gloria had left for her aunt's funeral, I found it odd to depart her home without my staff, pack, and hat, which couldn't be worn in Canterbury Cathedral. Without these symbols of pilgrimage, I was but another passerby to those on the street, who would otherwise have looked me over like a human relic from another time.

The closer I got to the cathedral, the thicker the festive crowd became, speaking German, Italian, and Spanish as well as English. Voices were loud and excited, as if a rock concert or football game were starting. The smell of fish-and-chips, pizza, and burgers filled the carnival air, and a violin player tapped her foot to an Irish jig as a rubber elf sat on her shoulder, his little legs dangling. A Japanese couple took pictures of a bearded man juggling three balls. With a cigarette dangling from his mouth, he blew smoke rings for the better-aimed balls to leap through like trained animals or birds. And just as in Chaucer's time, the streets were scattered with beggars.

"Spare a little change for Cat?" said a teenage girl, holding a dog in her lap as she sat on a blanket outside one of many cafés.

"Cat?" I said, eyeing the dog.

"Cat's his name," she said. "Instead of a cat in a hat, it's a cat in a dog."

Big Head, Red Top, and the other street kids back in Rochester were days ago, and yet I felt them in my heart as if we had talked the past hour. This girl with her dog named Cat now found the same soft spot.

"Sure," I said, pulling some coins from my pocket. "A dog did me a favor a couple of days ago."

She smiled when I gave her the money, and the dog licked her face.

"What kind of favor?" she said. Her wondrous British accent was just as rich to my ears as the words of someone affluent.

"He connected me to people in the past," I said, and went on to explain what had happened at the Old Stone Church.

Her eyes beamed. "That's a better trick than fetching a stick," she said.

When Henry II walked barefoot along these same streets and entered the cathedral, he was flogged by monks bearing branches, as part of his penance for his hand in the murder of Becket on December 29, 1170. Saint Thomas was born in London, December 21, 1118, to parents who came from Normandy. After studying in Paris, Becket became a secretary for his kinsman Osbert Huitdeniers, who was "justiciar" of London. In 1141 he became a favored clerk of Theobald, archbishop of Canterbury.

Theobald sent Becket to study civil and canon law for a year at Bologna and Auxerre and in 1154 ordained him deacon. "Thomas of London," as Becket was called during this period, became—at the age of thirty-six—chancellor under Henry II. The friendship between the king and Becket deepened along with the new chancellor's appreciation of the riches surrounding him. In 1158, when Becket traveled to France to negotiate a marriage treaty, onlookers marveled at his decadence.

A French chronicler, Garnier, noted that Becket was a notorious fighter and had seen him unhorse many French knights. Deacon though Becket was, he had led many attacks himself. This dichotomy of holy man and warrior in the Middle Ages was not uncommon. An order of weapon-toting clerics, the Knights Templar, had been established in the twelfth century in Jerusalem to protect pilgrims and the Holy Sepulcher. While blood may have stained Becket's hands in battle, his speech stayed clean of profanity, and he punished others for using it as well as for lying.

Archbishop Theobald died in 1161. On Saturday, June 2, 1162, Becket was ordained a priest and the next day consecrated bishop. By the end of the same year, the new archbishop underwent a transformation, rejecting the decadent lifestyle he had enjoyed as the king's chancellor. He began fasting and wearing hair shirts to keep his skin pricked with the suffering of mankind. Becket walked barefoot to greet those who brought him the pallium from Rome. This cloak of authority, draping his shoulders, would take him another step closer to his violent death.

Trouble first surfaced between Henry II and Becket when the archbishop reclaimed estates belonging to his see. The tightrope friendship unraveled further as Becket refused to embrace the "avitae consuetudines," which was a series of unspecified articles Henry derived from his grandfather's customs. Among them, however, one point was boldly clear: the king insisted on trying clerics charged with crimes in the secular courts. Becket fought this tooth and nail, and Henry II retaliated by requiring the archbishop to surrender castles that had come under the church's domain.

The king tightened the political thumbscrews by demanding that Becket account for all the moneys that had passed through his hands as chancellor. He was ultimately ordered to pay £30,000. His fellow bishops begged Becket to end the quarrel by beseeching the king's mercy. Becket not only refused, he threatened the advisers and paraded into the royal council chamber with his archiepiscopal cross held overhead as if he were again on the battlefield. Henry, equally infuriated, yelled that Becket be sentenced, but the archbishop, yet brandishing the cross, pushed through the confused courtiers to make his escape.

Less than three weeks later, November 2, 1164, Becket disguised himself and fled to a ship docked at Sandwich. Sailing to France, where Louis VII welcomed him, Becket threw himself at the feet of Pope Alexander III, who refused to accept his resignation of his see.

On November 30 Becket took refuge at the Cistercian Abbey of Pontigny in Burgundy. Within a year Henry confiscated the archbishop's property and exiled Becket's kinsfolk. When the king swore to topple the whole Cistercian order for harboring Becket, he left the abbey.

Becket expressed his sorrow and anger in 1165 in "The Address of the Blessed Thomas, Archbishop of Canterbury, to Henry, King of England, at his Council Held at Chinon," which was included in *History of England,* written in the thirteenth century by Roger of Hoven, a royal clerk with access to invaluable documents and letters.

With great longing have I longed to see your face, and to converse with you; much, indeed, on my own account, but more especially on yours. On my account that, on seeing your face, you might recall to mind the services which, in my obedience to you, I have devotedly rendered to you to the best of my conscience; as God may help me at the last

judgment, when all shall stand before His tribunal to receive according to what they have done in the body,
whether good or whether evil; also, that I might move you
to take compassion upon me, who am obliged to live on
charity among the people of a foreign land; although, by
the grace of God, I still have sufficient provision and in
abundance. It is also my great consolation that the Apostle says "All that will live godly in Christ shall suffer persecution," and the words of the Prophet are, "I have not
seen the righteous man forsaken, nor his seed begging
bread." Again, for your own sake for these three reasons:
because you are my lord, because you are my king, and because you are my son in Spirit. Because you are my lord, I
owe and offer to you my counsel, as is due from every
bishop to his lord, in accordance with the honor of God
and of the Holy Church; because you are my king, I am
bound to respect and to admonish you; because you are
my son, I am bound by the duties of my office to chastise
and to correct you. For a father corrects his son, sometimes in kind words and sometimes in harsh, that, by one
means or the other, he may recall him to do what is right.
You ought to understand that by the grace of God, you
are a king for the following purposes: first, because it is
your duty to govern yourself, and to amend your life with
the practice of good manners, in order that by your example others may be induced to reform their lives, according
to the saying of wise men, that the world is formed after
the example of a king. In the second place, for encouraging some and punishing others, by virtue of the power
which you have received from the Church with the sacra-
ment of anointing, and with the sword which, in virtue of
your office, you wield for the destruction of evil-doers to
the Church. For kings are anointed in the three places: on
the head, on the breast, and on the arms, thereby signify-

ing glory, knowledge and strength. The kings who, in
ancient times, did not observe the judgments of God,
but sinned against His commandments, were deprived of
both glory, knowledge and strength. . . . And, inasmuch as
it is certain that kings receive their power from the
Church, and not it from them, but (with your leave I say
it) from Christ, you ought not to give your commandments to bishops to absolve or to excommunicate any
person, to bring the clergy before secular courts, to pro-
nounce judgment relative to tithes and churches, to forbid bishops taking cognizance of breaches of faith or
vows in such manner as is here set forth in writing among
your customs, which you style the laws of your grandfather. . . . Do not then attempt, my lord, if you wish for
the salvation of your soul, in any way to withdraw from
that Church what is its own, or in any degree to contra-
vene justice in acting towards it; but rather allow it to enjoy the same freedom in your kingdom which it is known
to enjoy in others. Keep in remembrance also the profession which you made and placed in writing upon the altar
at Westminster, to preserve its liberties to the Church of
God, at the time when, by my predecessor, you were consecrated and anointed king. Restore, also, the church of
Canterbury, in which you received your promotion and
consecration, to that state and dignity which it enjoyed in
the days of your predecessors and mine. Restore, also, the
possessions which belong to that church, the towns, the
castles, the estates, of which you have made distribution
at your will, and replace in full all the things which have
been taken from either me as well as my clerks and laymen. Likewise, allow me freely and in peace to return to
my see, and I am ready to serve you loyally and duteously,
as my most dear lord and king, in so far as I can, saving
always the honor of God and of the Roman Church

and my orders. But if you will not do thus, then know, for a certainty, that you will feel the severity of God's vengeance.[4]

A series of letters from Pope Alexander and Becket, echoing the grief of "The Address," was sent to Henry II in the following years without success. On January 6, 1169, the kings of England and France held a conference at Montmirail. There Becket threw himself at Henry's feet, only to be pushed away since he yet refused to accept the customs of Henry's grandfather.

In 1170 Becket returned to Canterbury when it appeared that he and the king might make amends. But when the archbishop objected to the coronation of Prince Henry, the king again became outraged, questioning what could be done to rid himself of the renegade Thomas once and for all. Four knights interpreted the king's anger as instruction to kill Becket. Gervase, a Canterbury monk, observed the murder and recorded it. His account was translated in 1853 by Joseph Stevenson in *The Church Historians of England*.

But on the fifth day of the nativity, which was the third day of the week, there arrived four courtiers, who desired to speak with the archbishop, thinking by this to discover the weak points [of the monastery]. These were Reginald Fitz-Urse, Hugh de Morville, William de Traci, and Richard Brito. After a long discussion, they began to employ threats; and at length rising up hastily, they went out into the courtyard; and under the spreading branches of a mulberry-tree, they cast off the garments with which they had covered their breastplates, and, accompanied by those persons whom they had summoned from the province, they returned into the archbishop's palace. Yet he, unmoved by the exhortations, the prayers, and the tears of his followers, remained firm in his place, until the time had arrived for the performance of the evening service in the church; towards which he advanced with a slow and deliberate step, like one who of his own free-will prepares himself for death. Having entered the church, he paused at the threshold; and he asked his attendants of what they were afraid. When the clerks began to fall into disorder, he said, "Depart, ye cowards! Let these blind madmen go on in their career. I command you, in virtue of your obedience, not to shut the door."

While he was thus speaking, behold! The executioners, having ransacked the bishop's palace, rushed together through the cloisters; three of whom carried hatchets in their left hands, and one an axe or a two-edged glaive, while all of them brandished drawn swords in their right hands. But after they had rushed through the open door, they separated from each other, Fitz-Urse turning to the left, while the three others took to the right. The archbishop had already ascended a few steps, when Fitz-Urse, as he hurried onwards, asked one whom he met, "Where is the archbishop?"

Hearing this, he turned round on the step, and, with a slight motion of the head, he was the first to answer, "Here I am, Reginald. I have conferred many a benefit on you, Reginald; and do you now come to me with arms in your hands?"

"You shall soon find out," was the reply. "Are you not that notorious traitor to the king?" And, laying hold on his pall, he said, "Depart hence;" and he struck the pall with his sword.

The archbishop replied, "I am not a traitor; nor will I depart, wretched man!" and he plucked the fringe of his pall from out of the knight's hand.

The other repeated the words, "Flee hence!"

The reply was, "I will not flee; here your malice shall be satisfied."

At these words the assassin stepped back as if smitten by a blow. In the meantime the other three assailants had arrived; and they exclaimed, "Now you shall die!"

"If," said the archbishop, "you seek my life, I forbid you, under the threat of an anathema, from touching any of my followers. As for me, I willingly embrace death, provided only that the church obtains liberty and peace at the price of my blood." When he said these words, he stretched forth his head to the blows of the murderers.

Fitz-Urse hastened forward, and with his whole strength he planted a blow upon the extended head; and he cried out, as if in triumph over his conquered enemy, "Strike! Strike!"

Goaded on by the author of confusion, these butchers, adding wound to wound, dashed out his brains; and one of them, following up the martyr (who at this time was either in the act of falling, or had already fallen), struck the pavement with his sword but the point of the weapon broke off short. They now returned through the cloister, crying out "Knights of the king, let us go; he is dead!" And then they pillaged whatever they found in the archbishop's residence.

See here a wonder. While he was yet alive, and could speak, and stand on his feet, men called him a traitor to the king; but when he was laid low, with his brains dashed out, he was called the holy Thomas, even before the breath had left his body.

This blessed martyr suffered death in the ninth year of his patriarchate, on the fourth of the calends of January [December 29], being the third day of the week, A.D. 1170, while the monks were singing their vespers. His dead body was removed and placed in the shrine before the altar of Christ. On the morrow it was carried by the monks and deposited in a tomb of marble within the crypt. Now, to speak the truth—that which I saw with my eyes, and handled with my hands—he wore hair-cloth next his skin ... over that a black cowl, then the white cowl in which he was consecrated; he also wore his tunic and dalmatic, his chasuble, pall and miter; lower down, he had drawers of sack cloth, and over these others of linen; his socks were of wool, and he had on sandals.[5]

As I made my way through the carnival crowd toward Canterbury Cathedral, the words of Gervase, describing Becket's murder, seemed timid compared to today's raw and brutal media coverage of such an event. If Becket were killed in America today, TV news shows would blast viewers with pictures of the bloodstained cathedral, close-ups of the scattered brains, note what the archbishop ate that day, grill the monks about his most personal habits ("Where did he get that hair-cloth shirt, anyway?"), probe whether he had a mistress or boyfriend or had ever visited a sexual site on the Internet, show pictures of him clenching his teeth in battle and crying at mass. Wild rumors would fly on the street and through callers to *Larry King Live*: Was the assassination a mafia hit? The work of the CIA or the FBI? (Such a murder would be akin to President Bush's being linked to the death of Billy Graham.) Members of the media would talk to friends and family of the killer knights and present a wide assortment of political and religious experts ready to swear what could have prevented the murder. TV ratings would soar as the four knights came to trial, defended by Johnnie Cochran or Jerry Spence, and Geraldo Rivera would spend the night in the very spot where the archbishop lost the top of his head. Rap and pop songs about the brutal death would rock the charts, and book and movie deals would be made over lunch as the public hungered for more details of gore, intrigue, thrills, and betrayal. Religious fanatics would warn us all that such murder was a sign from God not only that our country's on a fast train to hell but that THE END IS NEAR.

But without even the printing press in 1170, the story of Becket's death and the miracles that followed was to move across England and Europe by word of mouth and handwritten accounts carried by horses, ships, and homing pigeons. My own steps moved equally slowly as the entrance to Canterbury Cathedral now appeared only a block away. It loomed over me like some colossal medieval wave about to crest and pull me into its undertow.

CHAPTER

12

Inside, the mammoth cathedral smelled of another world, a dusty, cavelike chamber linking the dead to the living. The arched stone ceilings were so high that they taunted me for my lack of wings, and stained-glass windows—made of melted ash and sand—depicted miracles and filtered sunlight through bigger-than-life human figures, showing history to illiterate medieval pilgrims.

Tombs of Henry IV and Edward, the Black Prince, rested among carved stone sarcophagi, which encased the remains of archbishops from centuries ago, their faces so lifelike that it seemed they might rise at any moment to conduct a mass in Latin. They intrigued me as much as they made me uneasy, their pomp and power reduced to bones and ashes.

Though no one sat in the throne of the archbishop, the seat was not empty. Onlookers filled it with stares. Everyone appeared to be under a spell as they gawked, pointed, and whispered.

Mysterious sound flowed through the building, as if vibrations from millions of pilgrims' prayers from the past eight hundred years yet drifted overhead like a flock of invisible swallows, whistling as softly as a breeze in treetops. For the first time in my life, I glimpsed how a monk, feeling God in a place like this, could wish to live in a brotherhood free of the outside world—even if some would accuse him of escapism.

Any dread I had had of not feeling comfortable here because of my Native American spirituality was put to rest. The God I envisioned did not want me in the autumn of my life to draw lines in the sand about differences in beliefs but to dig deep enough in the sand to find water for all of humanity to drink.

Cool, moist air rose up stone steps descending to the spot where Becket was murdered, now marked with three swords on the wall and surrounded by a black chain. Here the monks mopped his blood from the floor with cloth and prepared his body for the nearby crypt. That very night a townsman who had gathered some of the blood hurried home, and the first Becket miracle occurred when the man healed his paralyzed wife by touching her with the bloodstained cloth. That which the monks had saved would be diluted in water—"Canterbury water," or "the water of Saint Thomas"—and sold in vials, ampullae, worn on chains around the neck of pilgrims as a kind of badge. The diluted water was also drunk and smeared on the eyelids of the blind. Benedict of Peterborough wrote that, "just as St. Thomas in his lifetime sought to achieve the same perfection as the Son of Man, so, after his death, he was honored in the same fashion, by the partaking of his blood." Not everyone could stomach such a thing. An ill monk of Mont-Saint-Michel rejected a swallow of wine that had been poured over the skull of Saint Aubert, "preferring to die than drink wine swilled in the head of a corpse."[1]

A woman in front of me squatted and rubbed her hand across the stone floor as though she saw Becket's blood. When she arose, she examined her palm.

"I don't mean to intrude," I said, stepping closer. "But are you hoping for a miracle?"

Looking me over, she lowered her hand as though to hide what she had just done.

"I just need some strength right now," she said. "My daughter is going through a hard time."

She headed up the stairs. Standing over the murder site, I beheld the floor, smudged with her troubled heart.

Only a few steps later, I entered the crypt. Its low arched ceiling with narrow stone ridges looked like the skeleton of some prehistoric creature, and I felt swallowed by it, taking me deeper into an already altered reality. If spirits and ghosts are more than archetypical products of an imagination trying to make sense of the human soul, some surely lived here. They peeked from inside the stone columns and whispered about human beings, the living, as if we were yet children, so ignorant of what awaited us. The crypt's eerie beauty made the very air itself stir with mysticism, and I took a deep breath, the way people sometimes do after a forest rain.

Their soft voices drifting through the crypt, the visitors were like members of a tribe gathered around a nightly fire, and I felt part of them. The same universal force had brought us together, and here in this subterranean twilight, we shared awareness of our own splendor and vulnerability, like passengers on a ship who could not see land. The vast, deep ocean beneath us was the crypt's question of afterlife as well as the meaning and purpose of our lives.

Candles flickered around the site of the tomb of Saint Thomas from 1170 to 1220 and at the Chapel of the Holy Innocents. Nearby a man on a wooden bench with a Bible lowered his head and prayed. Then he looked to Jesus on the cross as if some answer would surely appear in his face. The whole time he fidgeted with a rosary. When we made eye contact, I started to look away. But I couldn't because his stare cut right into my core. Whatever he suffered I also knew in myself sometime in the past. There was no illusion that I would not see it in one form or another again in the future.

A sign over a table where candles burned read: YOUR

PRAYERS WILL BE PLACED UPON THE ALTAR TOMORROW AT
8 A.M. FOR HOLY COMMUNION SERVICE. Candles were available by dropping a coin into a box, and a stack of note cards
rested on the table along with pens. Several of the prayers had
been posted on a board:

> Please stop school violence in America, the starvation in
> Africa. Bring peace to the Middle East.

> Lord, I pray that Sam be made well. Please don't take him
> from us just yet.

> Please help Helen calm down and help me lose weight.
> I'm so tired of being fat.

> Father, please don't let me be pregnant again. And forgive
> me for what I said to Jim.

> Help Bill understand that he is drinking too much. Give
> me the strength I need to love him just the same.

> God, I beg You. Take this cancer away.

The last one appeared to be the writing of a child:

> Jesus, have you seen my rabbit in heaven? If you bring
> him home, I won't let him out of the cage again.

The retired hairstylist in Rochester had asked that I pray for
her ailing husband while placing the rose petals by a lighted
candle. I was doing just that when a woman in her early
twenties and dressed like a monk appeared. Her hair was story-
book-angel blond. She began to gather the prayer cards.

"Do you collect them every day?" I asked.

"Several times a day," she said. "Fifty to a hundred each time. The bishop will hold them up as a mass prayer." She lifted the cards like a winning hand at poker.

"Does he read them?" I asked, thinking of the lost rabbit and the woman begging God to cure her cancer.

"Not usually," she said, in a sheepish voice. "Once a year a priest reads three weeks' worth to see what people are wanting."

"What becomes of the cards that aren't read?" I said.

Her strained grin was apologetic. "They get tossed."

"Into the trash?" I said, questioning if they weren't humble but important documents shedding light on mankind at that point in history.

She nodded as she pulled strands of blond hair from over her eyes and disappeared behind a stone column with the cards. The prayer board was then empty, and one of the candles fought for its life. Seconds later it went out, and smoke drifted over it. Medieval pilgrims sometimes ate the candles and their charred wicks left at shrines, hoping to receive a miracle.

Exiting the crypt, I walked past where Becket had been murdered and approached the stone stairs that led to his shrine in the Trinity Chapel, to which his remains had been translated from the crypt in 1220. Subtle silver light reflected from indentations in the stairs, worn smooth by thousands of pilgrims climbing them on their knees.

In 1538 Henry VIII, enraged that the pope in Rome disapproved of his constant marrying and divorcing—he had six wives—decided to form his own church for all of England. Priests were required to join it, and monasteries were dissolved. All saints' shrines, including Becket's, were to be destroyed and the saints' bones burned. Henry VIII ordered a blue diamond from Becket's shrine to be set into a ring he wore. He renamed the cathedral Christ Church.

Taking one final step closer to medieval pilgrims, I lowered myself to my knees and began to climb the stone stairs toward the site of Becket's shrine. Each step forward forced me to lean on my hands to prevent falling. My knees hurt. Onlookers whispered, and one woman made the sign of the cross. A boy around five or six years old jerked his mother's dress.

"What's he doing?" he said.

The woman put a finger to her lips: "Quiet."

Becket's shrine, made of gold and decorated with all kinds of jewels, had a stone base and was supported on marble pillars. Its wooden cover, ornately carved, was suspended from the ceiling. In 1428 two monks, John Vyel and Edmund Kyngyston, were guardians of the shrine and recorded their duties in Latin in "The Customary of the Shrine of St. Thomas Becket." It was mandatory that one of the guardians be at the shrine at all times, except during a meal. After the monastery's mass every day, the shrine precincts' doors were shut, and the guardians' first assistant clerk, carrying an "offensive and defensive instrument," searched all dark corners where thieves or dogs could hide. After the guardians dined in the refectory, the shrine was opened to the public again, and the pilgrims were urged to enter ringing bells.

The guardians were required to clean all the shrine's jewels and every fourth year had to replace its twelve red and green candles, weighing thirty-one pounds each. Every third year they renewed a candle stretched around a drum. The length had to equal the circumference of Dover and was paid for by the town's mayor and other barons there. The enormous candle was lit daily at the mass of Saint Thomas, during vespers, matins, high mass, and for all processions to the shrine. On July 6 the guardians received seven monks' allowances of bread, seven pounds of cheese, and seven measures of beer, which they ate from and shared with pilgrims who were exhausted and hungry from their journeys. They coaxed the pilgrims to make generous offerings and kept the area around the shrine swept clean

Monk drinking beer. (B.M. MS. Sloane 2435. f.44v.)

to guard against infections brought on the travelers' feet. Taking his turn as president of the common room for a week, a guardian gave a measure of wine to the other monks "for the increase of recreation," so that "his companions might rejoice at his presence among them."[2]

The arrival of medieval pilgrims was not as orderly as the lives of the guardian monks. Coughing, shivering, and bleeding from the feet, the pilgrims ached to touch the shrine that would heal them and save them from hell. Sweaty and dirty from their long journeys, during which they often didn't sleep well from fear of being robbed or murdered, they smelled of sweat and excrement, and their patience had worn thin. Pus oozed from the sores of lepers, pushed aside by the stronger travelers as if the shrine were the last morsel on earth. Those on crutches hobbled as best they could, while those on hand trestles, pulling their bodies behind them, fought to near the shrine by the mercy of others' lifting them up the stairs. Thread with which the ill members of a family had been measured dangled from

A cripple in a pushcart. (B.M. MS. Luttrell Psalter. f.186v.)

the pilgrims' hands as they longed to place it around or upon the covering of the shrine to ensure answered prayers. Others brought their bent coins or wax images of children, teeth, hands, hearts, and eyes. Some of the pilgrims, suffering from mental disorders, cried or laughed hysterically, while others howled like kicked dogs. At times the entrance to the shrine appeared more like a door to a hellish carnival than to God's pearly gates.

Some pilgrims, not receiving the miracle they sought, could not pull themselves away from a saint's bones. They would stick to a shrine for weeks or even months at a time as they lay on makeshift beds or wrapped themselves in blankets, praying for salvation, for healing, while they survived on scraps or alms. Physicians attended the wealthier pilgrims as they awaited a cure from a shrine. Others never got to touch a saint's resting place at all. They died within sight of it.

Monks at every medieval shrine kept a book in Latin to register the pilgrims' cures, and this was true for the Canterbury Cathedral in *Miracles of St. Thomas*. Robert of London recovered the sight of his right eye only. Walter, a knight of Lisors, was cured of leprosy. A mute Welsh acquired speech and could talk in both Welsh and English. Eilwin of Berkhampstead was cured of lameness. Godiva of Stratford was healed of noises and pain in her head. Beatrice, daughter of William of Ramsholt, forgot where she had placed the cheese. Her brother suggested that she pray to Saint Thomas, and she was given the answer in a dream. John of Bennington was cured of swelling in the throat.

In some cases the *Miracles of St. Thomas* recorded not only the symptoms and cures of pilgrims but what happened to them later. Relapses were common. A disturbed woman from Rouen regained her sanity at Becket's shrine but lost it again when she entered her home. A monk from Poitiers rejoiced that his leprosy was cured at Canterbury only to find the disease reappearing when he left town. Gerard, a Fleming, was only temporarily cured of an ulcer. Such relapses were usually blamed on a pilgrim's not giving sufficient thanks to the saint or not leaving enough money at the shrine. The failure was also attributed to the pilgrim's committing a huge sin. Ralph of Langton was cured of leprosy in May but had a relapse in December, "owing to some hidden judgment of God, . . . for the cause of this relapse only He can know."[3]

Relapses were not confined only to those making pilgrimages to Canterbury. Ralph Attenborough was healed of mental defects upon accepting the staff of a pilgrim of Saint James from a priest. But his problems reappeared three months later, when he returned from Santiago. In September 1201 he was cured at Sempringham. The shrine of Saint Aldhelm relieved Hubald, archdeacon of Salisbury, of neck pains. But they began again upon his return home and continued till his pilgrimage to Malmesbury.

In some cases a cure began while a pilgrim was en route to Canterbury and was completed upon touching the shrine. Other cures did not begin until a pilgrim headed home. One woman was cured when Saint Thomas in a dream told her to drink the juice of certain herbs in her garden and take a long nap. Many of the illnesses cured were probably self-induced as a result of a pilgrim's feeling guilt over a sin he had committed. Helen of Luttershall in the 1180s became a priest's mistress for three months and began to suffer insomnia and exhaustion. When she confessed her sin and prayed at the shrine of Saint Frideswide at Oxford, she recovered.

Stress, the heartbeat of most self-induced ailments, almost

killed Nicholas of Dover when he lost all appetite and didn't eat or drink anything for eighteen days. He regained the will to live only after friends carried him to Becket's shrine. Stress crippled a woman in Malmesbury, recorded William of Malmesbury. After she was bedridden for five years, her husband left her when all their money was gone, and she was driven to depend on charity. She was finally cured at the shrine of Saint Aldhelm in Malmesbury.

Faith healing undoubtedly cured most pilgrims, giving them what they expected through a subtle form of self-hypnosis. Benedict of Peterborough recorded the story of a young man who begged his friends for "water of Saint Thomas" as he lay on his deathbed.

> But unfortunately none of them had any, so one of the friends ran to a nearby fountain and filled a glass with fresh water. "Here," he said, "here is the saint's water for which you asked." The sick man believed it and drained the glass. Happily deceived, he immediately felt himself much improved; and thus, he who had lately been staring death in the face, got out of bed feeling nothing worse than a slight stiffness.[4]

Fraud was as common in the Middle Ages as it is in the modern world, and many pilgrims who claimed to have received miracles proved to be liars. Geoffrey Musard, a knight of Gloucestershire, faked his blindness when asking for "water of Saint Thomas" to be rubbed on his eyelids. A Lichfield woman swore that her son, crushed to death beneath a millstone, was resurrected by Saint Thomas, but she couldn't produce witnesses to confirm her story. It was next to impossible for the keepers of miracle books to determine who was fabricating their tales, who merely believed they had been cured, and who had truly experienced a miracle. A pilgrim returning to his village with the story of a miracle was far more interesting to family and friends than one who had simply made the trip back home safely. He was a kind of victorious hero, who had been embraced by God himself via his saints. To receive a miracle was usually the one and only thing in his entire life that could make him stand out in a crowd. Two blind women who traveled to Canterbury were not among those who received miracles, and in the streets of Leicester, people openly laughed at their failures. The peer pressure to experience a medieval miracle was akin to today's pressure to succeed financially.

In some cases monks questioned evasive or inarticulate pilgrims for hours before admitting their miracles into their records. The church was torn about so many miracles' being reported. Those in the clergy who were honest wanted only the truth to reflect the power, mercy, and glory of God. Others couldn't have cared less because the pilgrims' visits filled their coffers.

Halfway up the slick stone stairs on my knees, I lost my balance, and a man walking down the stairs grabbed my arm.

"There you go," he said, as I repositioned myself. He studied me as though he wanted to talk but didn't dare intrude.

"You came by at a good time," I said, offering my hand in thanks.

His hand was strong and callused like that of a carpenter or a stonemason. Though he didn't speak another word before continuing on down the stairs, I would remember the warmth and strength of his grip for the rest of my life. He was, in that rare given moment, everyone I had met and would meet who reached out when I was not standing as tall as I would at other times. How freeing it became to put my ego and vanity away and admit that my spirit, like my body now, was sometimes down on its knees and needed others. I did not always have to be the strongest, lift the heaviest weight, or even hold my head high to feel gratitude for being alive. Funny thing—a man can sometimes see higher from the knees, resting on the mountain of his soul, than he can upright and proud while looking to be above it all.

Reaching the top of the stone stairs, I walked on my knees to the site of Becket's shrine, where eight or ten people moved aside. In place of the gold and jeweled shrine, destroyed in 1538, now stood a lone candle. Its flame was as beautifully golden as the light in my dream at the monastery, which had connected an illuminated shaft from my hands to heaven. In that dream I had felt an extraordinary connection with my British and Native American ancestors as we made stone spearheads together. Now, here at the end of my pilgrimage, I felt an equally archetypical bond with the medieval pilgrims because we had traveled the same trail. Their spirits seemed to linger here, crying out in joy and sorrow for Saint Thomas to deliver them.

Prayer for Saint Thomas's Day from the Roman Missal

Oremus. Deu, pro cuius Ecclesia gloriosus, Pontifex Thomas gladiis impiorum occubuit: praesta quaesumus; ut omnes qui implorant auxillium, petitionis suae salutarem consequamur effectum. Per Dominum nostrum Jesum Christum, qui Tecum vivit et regnat in unitate Spiritus Sancti Deus, per omnia saecula saeculorum. Amen.

Let us pray. O God, for the sake of Whose Church the glorious Bishop Thomas fell by the sword of ungodly men: grant, we beseech Thee, that all Who implore his aid, may obtain the good fruit of his petition. Through our Lord Jesus Christ, Who livest and reignest with Thee in the unity of the Holy Ghost, Forever and ever. Amen.

No one knows for certain what became of Becket's bones. Though Henry VIII ordered that they be burned when the shrine was destroyed, the monks may have moved them to another tomb and replaced them with other bones. Yet on my knees before the flickering candle, I was not concerned about whether the saint's earthly remains had gone up in smoke or not. There are, after all, two kinds of human bones. One is of flesh and blood, and the other is encased in that slippery, inflammable matter called legend.

Upright again, I walked from the twilit cathedral back to the bustling streets, where more than the bright sun jolted me. The beggar with the dog named Cat was gone, but the fiddle player with the rubber elf sitting on her shoulder stomped her feet as she played a new Irish jig. Just up the street a man blew a bagpipe with all the passion of the Miller in *The Canterbury Tales* when Chaucer's pilgrims paraded from Tabard Inn to begin their whimsical journey to Becket's shrine. Halfway between the fiddle and the bagpipe, a man strummed a guitar and sang "Blowin' in the Wind" Bob Dylan–style. The shoulder-to-shoulder crowd dropped tips to the musicians. Some of the tourists clapped, and a couple of barefoot teenagers with bells around their ankles danced before the fiddle player. Everyone looked happy, smiling with that we're-on-vacation glow.

But I did not feel part of the merrymakers. No, my journey had ended, except for one last thing I needed to do when darkness came, and a kind of melancholy was setting in. My flight back to the United States left tomorrow afternoon out of Heathrow Airport, and I didn't want to be on it. England was in my blood now in more ways than one, and I wanted Pilgrims' Way to stretch on for days and weeks, winding around new curves and up and down lush hills, where history stood bigger than life and strangers' stories fed me what no stores could sell.

Determined not to sink deeper into sweet sorrow over leaving England, I decided to visit The Canterbury Tales, an amusement center where one can take a pilgrimage alongside life-size characters from Chaucer's *Tales* made of wood and plastic. Five Cub Scouts and their den mother were buying tickets when I arrived at the Disneyland-like pilgrimage route.

"Are you all alone, sir?" said the Cub Scout with blond hair who looked a lot like Prince Philip.

"Not if you guys are here," I said, winking.

"Want to make the pilgrimage with us?" said the boy.

The den mother nodded that that was a fine idea, and I accepted the invitation. These kids were just what I needed, and within minutes I began to feel a bit like one myself. The admission charge included the rental of electric "wands" that we had to hold a certain way to hear the *Tales*, told by the wood and plastic pilgrims, as we passed from room to room. Each scene represented a facet of *The Canterbury Tales*, complete with the odors of medieval stables.

"Gross," said one of the scouts. "What's that smell?"

A trained bear. (B.M. MS. Burney 275. f.359v.)

"Cow and horse shit," whispered the blond boy. "Careful where you step."

The den mother looked embarrassed as one of the boys picked Chaucer's nose. When the Wife of Bath told her story, another fondled her.

"Give her a kiss," said the blond.

"I will not," said the scout, who pulled his hand from the Wife of Bath. "She's been with other boys." Their youthful giggles were as timeless as those in the Middle Ages.

It was strange to hold an electric wand instead of my oak staff and to complete the electronic pilgrimage in only forty-five minutes, instead of a week by foot. When we turned in our wands, the exit naturally took us through the gift shop. There I bought the scouts pilgrim badges, which they pinned on their shirts along with scout badges they had earned from playing sports, and—

"I got this badge for building a clay castle," said the blond. "But I smashed it and turned it into a soccer player."

"Yeah, you gave him a nose out to here," said the blond's friend.

The kids' youthful spirits stayed with me as we parted, and I walked back to The Bishop's Finger to eat dinner. The sun was setting, and the place began to fill with college students drinking ale and glasses of "Holy Madness" and "Heaven's Gate." In the midst of the approaching party, a girl wearing pink sunglasses sat alone in the corner reading a book with such an intense expression that she seemed to hold the very love of her life. The cover of the book had been removed, and I couldn't read the title, which made it and her all the more intriguing. One second she chuckled. The next she squirmed, running her fingers through her hair as if courted by written words, whispering what only she could hear.

The word *book* evolved from the Anglo-Saxon word *boc*,

which meant "beech." The Anglo-Saxons used the tree's outer bark and slabs of thin inner bark as writing materials. In the Middle Ages a book was considered a sacred object, a kind of holy relic in itself, because it housed ancient knowledge, the road to wisdom, the doorway to God. If one book did not contain the answers a person sought, he believed he could find them in another book in a different part of the world. Travel, like pilgrimage, became one with the process of learning.

Scholars wandered medieval roads throughout England and Europe, seeking that next written piece of human understanding to accompany any books they already possessed. The illiterate masses, starved for enlightenment, sought the scholars' vagabond teachings as if they were secrets. The church condemned such scholars because it foresaw the seeds of individuals' thinking for themselves, robbing the church of its power and control. But with the invention of the printing press, those fateful seeds sprouted beyond the clerics' greatest imagination. The Renaissance's communications revolution would spread to the New World, where it was believed that the next grand piece of the human puzzle would be found. Though it was, it was also soon discovered—as we all know so well today—that the puzzle itself increased not only in size but in complexity: America is more than just a melting pot. It is the dinner table of the most powerful culture on earth, where everyone around the globe wants to take a bite, one way or the other.

It disappointed me when the girl in pink sunglasses closed her book and exited The Bishop's Finger. But only minutes later the cook won my attention. Learning that I had just walked to Canterbury from London, he prepared a special dish, pasta with pesto, and flippantly named it Pilgrim's Reward. I was relieved to see that he didn't have an open sore, as the Cook did in Chaucer's *Tales*:

A COOK they hadde with hem for nones,
To boil the chickens with the marybones [marrowbones],
And powdre-marchant tart, and galingale [spices].
Well could he know a draught of London ale.
He could rost, and seeth [boil], and frye,
Maken mortreux [stew], and well bake a pie [meat pie].
But greet harm was it, as it thoughte me,
That on his shin a mormăl [open sore] hadde he.

"If you can correctly name The Bishop's goldfish," the cook said, "I'll give you a desert on the house."

"Goldfish?" I said, looking about for an aquarium.

"I'll bring the fish out for your observation."

As the cook headed back into the kitchen, Neil, the bartender who had helped me find a B and B earlier that day, shook his head.

"Beware the spicy cook," said Neil.

Sean, the bartender who had suggested the Canterbury Cathedral Condos, looked on like the canary-eating cat.

"Find what you were looking for at the shrine?" he said, his tone salty but not mean-spirited.

"It's been the trip of a lifetime," I said. "I don't want to leave England."

"Tell you what," he said, "you take my job here and let me go to the States instead."

The cook paraded from the kitchen with a plastic bag filled with water and what appeared to be an orange fish about a foot long and only as big around as my thumb. He held it overhead as though it were royalty, splashing in pomp and glory. While medieval folks believed in some exotic sea creatures, they had never laid eyes on the likes of this.

"The one that got away, I dare say," said Sean.

When the cook dangled the fish before me, it became even stranger, because it had no scales and its eyes were as orange as its body. A single green fin ran down its back. A second later it became clear, however, that it was no fish at all but a carrot the cook had carved. The fin was a slice of cucumber.

"I caught him just before he swam upstream into a pot of vegetable soup," said the cook.

Moments later the carrot fish was passed around The Bishop's Finger as though it were some rare catch, at least from the sea of silliness. I had come to appreciate the British eccentricity—recognized it in myself and my fellow Americans—and it seemed most appropriate now that my last evening in England be spent among a fun-loving crowd, downing glasses of "Holy Madness" and "Heaven's Gate." Yes, my journey had come full circle now, for I had started out in Southwark at the site of Tabard Inn, where Chaucer's ale-drinking pilgrims began their festive trek to Becket's shrine.

> In Southwerk at the Tabard as I [Chaucer] lay,
> Redy to wenden [go] on my pilgrimage
> To Canterbury, with full [very] devout corage,
> At night was come into that hostelrye,
> Well nine and twenty in a compaignye
> Of sundry folk, by aventure [chance] y-falle,
> In fellawship, and pilgrims were they alle
> That toward Canterbury wolden [would] ride.

Only ten minutes after the carrot fish circulated The Bishop's Finger party crowd, the bag was opened, and two of the college students nibbled on it. Two tables away, as the jukebox blared and cigarette smoke filled the room like a fog, three other youths were having their own brand of fun. Each took a turn blowing foam from his glass of ale to try to extinguish a match flame held at arm's length. Foam flew everywhere but on the target, which was more entertaining for the players because it landed on a friend's face.

As the evening wore on, laughter grew louder, and eyes became more lustful, while body language loosened like carefree tongues. Chaucer's pilgrims at the Tabard Inn could've fit right in, and the Wife of Bath might've found a fling or husband number six.

But even a ripsnorting party can't top hearing strangers' stories, and I soon circulated the crowd till someone recognized my calling in life. His name was Ted, and his hair had been burred. Small, with dark skin, he was in his thirties, a wolf's head tattooed on his forearm. He kept looking at his cell phone as if his very life depended on it.

"Pretty wild place," I said, watching the foam blowers.

His hand dismissed them.

"I have to be around people," said Ted. "It helps keep my mind off my troubles. It helps a little, anyway. Nothing can really make you forget your pain." He glanced at the phone in his hand.

"We all hurt sometimes," I said, and his eyes melted as if he had just found a new friend. I told him what had brought me to England and that I dreaded leaving tomorrow.

"You're a lucky man," he said. "Now you have two countries to call home. You're free to come and go, and England will be here when you return. Wish I wore your shoes. I can't leave here. Not legally, anyway."

He lifted the cell phone and passed it to his other hand, his eyes on it like a door to freedom.

"Why can't you leave England?" I said.

"Trouble," he said. "Something stupid I did a while back when I was down and out. The Irish are not the only ones who had to lick rocks to get a taste when they were growing up." He clicked his cell phone on and off. "I'm not bitter, just realistic. I did what I did, and no one made me."

"What happened?" I said.

"Do you have children?" he said, and I shook my head. "People you love, though, right?" I nodded. "I live for my two girls, but I'm not even allowed to visit them. Their mother has them in London."

"Why can't you visit them?" I said.

"That's what the judge ordered," he said. "My wife's wishes. I went to prison for robbing a bank."

"You robbed a bank?" I said.

"I was out of work," he said. "My girls needed things. I had a few pints and got inspired."

With all my years on the road, I had met several ex-cons and knew they could be as manipulative as the shrewdest salesman. But I was also acutely aware that they could be more honest and to the point than most people. Ted seemed so desperate in telling his story—a tale as timeless and universal as one told by Chaucer's pilgrims—that I found it difficult to envision him holding a pistol on a knee-knocking bank teller.

"Was this an *armed* robbery?" I said.

He looked caught somewhere between being embarrassed and ashamed, and yet an impish pride darted through his eyes.

"Yes," he finally said. "I robbed the place with a can of bug spray."

"Bug spray?" the words leaped from my mouth.

"Had a range of twenty feet," he said. "Twenty feet and two years behind bars." He lifted his cell phone yet again. "I'm waiting on my daughters to phone."

Twenty minutes later the girls had still not called, and I so wanted to hear the phone ring—to see his troubled eyes brighten. I told Ted the same in more subtle terms.

"You've helped by just listening," he said. "Everybody else is just in here to escape. They don't care anything about my life."

Night had fallen when Ted ordered another glass of "Holy Madness," and I told him good-bye.

"Don't take your freedom for granted," he said. "It's the one cliché that's a real blessing, and we don't recognize it till it's gone."

His words stayed with me as I left The Bishop's Finger and made me realize all the more how much I had to be grateful for. My cup overflowed, not only within my spirit after the journey's end but even, it seemed, in the river Stour as it ran through Canterbury in the moonlit night. There, along the grassy banks beneath trees, I carved a small, plain boat from a piece of bark gathered from the medieval grounds of the monastery just outside where Becket had been murdered. When I was in the crypt reading the posted prayers, I took a candle and now placed it on the boat with a dove feather from my hat—the Cherokee bird sent from the Spirit World to tell us we are not alone. Lighting the Christian candle, I eased the boat down into the river and thought how life flows as well from person to person, place to place, and event to event, no matter what our religious or spiritual convictions.

The boat's gentle glow drifted downstream toward the sea, and at least for the night, all my prayers had been answered. God was only an arm's length away, right there in the water, the earth, the trees, the moon, all those I had met along the way, and the historic cathedral itself, towering over Canterbury as tall as Becket's legend.

EPILOGUE

My first week back home in the mountains of north Alabama was difficult after such an extraordinary journey to Canterbury. Driving a car instead of walking speeded everything up way too much, sucking away that special air the soul again learns to breathe when traveling by foot so close to the earth. The pebble we will never see at seventy miles an hour becomes a boulder on a sacred walk.

TV shows and news reports depicting violence disturbed me, and America's emphasis on materialism and competition saddened me. While the medieval church may have controlled the ignorant masses, the modern American world is also a bit brainwashed. But instead of the church doing it on the great scale it once celebrated, it has been replaced with advertisements on TV: every other ad caters to people's fear of death, just as profound now as it was in the Middle Ages. But instead of taking pilgrimages for our spiritual and physical health, we have turned to "miracles" in the form of every pill imaginable. Don't forget to buy that new car, the latest fashion, and diet food—guaranteed to give heaven on earth.

Often in debt up to our necks and working at jobs that we don't truly love, we have become modern-day serfs, bowing to a lord whose face we can't quite see there in the shadows between paychecks. We just know down in our guts and hearts that something isn't right, and we dare not talk about it too openly for fear it will become more real than we can dare bear.

My pain upon returning to America, however, began to subside when I walked with my Christ and Sequoya staff into the woods behind my cottage to the circle of stones placed there by Native Americans at the same time medieval pilgrims journeyed to Canterbury. There I spent the night on a blanket by a campfire after fasting for three days, asking the Great Spirit to help me make the transition back to the country where I was born. Overhead the Milky Way, the "Way of Saint James," glittered with its cosmic beauty, but I could not deny the report that evening on National Public Radio that two-thirds of Americans can no longer see the Milky Way because of pollution.

Still, the night proved to be just the medicine I needed. In the days that followed, my sorrow was replaced with compassion and joy, and I was already making plans to return to England the next year. As Ted the bug-spray bank robber said, "You have two countries now to call home." I also began to see Americans with a new point of view and cherished them more deeply than before my pilgrimage to Canterbury. Many of them, like myself, had British roots. We shared more than the same language and DNA. We were shaped and formed to a great extent by the stories passed on to us, generation after generation, from our Christian medieval ancestors. Their experiences live in our collective minds, and we sense them moving about in our lives like subtle emotions between the lines. Our hearts carry their misdeeds as well as their splendors, their weaknesses as well as their strengths.

Just as our forefathers came to America to seek a better life, I grasped more clearly in digesting my trek to Canterbury that we are still searching for meaning and purpose in a complex and constantly changing society. We are all on a testing pilgrimage through life, whether we carry a staff, a hammer, or a laptop. All roads do not lead to Rome, the empire that built Pilgrims' Way. Rather, they lead to the human condition, where soul and spirit await our daily judgment to acknowledge them or turn our heads, pretending that we don't see.

Five months have passed since I spent the night by the circle of stones. The autumn leaves have turned bright red and yellow, falling to the earth while orange pumpkins are scattered in fields among late corn. Owls hoot just beyond my door at night, and at dawn flocks of geese fly overhead to a nearby lake. A hive of wild honeybees thrives in the hollow section of my front-yard oak. It's now impossible to see the bees, coming and going from the tree's hole, without envisioning just how sacred beeswax was to medieval pilgrims. Their wax candles and their images of hearts and other body parts left at shrines were prayers of the highest order, and today each bee is a thread in a tapestry weaving the past to the present.

The tiny urn of English soil—my last pinch of earth came from the monastery grounds around Canterbury Cathedral—was buried beneath the oak alongside the items given to me when I walked the Trail of Tears. The Canterbury staff leans in the corner of the cottage by the fireplace, and the shell discovered at the Old Stone Church rests in my hatband with the feathers and snake rattle. The hat hangs on a deer-antler hook by the front door. The handful of wheat gathered in the English field two days before my journey's end dried and has been added to my medicine pouch. I placed it there that it might help me measure my day-to-day life, separating the wheat from the chaff as I make my daily bread.

When I hold that medicine and close my eyes, I yet smell the plowed English soil and freshly mown hay, feel the cool stream running over my bare feet, hear the crows squawk, and see rolling, lush green hills, ancient stone cottages, and the faces of those I met. Ah, the people ... Each lifts me in his or her unique way. But the face I see most often is that of the boy on his bike right before I gave him the good-luck feather. His words ring like a time-tested bell: "You and I are miracles, aren't we?" My heart always answers the same: "I do believe we are."

NOTES

CHAPTER I

1. Shirley Du Boulay, *The Road to Canterbury* (Harrisburg, PA: Morehouse Publishing, 1994), 13.

2. Elizabeth Kimball Kendall, ed., *Source Book of English History* (New York: Macmillan Company, 1900), 66–71.

3. Unless otherwise stated, all quotes from *The Canterbury Tales* are taken from Geoffrey Chaucer, *The Canterbury Tales: A Selection* (London: Penguin Popular Classics, 1996).

4. Donald R. Howard, *Chaucer: His Life, His Works, His World* (New York: Dutton, 1987), 13.

5. Ibid., 391.

6. Robert Lacey and Danny Danziger, *The Year 1000: What Life Was Like at the Turn of the First Millennium—An Englishman's World* (London: Little, Brown and Company, 1999), 137.

7. Ibid., 138.

CHAPTER 2

1. 13 Henry IV A.D. 1412 Letter-Book I. Fol. CXII. (Latin) from Henry Thomas Riley, ed. and trans., *Memorials of London and London life, in the XIIIth, XIVth, and XVth centuries. Being a series of extracts, local, social, and political from the early archives of the City of London, A.D. 1276–1419* (London: Longmans, Green and Company, 1868), Hilles: 942.1 2.

2. From the accounts translated in J. H. Robinson, *Readings in European History* (Boston: Ginn, 1905), 97–105.

3. Ibid.

4. Lacey and Danziger, *The Year 1000*, 159.

CHAPTER 3

1. Frances Gies and Joseph Gies, *Life in a Medieval Castle* (New York: Harper & Row, 1974), 196–197.

2. Ibid., 157–158.

CHAPTER 5

1. Gies and Gies, *Life in a Medieval Castle*, 190–191.
2. Ibid., 73.
3. Ibid., 97–98.
4. Ibid., 98–99.
5. Ibid., 99–100.
6. Ibid., 101.
7. Ibid., 101.
8. Ibid., 116–117.
9. Ibid., 113–114.

CHAPTER 6

1. Jonathon Sumption, *Pilgrimage—An Image of Medieval Religion* (Totowa, NJ: Rowman and Littlefield, 1975), 101.
2. Ibid., 75.
3. Ibid., 79.
4. Ibid., 106.
5. Charles W. Kennedy, trans., *Riddles from the Exeter Book—An Anthology of Old English Poetry* (New York: Oxford University Press, 1960), 43.
6. Ibid., 64.

CHAPTER 7

1. Marjorie Rowling, *Everyday Life in Medieval Times* (New York: Dorsett Press, 1987), 113, 118, 133.
2. Ibid., 117.
3. Ibid., 119.
4. Ibid., 120.
5. Ibid., 122.
6. Ibid.
7. Ibid., 128.
8. Ibid., 129.
9. Ibid., 132.
10. Sumption, *Pilgrimage*, 66.
11. Rowling, *Everyday Life in Medieval Times*, 124.
12. Ibid., 124.

CHAPTER 8

1. Frances Gies and Joseph Gies, *Women in the Middle Ages* (New York: Barnes & Noble, a Division of Harper & Row, 1980), 68.
2. Ibid., 71.
3. Ibid., 74.
4. Margaret Wade Labarge, *Women in Medieval Life* (London: Penguin Books, 2001), 107.
5. Gies and Gies, *Women in the Middle Ages*, 84.
6. Ibid., 76.
7. Ibid., 81.
8. Ibid., 78.

9. Ibid., 85.
10. Ibid., 86–87.
11. Ibid., 92.
12. Ibid., 93.

CHAPTER 9
1. Ronald C. Finucae, *Miracles and Pilgrims—Popular Beliefs in Medieval England* (New York: St. Martin's Press, 1977), 95.

CHAPTER 10
1. Richard Kieckhefer, *Magic in the Middle Ages* (Cambridge, England: Cambridge University Press, 1989), 71.
2. Ibid., 74.
3. Ibid., 73.
4. Ibid., 77.
5. Ibid., 78.
6. Frances Gies and Joseph Gies, *Cathedral, Forge, and Waterwheel: Technology and Invention in the Middle Ages* (New York: HarperCollins, 1994), 213.
7. Kieckhefer, *Magic in the Middle Ages*, 91.
8. Sumption, *Pilgrimage*, 23.
9. Ibid.
10. Ibid., 23–24.
11. Ibid., 24.
12. Ibid., 27.
13. Ibid., 29.
14. Ibid.
15. Ibid., 30–31.
16. Ibid., 33–34.
17. Ibid., 36.
18. Ibid., 40.
19. Ibid.

CHAPTER 11
1. Howard, *Chaucer: His Life, His Work, His World*, 482.
2. Kendall, *Source Book of English History*, 56–58.
3. Ibid., 59.
4. Henry T. Riley, trans., *The Annals of Roger de Hoveden*. 2 vols. (London: Bohn, 1853).
5. Joseph Stevenson, trans., *The Church Historians of England* (London: Seeley's, 1853), Vol. V, part 1, 329–336.

CHAPTER 12
1. Sumption, *Pilgrimage*, 83.
2. D. H. Turner, trans., "The Customary of the Shrine of St. Thomas Becket." *Canterbury Cathedral Chronicle* (Canterbury, England), April 1976, 16–22.
3. Sumption, *Pilgrimage*, 87.
4. Ibid., 86–87.

BIBLIOGRAPHY

Banham, Debby, ed. and trans. 1991. *Monasteriales Indicia, The Anglo-Saxon Monastic Sign Language*. Norfolk, England: Anglo-Saxon Books.

Bede. 1955. *Ecclesiastical History of the English People*. Edited by D. H. Farmer and translated by Leo Sherley-Price. London: Viking Penguin.

Chamberlin, E. R. 1993. *The Bad Popes*. New York: Barnes & Noble Books.

Chaucer, Geoffrey. 1934. *The Canterbury Tales*. Modern English by J. U. Nicolson. New York: Garden City Publishing Company.

———. 1996. *The Canterbury Tales*. London: Penguin Popular Classics.

Davies, R. Trevor. 1926. *Documents Illustrating the History of Civilization in Medieval England 1066–1500*. London: Methuen & Company.

Finucane, Ronald C. 1995. *Miracles and Pilgrims: Popular Beliefs in Medieval England*. New York: St. Martin's Press.

Geary, Patrick J. 1990. *Furta Sacra: Thefts of Relics in the Central Middle Ages*. Princeton, N.J.: Princeton University Press.

Gies, Frances and Joseph Gies. 1994. *Cathedral, Forge and Waterwheel: Technology and Invention in the Middle Ages*. New York: HarperCollins.

———. 1974. *Life in a Medieval Castle*. New York: Harper & Row.

———. 1987. *Marriage and the Family in the Middle Ages.* New York: Harper & Row.

———. 1980. *Women in the Middle Ages.* New York: Barnes & Noble, a Division of Harper & Row.

Goldberg, P. J. P., ed. and trans. of documentary sources. 1995. *Women in England, c. 1275–1525.* Manchester, England: Manchester University Press.

Hartley, Dorothy, and Margaret M. Elliot. 1931. *Life and Work of the People of England.* Vol. 1. London: B. T. Batsford.

Hendrickson, Robert. 1997. *QPB Encyclopedia of Word and Phrase Origins.* New York: Facts on File.

Hieatt, Constance B., and Sharon Butler. 1985. *Curye on Inglish: English Culinary Manuscripts of the Fourteenth-Century.* New York: Oxford University Press, for The Early English Text Society.

Howard, Donald R. 1987. *Chaucer: His Life, His Work, His World.* New York: E. P. Dutton.

Jacobus de Voragine. 1969. *The Golden Legend.* Translated by Granger Ryan and Helmut Ripperger. New York: Arno Press.

Kendall, Elizabeth, ed. 1900. *Source-Book of English History.* New York: Macmillan Company.

Kennedy, Charles W., trans. 1960. *Riddles from the Exeter Book: An Anthology of Old English Poetry.* New York: Oxford University Press.

Kieckhefer, Richard. 1989. *Magic in the Middle Ages.* Cambridge, England: Cambridge University Press.

Labarge, Margaret Wade. 2001. *Women in Medieval Life.* London: Penguin Books.

Lacey, Robert, and Danny Danziger. 1999. *The Year 1000: What Life Was Like at the Turn of the First Millennium—An Englishman's World.* London: Little, Brown and Company.

Leed, J. Eric. 1991. *The Mind of the Traveler: From Gilgamesh to Global Tourism.* New York: Basic Books.

Manchester, William. 1992. *A World Lit Only by Fire: The Medieval Mind and the Renaissance—Portrait of an Age*. London: Little, Brown and Company.

Peter of Blois. 1847. *Epistola*. Edited by J. A. Giles and translated by A. B. Hawes. Oxford, England.

Ravensdale, Jack. 1989. *In the Steps of Chaucer's Pilgrims: From Southwark to Canterbury from the Air and on Foot*. London: Souvenir Press.

Reeves, Compton. 1995. *Pleasures and Pastimes in Medieval England*. New York: Oxford University Press.

Riley, Henry Thomas, ed. and trans. 1868. *Memorials of London and London Life in the 13th, 14th and 15th Centuries. Being a series of extracts, local, social, and political, from the early archives of the City of London, A.D. 1276–1419*. London: Longmans, Green and Company.

Robertson, James, ed. 1876. *Materials for the History of Thomas Becket*. London: Longman and Company.

Robinson, J. H., trans. 1905. *Readings in European History*. Boston: Ginn.

Roger of Hoveden. 1853. *The Chronicle*. Published as *The Annals of Roger of Hoveden*. Translated by Henry T. Riley. London: Bohn.

Rowling, Marjorie. 1987. *Everyday Life in Medieval Times*. New York: Dorsett Press.

Sumption, Jonathan. 1975. *Pilgrimage: An Image of Medieval Religion*. Totowa, N. J.: Rowman and Littlefield.

Thorpe, Benjamin, ed. 1840. *Ancient Laws and Institutes of England*. London: Eyre & Spottiswoode.

Tuchman, Barbara W. 1978. *A Distant Mirror: The Calamitous 14th Century*. New York: Ballantine Books.

Turner, D. H. trans. 1976. "The Customary of the Shrine of St. Thomas Becket." *Canterbury Cathedral Chronicle* (Canterbury, England), April, 16–22.

Willeford, William. 1969. *The Fool and His Scepter*. Evanston, Ill.: Northwestern University Press.

ABOUT THE AUTHOR

In 1989, JERRY ELLIS became the first person in modern history to walk the nine-hundred-mile route of the Cherokee Trail of Tears. He wrote about that journey in his book *Walking the Trail*. He is also the author of *Marching Through Georgia* and *Bareback!* A graduate of the University of Alabama, Ellis has had four plays produced and has written for *The New York Times*. He lives in Alabama.